Finding What You Need

The handbook provides many ways to reach its information:

Use a table of contents.

Inside the front cover, a brief contents gives an overview of the handbook. Inside the back cover, a detailed outline lists all the book's topics.

Use the index.

At the end of the book (p. 262), this alphabetical list includes all topics, terms, and problem words and expressions.

Use the glossaries.

The Glossary of Usage (p. 239) clarifies words and expressions that are often misused or confused, such as *hopefully* or *affect/ effect*. The Glossary of Terms (p. 249) defines grammatical terms, including all terms marked ° in the text.

Use the elements of the page.

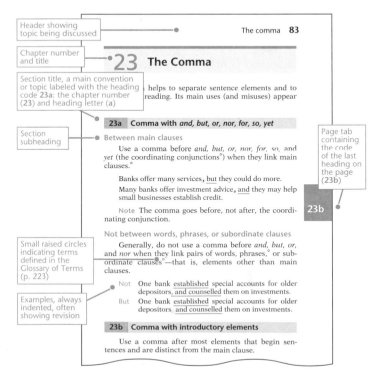

Header showing topic being discussed ● — The comma **83**

Chapter number and title — ●**23** **The Comma**

Section title, a main convention or topic labeled with the heading code **23a**: the chapter number (23) and heading letter (a) — helps to separate sentence elements and to reading. Its main uses (and misuses) appear

23a   Comma with *and, but, or, nor, for, so, yet*

Section subheading — ● Between main clauses

Use a comma before *and, but, or, nor, for, so,* and *yet* (the coordinating conjunctions°) when they link main clauses.°

Banks offer many services, but they could do more.

Many banks offer investment advice, and they may help small businesses establish credit.

Note The comma goes before, not after, the coordinating conjunction.

Page tab containing the code of the last heading on the page (23b)

23b

Not between words, phrases, or subordinate clauses

Generally, do not use a comma before *and, but, or,* and *nor* when they link pairs of words, phrases,° or subordinate clauses°—that is, elements other than main clauses.

Small raised circles indicating terms defined in the Glossary of Terms (p. 223)

Examples, always indented, often showing revision

Not One bank established special accounts for older depositors, and counselled them on investments.

But One bank established special accounts for older depositors and counselled them on investments.

23b   Comma with introductory elements

Use a comma after most elements that begin sentences and are distinct from the main clause.

THE

Jane E. Aaron
Elaine Bander

LITTLE,

BROWN

ESSENTIAL

HANDBOOK

FOURTH CANADIAN EDITION

Pearson Canada
Toronto

Library and Archives Canada Cataloguing in Publication

Aaron, Jane E.
  The Little, Brown essential handbook / Jane E. Aaron, Elaine
Bander.—4th Canadian ed.

Previous Canadian eds. published under title: The Little, Brown
  essential handbook for writers.
Includes index.

ISBN 978-0-205-78433-2

  1. English language—Grammar—Handbooks, manuals, etc.
2. English language—Rhetoric—Handbooks, manuals, etc.
I. Bander, Elaine, 1946– II. Title.

PE1112.A27 2011   808′.042   C2010-905517-9

ISBN 978-0-205-78433-2

Vice-President, Editorial Director: Gary Bennett
Editor-in-Chief: Ky Pruesse
Acquisitions Editor: David S. Le Gallais
Marketing Manager: Loula March
Supervising Developmental Editor: Suzanne Schaan
Project Manager: Richard di Santo
Production Editor: Avivah Wargon
Copy Editor: Kelly Coleman
Proofreaders: Judith Turnbull, Sharon Kirsch, Claudia Forgas
Compositor: Joan Wilson
Permissions Researcher: Karen Hunter
Art Director: Julia Hall
Cover and Interior Designer: Kerrin Hands

For permission to reproduce copyrighted material, the publisher gratefully
acknowledges the copyright holders listed on page 279, which is considered
an extension of this copyright page.

Statistics Canada information is used with the permission of Statistics
Canada. Users are forbidden to copy the data and redisseminate them, in
an original or modified form, for commercial purposes, without permission
from Statistics Canada. Information on the availability of the wide range
of data from Statistics Canada can be obtained from Statistics Canada's
Regional Offices, its World Wide Web site at **www.statcan.gc.ca**, and its
toll-free access number 1-800-263-1136.

2 3 4 5   15 14 13 12

Printed and bound in Canada.

Preface

This small book contains essential information about academic writing, the writing process, usage, grammar, punctuation, research writing, and source citation—all in a convenient, accessible format.

You can use this book at any level of writing, in any discipline, and in or out of school. The explanations assume no special knowledge of the terminology of writing: needless terms are omitted, and essential terms, marked °, are defined in the Glossary of Terms. Material especially for writers using English as a second language is marked ESL. Examples come from a wide range of subjects, from science to literature to business.

The guide facing the title page shows how the book works, and the complete table of contents inside the back cover details the coverage. The book has three main components.

The big picture

An overview of academic writing, the writing situation, the writing process, and document design begins the book. These chapters can help you define the context for your writing and make decisions about purpose, audience, research, revision, format, and other matters.

Editing

Many of this book's chapters will help you write clearly and correctly. You'll never need or use every chapter because you already know much of what's here, whether consciously or not. The trick is to figure out what you *don't* know, focus on those areas, and back yourself up with this book.

Checklists for editing appear on pages 24 (effective sentences), 46 (grammatical sentences), 82 (punctuation), and 104 (spelling and mechanics). You can develop a personal editing checklist as well by keeping a list of mistakes and other writing problems that your readers point out to you.

Research and documentation

When you need to consult sources for your writing, this book can help you find them, evaluate them, and acknowledge them. Chapters 39–43 guide you through the process of research writing, and 40–43 detail the five most widely used styles for citing sources: Modern Language Association (MLA), American Psychological Association (APA), Chicago Manual of Style, Council of Science Editors (CSE), and IEEE (formerly Institute of Electrical and Electronics Engineers).

The following aids are also available:

CourseSmart

CourseSmart goes beyond traditional expectations—providing instant, online access to the textbooks and course materials you need at an average savings of 60%. With instant access from any computer and the ability to search your text, you'll find the content you need quickly, no matter where you are. And with online tools like highlighting and note-taking, you can save time and study efficiently. See all the benefits at **www.coursesmart.com**.

Technology specialists

Pearson's Technology Specialists work with faculty and campus course designers to ensure that Pearson technology products, assessment tools, and online course materials are tailored to meet your specific needs. This highly qualified team is dedicated to helping schools take full advantage of a wide range of educational resources, by assisting in the integration of a variety of instructional materials and media formats. Your local Pearson Education sales representative can provide you with more details on this service program.

Acknowledgments

The publisher and Canadian author would like to thank all the reviewers of the Canadian edition, including those listed below, whose comments were helpful in preparing this edition:

Wendy Morgan, Fleming College
Nancy Rishor, Fleming College
Kent Walker, Brock University
Lorraine York, McMaster University

Visit **MyCanadianCompLab** to access diverse resources for composition in one easy-to-use place:

- Sections on **writing**, **research**, and **grammar** cover all the key topics in the text, providing additional instruction, examples, and practice. **Exercises** offer the opportunity to practise the skills learned in class and include both self-grading quizzes and writing activities. **Writing samples** provide examples of different types of writing and different documentation styles; some are annotated to highlight key aspects or to stimulate reflection and discussion. **Videos** illustrate aspects of the writing process through scenarios, or provide grammar and editing tutorials through on-screen revision.

- **Pearson eText** gives you access to the text whenever and wherever you have access to the Internet. eText pages look exactly like the printed text, offering powerful new functionality for students and instructors. Users can create notes, highlight text in different colours, create bookmarks, zoom, click hyperlinked words and phrases to view definitions, and view in single-page or two-page view. Pearson eText allows for quick navigation to key parts of the eText using a table of contents and provides full-text search.

  Icons in the eText are hotlinked to related material within MyCanadianCompLab:

  - Explore icons link to writing samples
  - Watch icons link to video simulations and animated lessons
  - Listen icons link to instruction and practice questions that can be downloaded and listened to on an MP3 player.

- An online **composing** space includes tools such as writing tips and editing FAQs, so you can get the help you need when you need it, without ever leaving the writing environment. Within this space, you'll find access to **EBSCO's ContentSelect**, a database of articles from academic journals that can be used for research and reference.

- The **portfolio** feature allows you to create an e-portfolio of your work that you can easily share with your instructor and peers.

Use the access code packaged with new copies of this textbook to log on to MyCanadianCompLab, or purchase separate access through your campus bookstore or directly through the website.

P A R T   I

Academic Writing

PEARSON
mycanadiancomplab

Visit the **Composing** space in MyCanadianCompLab to research, draft, and revise your written work and assignments. You can view instructor, peer, and tutor comments on your work, pulling together all the feedback you will need to produce better writing samples and get better marks.

CHECKLIST

Revising Academic Writing

This checklist covers the main considerations in academic writing. For a detailed list of the contents of Part I see inside the back cover.

Purpose and audience
☑ What is your purpose? Does it conform to the assignment?
☑ Who are your readers? Will your purpose be clear to them?

Thesis
☑ What is your thesis, or central claim?
☑ Where in the paper does your thesis become clear?

Development
☑ What are the main points supporting the thesis?
☑ How well do the facts, examples, and other evidence support each main point?

Use of sources
☑ Have you used sources to support—not substitute for—your own ideas?
☑ Have you integrated borrowed material into your own sentences? (See pp. 145–53.)
☑ Have you fully cited each use of a source? (See pp. 158–64.)

Unity
☑ What does each paragraph contribute to the thesis?
☑ Within paragraphs, what does each sentence contribute to the paragraph's idea? (This paragraph idea is often expressed in a **topic sentence**.)

Coherence
☑ Will the organization be clear to readers?
☑ How smoothly does the paper flow?
☑ Have you used transitions to link paragraphs and sentences? (See p. 260 for a list of transitional expressions, such as *first, however,* and *in addition*.)

Language
☑ Have you used standard English that is appropriately formal for your writing situation?
☑ Is your writing authoritative and neutral?

Format
☑ Have you used the appropriate format for the kind of writing you're doing? (See p. 15.)
☑ Have you included all necessary parts of the paper, such as your name, a title, and source citations?

1 Features of Academic Writing

Writing is both a way of discovering, recording, refining, and organizing your thoughts—a process—and a tool for communicating those thoughts in a way that others can read and assimilate—a product. Whether you are writing a letter of application, a case report, a market assessment, a family memoir, a research essay, or even an oral presentation (see Chapter 45), you engage in a similar process in order to produce a finished piece of writing that fulfills its purpose. Thus, by mastering the features of academic writing, you master the ability to communicate effectively in many other situations.

When you write in college and university, however, you work within a community of teachers and students who have specific aims and expectations. The basic aim of this community—whether in English, psychology, biology, or some other discipline—is to contribute to and to build knowledge through questioning, research, and communication. The differences among disciplines lie mainly in the kinds of questions asked, the kinds of research done to find the answers, and the ways of communicating the answers.

Across the disciplines, the broad goals of building and exchanging knowledge produce several key features.

1a The thesis

The **thesis** is the central idea or claim in a piece of writing: the entire work develops and supports that idea. It is the "message" that your readers should take away from your writing. Often, your thesis starts out as a question that guides your research and writing. In the final paper, the thesis will probably appear in a **thesis statement.**

Here are pairs of questions and answering thesis statements from various disciplines:

Literature question	What makes the ending of Kate Chopin's "The Story of an Hour" believable?
Thesis statement	The ironic ending of "The Story of an Hour" is believable because it is consistent with the story's other ironies.

Visit www.mycanadiancomplab.ca for added help and exercises on the writing process.

History question	What were the long-term effects of the deportations of the Acadians in 1755?
Thesis statement	Despite the catastrophic deportations of 1755, many Acadians eventually returned to, and thrived in, their traditional homelands.
Psychology question	How common is violence between partners in dating relationships?
Thesis statement	The survey showed that violence may have occurred in a fifth of dating relationships among students at this college.
Biology question	Does the same physical exertion have the same or different effects on the blood pressure of men and women?
Thesis statement	After the same physical exertion, the average blood pressure of female participants increased significantly more than the average blood pressure of male participants.

These thesis statements are concise, they make claims based on evidence, and they are arguable on the basis of evidence. The rest of your essay must logically support and develop your thesis.

ESL In some other cultures it is considered unnecessary or impolite for a writer to express an opinion or to state his or her main idea outright. When writing in Canadian academic situations, you can assume that your readers expect a clear idea of what you think.

1b Evidence, synthesis, and balance

Your contribution as an academic writer comes from your ability to develop, refine, and support your ideas.

ESL While students in some cultures may be expected to consult only well-known sources and to adhere closely to the sources' ideas, in Canadian colleges and universities, students are expected to look for relevant and reliable sources, whether well known or not.

Evidence

The thesis statement of your paper will be based on evidence, drawn sometimes from your analysis of your own experience but more usually from research. Depending on the discipline you're writing in and the type of paper you're working on, you'll use a mix of the following kinds of evidence:

- **Facts,** statements whose truth can be verified.
- **Statistics,** facts expressed as numbers.
- **Examples,** specific instances of the point being made.

- **Expert opinions,** the judgments formed by authorities on the basis of their own analyses of the facts.

Evidence must be reliable to be convincing. Ask these questions about your evidence:

- **Is it accurate**—trustworthy, exact, and undistorted?
- **Is it relevant**—authoritative, pertinent, and current?
- **Is it representative**—true to its context, neither under- nor overrepresenting any element of the sample it's drawn from?
- **Is it adequate**—plentiful and specific?

Synthesis

In academic writing, you do more than merely summarize the information and ideas you find in research sources. You put the sources to work for you, evaluating them and revising your emerging ideas in response to your evaluation of the sources' evidence and arguments. In a typical paragraph of source-based academic writing, you'll lead with your idea and then give the evidence from sources that support your idea, or draw logical inferences based on the evidence. See pages 138–45 for more on evaluating and synthesizing sources.

Balance

Part of synthesis is finding balance in your own and others' claims so that your presentation is reasonable. In argument, especially, you need to face opposing views squarely and make appropriate appeals to readers.

If your thesis is arguable, then others can marshal their own evidence to support different views. Dealing with these views fairly, giving them their due, shows your responsibility and gives you a chance to deal with objections your readers may have. Find out what the opposing views are and what evidence supports them. Then explain them, refute the ones you can, grant the validity of the others, and demonstrate why, despite their validity, the opposing views are less compelling than your own.

In presenting both opposing views and your own, you'll make three kinds of appeals to readers:

- A *rational appeal* calls on readers' sense of logic. You make reasonable claims and support them with reliable evidence and sound logic.
- An *emotional appeal* calls on readers' feelings. You strengthen support for your claims by encouraging readers to feel empathy, pride, anger, or some other emotion. Such appeals should be used sparingly or not at all in academic writing. They can never substitute for evidence and logic.

- An *ethical appeal* is the sense you give of being reasonable, fair, and competent.

Like the presentation of opposing views, appeals require balance. Emotional appeals in particular can be risky if they misjudge readers' feelings or are inappropriate to the argument (for example, fanning readers' fear to force agreement with a claim).

1c Source citation

Using the ideas and information in sources carries the responsibility to acknowledge those sources fully. Not acknowledging sources undermines the incremental construction of knowledge on which academic work depends. It also opens you to charges of plagiarism, which can be punishable. (See Chapter 39.)

Most disciplines have a preferred style of source citation. For lists of disciplines' style guides, see page 163–64. For documentation guidelines and samples, see pages 164–84 (MLA style), 184–99 (APA style), 200–213 (Chicago style), 214–21 (CSE style), and 221–22 (IEEE style).

ESL Cultures have varying definitions of a writer's responsibilities to sources. In some cultures, for instance, a writer need not cite sources that are well known. In Canada, in contrast, a writer is obligated to cite all sources.

1d Organization

Academic writing, like most written and spoken communication, is usually divided into an **introduction**, a **body**, and a **conclusion**.

The **body** is the heart of academic writing, with each paragraph providing accurate evidence, logical arguments, and pertinent examples to support your thesis. Each **body paragraph** has a single topic usually expressed in a **topic sentence**. The topic sentence often begins the paragraph, but it may also occur as a second or even concluding sentence. The topic sentence may even be implied rather than stated. The rest of the paragraph explains, supports, and develops the stated or implied topic sentence. Nothing should go into a body paragraph that does not support the paragraph's topic.

Body paragraphs are developed using different **patterns of organization**. These may include narration (telling a story), description (using vivid detail to help your reader to see, hear, smell, taste, and touch whatever you are describing), process (providing a step-by-step account of how to do something), definition and classification (explaining logically what something is and isn't), comparison (identifying similar elements in two or

1d

more items), contrast (identifying significantly different elements in two or more items that belong to a similar category), examples and illustrations, cause and effect, and problem-to-solution. Most body paragraphs use some combination of these organizational patterns, providing details and arguments to support the topic sentence.

Many writers only write the introduction and conclusion after they have written the body of their essay. If you begin by writing your introduction, however, be prepared to revise it after completing the rest of your essay. (No matter how carefully you plan, you will discover new insights as you write.)

Introductions and conclusions have special jobs to do and therefore take special forms.

The **introduction** establishes the subject of the essay, motivates the reader to continue reading, and presents the thesis statement, usually at the end of the paragraph. Your introduction may begin with an interesting, relevant statement about your subject that will orient readers to your discussion, but you should avoid sweeping generalizations that go beyond the scope of your specific subject. Then quickly narrow to your thesis statement. Save your detailed evidence and arguments for the body paragraphs that follow.

The **conclusion** ties together the parts of the body, usually by inverting the structure of the introduction. Begin by briefly reinforcing your thesis, reminding readers how you have substantiated your claims. Then you may open your arguments to larger concerns or implications, or suggest further developments, possibly alluding to material in your introduction to provide a sense of closure.

Beyond this basic scheme, organization in academic writing varies widely depending on the discipline and the task. In the experimental sciences and social sciences, for example, writing will often include special sections on methodology and results. **Oral communication** requires more explicit explanations of your organizational structure in order to help your audience follow the development of your thoughts. (See Chapter 45.) Whatever organizational framework you use, develop your ideas as simply and directly as your purpose and content allow, and clearly relate your sentences, paragraphs, and sections, using transitional expressions° so that your readers always know where they are in the paper's development.

° Words marked with the degree sign (°) are discussed elsewhere in the text and are defined in the Glossary of Terms at the back of this book.

1e Language

In ordinary conversation with friends, and in informal written communication such as notes, blogs, and text messages, you probably use slang or dialect words as well as nonstandard, ungrammatical sentences, confident that you will still communicate your message. But just as you probably change from torn jeans into a clean suit for a job interview, so too you should use a slightly more formal (or standard) version of English to communicate in an academic environment.

Formal does not mean pretentious or stuffy. You should aim to convey your ideas clearly and plainly so that your readers will focus on your arguments rather than on your style or your personality. To do so, follow the rules of the dialect called **standard English** used by academic writers throughout the English-speaking world. This handbook will help you to write clear and correct standard English.

This means avoiding words and expressions, such as slang and ethnic or regional dialect, that are labelled "nonstandard." As well, you should translate any essential terms from a language other than English. (Note, however, that in Canadian academic discourse, many writers assume that their readers can understand French.)

Academic writing has some further specific style conventions:

- **Write objectively, not subjectively,** maintaining some distance between you and your reader. Generally, use the third person (*he, she, it, they*) rather than the first (*I, me*) or second (*you*).
- **Write authoritatively and neutrally.** Do not apologize for, or overly qualify, statements that you intend to support with strong logic and evidence. (If your sentence begins, *I feel that* . . . , then your sentence is about your feelings rather than about an argument that can be demonstrated or debated.) Avoid gushing enthusiasm or hostile criticism.
- **Avoid contractions and false passives.** Write out contracted words like *didn't* or *he's* as *did not* or *he is*. Use the passive voice° (p. 56) only when you intend to convey that an outside agency has acted upon the passive subject, as in *He was prevented by the government* or *He was arrested*. Use active° rather than passive verbs to indicate who is performing the action: not *His actions were believed to be illegal* but *CSIS believed that his actions were illegal*.

CHECKLIST FOR ACADEMIC LANGUAGE

Rapid communication by e-mail and text or instant messaging encourages some informalities that are inappropriate in academic writing. Check your academic papers especially for the following:

- ☑ **Sentence fragments** Make sure every sentence has a subject and a verb. Avoid fragments such as *Observing the results* and *After the meeting*. For more on fragments, see pages 75–77.
- ☑ **Punctuation** Use standard punctuation between and within sentences. Check especially for missing commas and apostrophes. See pages 83–101.
- ☑ **Spelling** Use correct, standard spellings, avoiding spellings such as *enuf* for *enough, cuz* for *because, nite* for *night, u* for *you,* and *wl* for *will.* See pages 105–07.
- ☑ **Capital letters** Use capital letters at the beginnings of sentences, for proper nouns and adjectives, and in titles. See pages 109–11.
- ☑ **Abbreviations and contractions** Use standard abbreviations, avoiding short forms such as *2* for *to* or *too, b4* for *before, bc* for *because, ur* for *you are,* and *+* or *&* for *and.* See pages 113–15. Avoid contractions. Use *cannot* rather than *can't, I have* rather than *I've.* See page 92.

2 The Writing Situation

As an academic writer, you will always be communicating within a **writing situation:** the requirements and options that determine what and how you write. Considering your situation will tell you a great deal about how to proceed.

2a Subject, audience, and purpose

Whenever you write to be read by others, you are communicating something about a topic to a particular audience of readers for a specific reason.

Visit www.mycanadiancomplab.ca for
added help and exercises on the writing process.

Subject

When you receive a writing assignment, study its wording and requirements in order to focus on a subject:

- **What does your writing assignment tell you to do?** Words such as *discuss, analyze, report, interpret, argue, describe, compare,* and *evaluate* specify the way you are to approach your subject and what kind of thinking is expected of you.
- **What interests you about the subject?** A good subject is one that you care about. Consider what you already know or want to know more about.
- **What kind of research is required?** An assignment may specify the kinds of sources you are expected to consult.
- **Is your subject limited enough?** Choose a subject you can cover in the space and time you have, or narrow a broad topic by breaking it into as many specific subjects as you can think of.

Audience

As a writer, you should adapt each piece of writing to its intended audience. A business report, for example, may circulate among several readers, each of whom has a different level of knowledge and engagement with the subject, while a political or religious pamphlet may encounter readers who do not share your unstated assumptions. Awareness of your audience will help you to tailor your message effectively.

Most academic writing assignments ask you to assume an audience of educated readers or even experts in your subject. In academic writing, you are participating in a conversation about your subject with a community of informed scholars, some of whom wrote generations ago and some of whom (like you) have only recently joined the discussion. Use the questions below to adapt your writing to the needs and expectations of your readers:

- **Who will read your writing?** What can you assume your readers already know and think about your subject? How can your assumptions guide your writing so that you tell readers neither too little nor too much?
- **What are readers' expectations?** For the discipline you're writing in, what claims and evidence, organization, language, and format will readers look for?
- **What is your relationship to your readers?** How formal or informal should your writing be?
- **What do you want readers to do or think after they read your writing?**

Purpose

Writing can have many purposes: to convey information, stimulate debate, entertain, change people's minds, or persuade them to action. For most academic writing, your general purpose will be mainly explanatory or mainly argumentative. You will aim to clarify your subject so that readers understand it as you do, or you will aim to gain readers' agreement with a debatable idea about the subject. The following questions can help you think about your purpose:

- **What kind of writing does your assignment specify?** For instance, are you writing a case study, a review of others' writing, an analysis of causes, or a policy proposal?
- **What aim does your assignment specify?** For instance, does it ask you to explain something or to argue a point?
- **Why are you writing?** What do you want your work to accomplish? How do you want your readers to respond?
- **How can you best achieve your purpose?** What strategies will work best with your audience?

2b Research

Many academic writing assignments require you to consult one or more sources and to cite the sources you used. Ask these questions to determine the kind of research you may have to do:

- **What kinds of evidence will best suit your subject, audience, and purpose?** What do you need to learn in order to answer your research question? What combination of facts, examples, and expert opinions will generate and support your ideas?
- **Does your assignment require research?** Will you need to consult sources or conduct interviews, surveys, or experiments? Does your college or university have ethical guidelines for conducting interviews and experiments?
- **Even if research is not required, what information do you need for developing your subject?** How will you obtain it?
- **What documentation style should you use to cite your sources?** See pages 162–64 on source documentation in the academic disciplines.

2c   Deadline, length, and document design

3

The due date, the amount of writing expected, and the format all affect your options:

- **When is the assignment due?** How will you apportion the work you have to do in the available time?
- **How long should the paper be?** If no length is assigned, what seems appropriate for your subject, audience, and purpose? Note that longer is not necessarily better: good academic writing is selective, not exhaustive.
- **What format and illustrations does the assignment require?** See page 16 on format in the academic disciplines and pages 18–21 on using graphs, photographs, and other illustrations to support ideas.

3   The Writing Process

Like most writers (even very experienced ones), you may find writing sometimes easy but more often challenging. This chapter will help you anticipate the stages you will cycle through and the kinds of thinking involved along the way. The stages are not fixed, however. Writing is a recursive, or circular, process, and on any given project you may find that some other sequence helps you accomplish the same work.

3a   Development and focus

With a sense of your writing situation (Chapter 2), you can begin to gather and focus the ideas for your paper.

Exploration

Most writers start a project by exploring ideas. You might begin by trying to answer a question about a specific subject, as discussed in the next section, or you might need to explore ideas even to arrive at a specific subject.

- **Discover your own thoughts,** writing down ideas in a brainstorming list, a branching diagram, a journal

Visit www.mycanadiancomplab.ca for
added help and exercises on the writing process.

entry, or a freely written draft. Concentrate on opening up avenues: delay editing your ideas until you have seen how they come out in writing.

▪ **As appropriate, begin finding sources to support and extend your ideas.** See pages 126–45 for research tips.

Thesis and organization

To check your progress or find direction, try to pin down the central idea, or thesis, of your writing and to arrange your ideas and evidence.

The thesis is an important feature of academic writing, as discussed on pages 3–4. The following strategies can help you develop a thesis statement:

▪ **Focus your thoughts and information on a single dominant question you seek to answer.** Let the question guide your planning and research, but also allow it to change as information and ideas accumulate.

▪ **As your work continues, begin answering your question in a statement of your main idea.** Like your question, this thesis statement may change as your ideas do, but eventually it will be the focus of your final paper.

▪ **Classify (sort) your accumulated ideas and evidence** into categories or clusters, eliminating any that do not address your question, no matter how compelling or true they are. These clusters will suggest strategies for organizing your material, or will identify areas requiring further investigation and thought.

Even though your thesis is a debatable opinion, you should write it in a declarative sentence, using active verbs, as though it were a statement of fact:

> Not   I think that hip-hop could be seen to be like the Elizabethan sonnet.
>
> But   Hip-hop is like the Elizabethan sonnet because . . . .

The rest of your essay should then convince your reader that your thesis is valid. See pages 3–4 for examples of questions and thesis statements.

Many writers use a preliminary outline to see how they will support the thesis and where they need more research. Such an outline need not be very detailed: a list of the major points, with the most significant support for each point, often provides an adequate map for proceeding, especially if you indent subordinate points underneath the larger ideas they support or illustrate.

3d

3b First drafts

As you work, save all of your notes and drafts in separate files, and back them up. In your early drafts, try to compose freely so that you can work out what you want to say. Resist self-criticism until later.

You may find it helpful to draft in sections, devoting a paragraph or more to each major point that supports your thesis. State the point clearly, and support it with arguments and evidence. This approach will keep you moving ahead while it also helps you focus on making your evidence work for your ideas.

3c Revision

When you have a draft of your paper, let it rest for a while to get some distance from it and perhaps to gather comments from others, such as your classmates or instructor. Then revise the draft using the checklist on page 2, concentrating on the effectiveness of the whole. (Leave style, correctness, and other specific issues for the separate step of editing, discussed below.)

3d Editing and proofreading

Much of this book concerns editing—tightening or clarifying sentences, polishing words, repairing mistakes in grammar and punctuation. Leave this work until after revision so that your content and organization are set before you tinker with your expression. For editing guidelines, see the checklists on pages 24 (effective sentences), 46 (grammatical sentences), 82 (punctuation), and 104 (spelling and mechanics).

Most writers find that they spot errors better on paper than on a computer screen, so edit a printout if you can. And be sure to proofread your final draft before you submit it, even if you have used a spelling checker or similar aid (see below).

Spelling checkers

A spelling checker can be a great ally: it will flag words that are spelled incorrectly and will usually suggest alternative spellings that resemble what you have typed. However, this ally has limitations:

- **The checker may flag a word that you've spelled correctly,** just because the word does not appear in its dictionary, or because your checker is set to "Canadian" spelling but that you have typed the word using American spelling, or vice-versa. See page 105.

- **The checker may suggest incorrect alternatives.** Before accepting any highlighted suggestion from the checker, you need to verify that the word is actually what you intend. Consult an online or printed dictionary when you are not sure of the checker's recommendations.
- **Most important, a spelling checker will not flag words that appear in its dictionary but that you have misused.** It will not distinguish homonyms such as *whose* or *who's, their* or *there,* and *sight* or *site* or *cite,* nor will it recognize a wrong word or a missing word. Consult dictionaries and the Glossary of Usage on pages 239–48.

Grammar and style checkers

Grammar and style checkers can flag incorrect grammar or punctuation and wordy or awkward sentences. You may be able to customize a checker to suit your needs and habits as a writer—for instance, instructing it to look for problems with subject-verb agreement or for passive verbs.

Like spelling checkers, however, grammar and style checkers are limited:

- **They miss many errors** because they are not yet capable of analyzing language in all its complexity.
- **They often question passages that don't need editing,** such as an appropriate passive verb or a deliberate and emphatic use of repetition.

Each time a grammar and style checker questions something, you must determine whether a change is needed at all and what change will be most effective, and you must read your essay carefully on your own to find any errors the program missed.

4 Designing Documents

Legible, consistent, and attractive papers and correspondence serve your readers and reflect well on you. This chapter explains the basics of formatting any document so it will be clear and effective.

Visit www.mycanadiancomplab.ca for added help and writing samples.

4a Formats for academic papers

Many academic disciplines prefer specific formats for students' papers. This book details three such formats:

- MLA, used in English, foreign languages, and some other humanities (pp. 181–84).
- APA, used in the social sciences and some natural sciences (pp. 196–99).
- Chicago, used in history, art history, religion, and some other humanities (pp. 211–213).

The design guidelines in this chapter extend the range of elements and options covered by most academic styles. Your instructors may want you to adhere strictly to a particular style or may allow some latitude in design. Ask them for their preferences.

4b Clear and effective documents

Your papers, reports, and correspondence must of course be neat and legible. But you can do more to make your work accessible and attractive by taking care with margins, text, lists, headings, and illustrations (tables, figures, and images).

Margins

Provide minimum one-inch (2.5 cm) margins on all sides of a page to prevent unpleasant crowding. If your document will be presented in a binder, provide a larger left margin—say, 1½ inches (3.75 cm). In academic writing, avoid justifying the right margin (making the words even with the margin) as though your essay were printed.

Text

Line spacing

Double-space most academic documents, with an initial indention for paragraphs. Single-space most business documents, with an extra line of space between paragraphs. Double- or triple-space to set off headings in both kinds of writing.

Type fonts and sizes

The readability of text also derives from the type fonts (or faces) and their sizes. For academic and business documents, choose a standard font and a type size of 10 or 12 points.

10-point Times Roman

12-point Times Roman

4b

Highlighting

Within a document's text, underlined, *italic,* **boldface,** or even colour type can emphasize key words or sentences. Underlining is rarest these days, having been replaced by italics in business and most academic writing. In both academic and business writing, boldface can give strong emphasis—for instance, to a term being defined. More in business than in academic writing, colour can highlight headings and illustrations.

Lists

Lists give visual reinforcement to the relations between like items—for example, the steps in a process or the elements of a proposal. A list is easier to read than a paragraph and adds white space to the page.

When wording a list, work for parallelism among items—for instance, all complete sentences or all phrases (see p. 34). Set the list with space above and below and with numbering or bullets (centred dots or other devices, such as the small squares in the list on this page, below). Most word processors can format a numbered or bulleted list automatically.

Headings

Headings are signposts. In a long or complex document, they direct the reader's attention by focusing the eye on a document's most significant content. (Don't use them in essays of fewer than three thousand words unless instructed to do so.) Most academic and business documents use headings functionally, to divide text, orient readers, and create emphasis. Follow these guidelines:

- **Use one, two, or three levels of headings** depending on the needs of your material and the length of your document. Some level of heading every two or so pages will help keep readers on track.
- **Create an outline of your document** to plan where headings should go. Reserve the first level of heading for the main points (and sections) of your document. Use a second and perhaps a third level of heading to mark subsections of supporting information.
- **Keep headings as short as possible** while making them specific about the material that follows.
- **Word headings consistently**—for instance, all questions (*What Is the Scientific Method?*), all phrases° with *-ing* words (*Understanding the Scientific Method*), or all phrases with nouns (*The Scientific Method*).

4b

- **Indicate the relative importance of headings** with type size, positioning, and highlighting, such as capital letters, underlining, or boldface.

FIRST-LEVEL HEADING

Second-Level Heading

Third-Level Heading

- **Keep the appearance simple**, minimizing variations in type style and type size and avoiding extra-large letters or unusual styles.
- **Don't break a page immediately after a heading.** Push the heading to the next page.

Note   Document format in psychology and some other social sciences requires a particular treatment of headings. See page 197.

Tables, figures, and images

Tables, figures, and images can often make a point for you more efficiently and effectively than words can. Tables present data. Figures (such as graphs or charts) usually recast data in visual form. Images (such as diagrams, drawings, photographs, and clip art) can explain processes, represent what something looks like, add emphasis, or convey a theme.

Follow these guidelines when using tables, figures, or images in academic and most business writing:

- **Focus on a purpose for your table or illustration**—a reason for including it and a point you want it to make. Otherwise, readers may find it irrelevant or confusing.
- **Provide a source note for someone else's independent material**, whether it's data or a complete illustration (see p. 156). Each discipline has a slightly different style for such source notes; those in the table below and the figures on pages 20–21 reflect the style of the humanities. See also Chapters 40–43.
- **Number figures and images together**, and label them as figures: Figure 1, Figure 2, and so on.
- **Number and label tables separately from figures:** Table 1, Table 2, and so on.
- **Refer to each illustration** (for instance, "See Figure 2") at the point(s) in the text where readers will benefit by consulting it.
- **Determine the placement of illustrations.** The social sciences and some other disciplines require each illustration to fall on a page by itself immediately

after the text reference to it. You may want to follow this rule in other situations as well if you have a large number of illustrations. Otherwise, you can place them on your text pages just after their references.

Many organizations and academic disciplines have preferred styles for tables and figures that differ from those given here. Statistics Canada also offers a "Guide to creating and using graphs" at *http://www.statcan.gc.ca/edu/power-pouvoir/ch9/using-utilisation/5214829-eng.htm*. When in doubt about how to prepare tables and figures, ask your instructor or supervisor.

Tables

Tables usually summarize raw data, displaying the data concisely and clearly.

- **Provide a self-explanatory title above the table.**
- **Provide self-explanatory headings for horizontal rows and vertical columns.** Use abbreviations only if you are certain readers will understand them.
- **Lay out rows and columns for maximum clarity.** In the sample below, for instance, lines divide the table into parts, headings align with their data, and numbers align vertically down columns.

Table 1
Proportion of children aged six months to five years in child care, by age

Child age	% in child care	
	1994–1995	2002–2003
Six months to under one year	36.0	28.6
One year	43.3	56.1
Two years	44.5	58.1
Three years	42.4	57.7
Four years	41.5	55.7
Five years	40.8	53.1
Total	41.9	53.6

Source: Statistics Canada, "Child Care in Canada," Catalogue no. 89-599-MIE2006003, *The Daily*, 5 Apr. 2006, Web, 25 July 2006.

Figures

Figures represent data graphically. They include the three kinds presented on pages 20–21:

pie charts (showing percentages making up a whole), bar graphs (showing comparative data), and line graphs (showing change).

- **Provide a self-explanatory caption or legend below the figure.**
- **Provide self-explanatory labels for all parts of the figure.**
- **Draw the figure to reflect its purpose and the visual effect you want it to have.** In Figure 3 on page 21 shortening the horizontal date axis emphasizes the movement of the line over time.

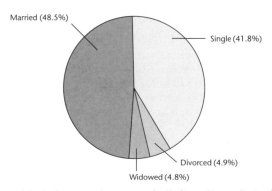

Fig. 1. Marital status in 2005 of all Canadians. Data from Statistics Canada, CANSIM, table 051-0010, 5 Apr. 2006, Web, 25 July 2006. <www40.statcan.gc.ca/l01/cst01/famil01-eng.htm>.

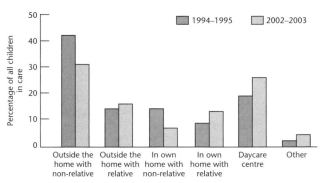

Fig. 2. Type of care for Canadian children in daycare, 1994–1995 and 2002–2003. Data from Statistics Canada, "Child care in Canada," Catalogue no. 89-599-MIE2006003, Table 3, *The Daily*, 5 Apr. 2006, Web, 25 July 2006.

Index (unadjusted)   (1992 = 100)

4b

Fig. 3. The Consumer Price Index, July 2001–July 2006. Data from Statistics Canada, Catalogue no. 62-001, Table 4, 5 Apr. 2006, Web, 25 July 2006. <http://www.statcan.gc.ca/pub/62-001-x/62-001-x2010009-eng.htm>.

Photographs and other images

Diagrams, photographs, and other images can add substance to an academic or business document. In a psychology paper, for instance, a photograph may illustrate a key experiment. But images cannot represent your ideas by themselves: you need to relate them to your text, explain their significance, and label, number, and caption them (see pp. 18–19).

Note When using an image prepared by someone else, you must always cite the source. Most copyright holders allow the use of their material for academic papers that are distributed only within a class. However, public use, such as on a website, requires permission from the copyright holder.

PART II

Effective Sentences

Effective Sentences

Emphasis

- ☑ Make subjects and verbs of sentences focus on key actors and actions. (See opposite.)
- ☑ Stress main ideas by placing them first or last in a sentence. (See pp. 26–27.)
- ☑ Link equally important ideas with coordination. (See pp. 27–29.)
- ☑ De-emphasize less important ideas with subordination. (See p. 29.)

Conciseness

- ☑ Use the active voice to focus on key actors and actions. (See p. 30.)
- ☑ Cut empty words and unneeded repetition. (See pp. 30–31.)
- ☑ Avoid unneeded *there is* and *it is* constructions. (See p. 32.)
- ☑ Reduce word groups to their essence, and combine sentences where appropriate. (See pp. 31–32.)

Parallelism

- ☑ Use parallel constructions to show the equivalence of elements connected by *and, or, not only . . . but also,* and similar words. (See pp. 32–34.)

Variety and details

- ☑ Vary sentence lengths and structures to stress your main ideas and hold readers' attention. (See pp. 34–36.)
- ☑ Provide details that make your sentences clear and interesting. (See p. 36.)

Appropriate words

- ☑ Use language appropriate for your writing situation. (See p. 37.)
- ☑ Avoid sexist and other biased language. (See pp. 39–42.)

Exact words

- ☑ Choose words that are suited to your meaning and are concrete and specific. (See pp. 42–43.)
- ☑ Make words correct in idiom and also fresh, not clichéd. (See pp. 43–44.)

5 Emphasis

Emphatic writing leads readers to see your main ideas both within and among sentences. Besides the following strategies for achieving emphasis, see also the discussions of conciseness (p. 30) and variety (p. 34).

5a Subjects and verbs

The heart of every sentence is its **subject**, which usually names the actor, and its **verb**, which usually specifies the subject's action: *Children* [subject] *grow* [verb]. When these elements do not identify the key actor and action in the sentence, readers must find that information elsewhere and the sentence may be wordy and unemphatic. In the following sentences, the subjects and verbs are underlined:

Unemphatic   The <u>purpose</u> of the Natural Sciences and Engineering Research Council (NSERC) <u>is</u> to fund talented Canadian researchers. <u>Grants</u> worth over $500 million <u>were awarded</u> this year to nearly nine thousand students and professors.

These sentences are unemphatic because their key ideas (NSERC's funding and awarding) do not form their grammatical subjects and verbs. Revised, the sentences are clearer and more concise:

Revised   <u>The Natural Sciences and Engineering Research Council (NSERC) funds</u> talented Canadian researchers. This year <u>the Council awarded</u> grants worth over $500 million to nearly nine thousand students and professors.

Ensure that the *intended* subject of your sentence is also the *grammatical* subject.

The constructions shown below usually drain meaning from a sentence's subject and verb.

Nouns made from verbs

Nouns made from verbs can obscure the key actions of sentences and add words. These nouns include *inten-*

tion (from *intend*), *proposal* (from *propose*), *decision* (from *decide*), *expectation* (from *expect*), *persistence* (from *persist*), *argument* (from *argue*), and *inclusion* (from *include*).

Unemphatic | The Minister of Industry made a <u>decision</u> to fund three thousand professors from across Canada. Her <u>intention</u> is to give them $4 million in Discovery Grants to support their research in the natural sciences and engineering.

Revised | The Minister of Industry <u>decided</u> to fund three thousand professors from across Canada. She <u>intends</u> to give them $4 million in Discovery Grants to support their research in the natural sciences and engineering.

Weak verbs

Weak verbs, such as *made* and *is* in the unemphatic sentences above, tend to stall sentences just where they should be moving and often bury key actions:

Unemphatic | NSERC <u>makes</u> a huge contribution to Canadian technological research. Its role is to invest in people and ideas.

Revised | NSERC <u>contributes</u> hugely to Canadian technological research. It <u>invests</u> in people and ideas.

Passive voice

Verbs in the **passive voice** state actions received by, not performed by, their subjects. Thus, the passive de-emphasizes the true actor of the sentence, sometimes omitting it entirely. In general, use the **active voice**, in which the subject performs the verb's action. (See pp. 56–57 for more on passive and active voice.)

Unemphatic | Because nearly four thousand <u>students were given</u> Undergraduate Research Awards, hands-on laboratory <u>research was experienced</u> by many undergraduates.

Revised | Because <u>NSERC gave</u> nearly four thousand students Undergraduate Research Awards, those <u>students experienced</u> hands-on laboratory research.

5b Sentence beginnings and endings

The beginning and ending of a sentence are the most emphatic positions, and the ending is usually more emphatic than the beginning. To emphasize information, place it first or last, reserving the middle for incidentals.

> Unemphatic   Education remains the single best means of economic advancement, despite its shortcomings.
>
> Revised   Education remains, despite its shortcomings, the single best means of economic advancement.

Generally, readers expect the beginning of a sentence to contain information that they already know or that you have already introduced. They then look to the ending for new information. In the unemphatic passage below, the second and third sentences both begin with new topics (underlined), while the old topics from the first sentence (the controversy and education) appear at the end:

> Unemphatic   Education almost means controversy these days, with rising costs and constant complaints about its inadequacies. The <u>value of schooling</u>, however, should not be obscured by the controversy. <u>The single best means of economic advancement</u>, despite its shortcomings, remains education.

In the revision below, the underlined old information begins each sentence and new information ends the sentence:

> Revised   Education almost means controversy these days, with rising costs and constant complaints about its inadequacies. The <u>controversy</u>, however, should not obscure the value of schooling. <u>Education</u> remains, despite its shortcomings, the single best means of economic advancement.

5c   Coordination and subordination

Clear sentences show the relationships between ideas and stress the more important ideas over the lesser ones. Two techniques, coordination° and subordination,° can help you achieve such clarity.

Coordination

Use **coordination** to show that two or more elements in a sentence are equally important in meaning.

- Link two complete sentences (main clauses°) with a comma and a coordinating conjunction° (*and, but, or, nor, for, so, yet*).

The first Calgary Stampede in 1912 <u>was a great success</u>, but <u>a second one was not held until 1919</u>. (*But* is a coordinating conjunction and must follow the comma.)

- Link two main clauses with a semicolon alone or a semicolon and a conjunctive adverb,° such as *however*, *indeed*, or *therefore*.

<u>The early Stampedes were cowboy shows</u>; <u>since 1923</u>, however, <u>the Stampede has included an agricultural exhibition</u>. (*However* is a conjunctive adverb and can move around within its clause. It usually sounds better in the middle of the clause, set off by a pair of commas. See pp. 78–79.)

- Within clauses, link words and word groups with a coordinating conjunction (*and, but, or, nor*) but not with a comma.

<u>Cowboys</u> and <u>city folk</u> alike <u>flocked to the bronco riding</u> or <u>thronged the chuckwagon racing events</u>.

- Link main clauses, words, or phrases° with a correlative conjunction° such as *not only . . . but also* or *either . . . or*.

Families not only <u>had fun</u> but also <u>learned about cattle ranching</u>.

Coordination clarifies meaning and smooths choppy sentences.

Choppy sentences	We should not rely so heavily on oil. Coal and uranium are also overused. We have a substantial energy resource in the moving waters of our rivers. Smaller streams add to the total volume of water. The resource renews itself. Coal and oil are irreplaceable. Uranium is also irreplaceable. The cost of water does not increase much over time. The costs of coal, oil, and uranium rise dramatically.
Ideas coordinated	We should not rely so heavily on coal, oil, <u>and</u> uranium, <u>for</u> we have a substantial energy resource in the moving waters of our rivers <u>and</u> streams. Coal, oil, <u>and</u> uranium are irreplaceable <u>and</u> thus subject to dramatic cost increases; water, <u>however</u>, is self-renewing <u>and</u> more stable in cost.

Notes A string of main clauses connected by *and* implies that all ideas are equally important and creates a dull, plodding rhythm. Use subordination (see the next section) to revise such excessive coordination.

Two punctuation errors, the comma splice and the fused sentence, can occur when you link main clauses. (See pp. 77–79.)

Subordination

Use **subordination** to indicate that some elements in a sentence are less important than others for your meaning. Usually, the main idea appears in the main clause,° and supporting information appears in subordinate structures:

5c

- Use a subordinate clause° beginning with a subordinating word such as *although, because, before, if, since, that, when, where, which,* or *who (whom).*

  Although production costs have declined, they are still high. [Stresses that costs are still high.]

  Costs, which include labour and facilities, are difficult to control. [Stresses that costs are difficult to control.]

- Use a phrase.°

  Despite some decline, production costs are still high.

  Costs, including labour and facilities, are difficult to control.

- Use a single word.

  Declining costs have not matched prices.
  Labour costs are difficult to control.

Subordination can transform a monotonous string of main clauses into a more emphatic and interesting passage. (See also p. 35.)

String of main clauses	In recent years computer prices have fallen, and production costs have fallen more slowly, and computer manufacturers have had to struggle, for their profits have been shrinking.
Revised	Because production costs have fallen more slowly than computer prices in recent years, computer manufacturers have had to struggle with shrinking profits.

Generally, subordinate clauses give the most emphasis to secondary information, phrases give less, and single words give the least.

Note A subordinate clause or a phrase is not a complete sentence and should not be set off and punctuated as one. See pages 75–77 on sentence fragments.

6 Conciseness

Concise writing makes every word count. Conciseness is not the same as mere brevity: detail and originality should not be cut with needless words. Rather, the length of an expression should be appropriate to the thought.

You may find yourself writing wordily when you are unsure of your subject or when your thoughts are tangled. It's fine, even necessary, to stumble and grope while drafting. But you should straighten out your ideas and eliminate wordiness during revision and editing.

6b

6a Focusing on the subject and verb

Using the subjects° and verbs° of your sentences for the key actors and actions will tighten sentences. See page 25 under Emphasis for a discussion of specific techniques:

- Avoid nouns made from verbs, such as *intention* (from *intend*) and *decision* (from *decide*).
- Strengthen weak verbs, such as *is* and *make*.
- Rewrite the passive voice as active—for instance, change *The star was seen* by astronomers to *Astronomers saw* the star.

6b Cutting empty words

Cutting words that contribute nothing to your meaning will make your writing move faster and work harder.

Wordy   In my opinion I think that the situation of the production of genetically modified food at this point in time is no different from the kind of plant breeding, namely through hybridization, for the purpose of improvement that has been going on more or less for centuries.

Concise   Today's genetically modified food is not so different from yesterday's hybridized plants.

The underlining in the wordy example above highlights the kinds of empty words described below.

- Some phrases add nothing to meaning:

all things considered   in a manner of speaking
a person by the name of   in my opinion

Visit www.mycanadiancomplab.ca for added help and exercises on usage and style.

as far as I'm concerned	last but not least
for all intents and purposes	more or less

- Some abstract or general words, along with other words they require (such as *the* and *of*), pad sentences:

area	element	kind	situation
aspect	factor	manner	thing
case	field	nature	type

6d

- Some word groups mean the same thing as single words:

For	Substitute
at all times	always
at the present time	now
at this point in time	now
for the purpose of	for
due to the fact that	because
because of the fact that	because
in the final analysis	finally

6c Cutting unneeded repetition

Repeating or restating key words from sentence to sentence can link the sentences and emphasize information the reader already knows (see p. 27). But unnecessary repetition weakens sentences and paragraphs.

> Wordy   Many unskilled workers <u>without training in a particular job</u> are unemployed and do not <u>have any work</u>.
>
> Concise   Many unskilled workers are unemployed.

Be especially alert to phrases that say the same thing twice. In the following examples, only the underlined words are needed:

<u>circle</u> around	<u>repeat</u> again
<u>consensus</u> of opinion	<u>return</u> again
<u>cooperate</u> together	<u>square</u> [round] in shape
<u>the future</u> to come	surrounding <u>circumstances</u>

6d Reducing clauses and phrases

Modifiers° can be expanded or contracted depending on the emphasis you want to achieve. (Generally, the longer a construction, the more emphasis it has.) When editing your sentences, consider whether any modifiers can be reduced without loss of emphasis or clarity.

> Wordy   The Channel Tunnel, <u>which runs between Britain and France</u>, bores through a bed of solid chalk that is thirty-seven kilometres across.

Concise	The Channel Tunnel <u>between Britain and France</u> bores through <u>thirty-seven kilometres of solid chalk</u>.

6e Cutting *there is* or *it is*

Sentences beginning *there is* or *it is* (called expletive constructions°) are sometimes useful to emphasize a change in direction, but usually they just add needless words.

Wordy	<u>There were delays and cost overruns that plagued</u> construction of the Channel Tunnel. <u>It is the expectation of investors</u> to earn profits at last, now that <u>there are trains passing</u> daily through the tunnel.
Concise	<u>Delays and cost overruns</u> plagued construction of the Channel Tunnel. <u>Investors expect</u> to earn profits at last, now that <u>trains pass</u> daily through the tunnel.

6f Combining sentences

Often the information in two or more sentences can be combined into one tight sentence.

Wordy	An unexpected problem with the Channel Tunnel is stowaways. The stowaways are mostly illegal immigrants. They are trying to smuggle themselves into England. They cling to train roofs and undercarriages.
Concise	An unexpected problem with the Channel Tunnel is stowaways, <u>mostly</u> illegal immigrants <u>who</u> are trying to smuggle themselves into England <u>by clinging</u> to train roofs and undercarriages.

7 Parallelism

Parallelism matches the form of your sentence to its meaning: when your ideas are equally important, or parallel, you express them in similar, or parallel, grammatical form.

Visit www.mycanadiancomplab.ca for
added help and exercises on usage and style.

The air is dirtied by <u>factories belching smoke</u> and <u>vehicles spewing exhaust</u>.

Parallelism can also work like glue to link the sentences of a paragraph as well as the parts of a sentence:

<u>Pulleys are ancient machines</u> for transferring power. Unfortunately, <u>they are also inefficient machines</u>.

7a   Parallelism with *and, but, or, nor, yet*

7b

The coordinating conjunctions° *and, but, or, nor,* and *yet* signal a need for parallelism.

The industrial base was <u>shifting</u> and <u>shrinking</u>.

Politicians seldom <u>acknowledged the problem</u> or <u>proposed alternatives</u>.

Industrial workers were understandably disturbed <u>that they were losing their jobs</u> and <u>that no one seemed to care</u>.

Nonparallel	Steel companies kept losing money because <u>their plants were inefficient</u>, <u>high labour costs</u>, and <u>foreign competition was increasing</u>.
Revised	Steel companies kept losing money because of <u>inefficient plants</u>, <u>high labour costs</u>, and <u>increasing foreign competition</u>.

Notes Parallel elements match in structure, but they need not match word for word. In the preceding example, each element consists of at least one modifier° and a noun,° but two of the elements also include an additional modifier.

Be careful not to omit needed words in parallel structures.

Nonparallel	Given training, workers can acquire the <u>skills</u> and <u>interest in</u> other jobs. [Idiom dictates different prepositions with *skills* and *interest*.]
Revised	Given training, workers can acquire the skills <u>for</u> and interest in other jobs.

7b   Parallelism with *both . . . and, either . . . or,* and so on

Correlative conjunctions° stress equality and balance between elements. Parallelism confirms the equality. The correlative conjunctions include *both . . . and, either . . . or, neither . . . nor, not only . . . but also,* and *whether . . . or.*

At the end of *The Stone Angel*, Hagar both <u>acknowledges her lifelong fear of love</u> and <u>affirms her feisty independence.</u>

With correlative conjunctions, the element after the second connector must match the element after the first connector.

7c   Parallelism with lists, headings, and outlines

8a

The items in a list or outline should be parallel. Parallelism is essential in the headings that divide a paper into sections (see pp. 217–18).

Nonparallel	Revised
Changes in Renaissance England	Changes in Renaissance England
1. Extension of trade routes	1. <u>Extension</u> of trade routes
2. Merchant class became more powerful	2. <u>Increased power</u> of the merchant class
3. The death of feudalism	3. <u>Death</u> of feudalism
4. Upsurging of the arts	4. <u>Upsurge</u> of the arts
5. Religious quarrels began	5. <u>Rise</u> of religious quarrels

8 Variety and Details

To make your writing interesting as well as clear, use varied sentences that are well textured with details.

8a   Varied sentence lengths and structures

In most contemporary writing, sentences tend to vary from about ten to about forty words, with an average of fifteen to twenty-five words. If your sentences are all at one extreme or the other, your readers may have difficulty locating main ideas and seeing the relations among them.

- Break a sequence of **long sentences** into shorter, simpler ones that stress key ideas.
- Combine a sequence of **short sentences** with coordination (pp. 27–29) and subordination (p. 29) to show relationships and stress main ideas.

Visit www.mycanadiancomplab.ca for
added help and exercises on usage and style.

A good way to focus and hold readers' attention is to vary the structure of sentences so that they do not all follow the same pattern.

Varied sentence structures

A long sequence of main clauses can make all ideas seem equally important and create a plodding rhythm, as in the unvaried passage below. Emphasize your key subjects and verbs, moving in each sentence from old information to new (see p. 26–27). Subordinating less important information (bracketed in the revised passage) can help you achieve this emphasis.

8a

Unvaried

The moon is now drifting away from the earth. It moves away about 2.5 cm a year. This movement is lengthening our days, and they increase about a thousandth of a second every century. Forty-seven of our present days will someday make up a month. We might eventually lose the moon altogether. Such great planetary movement rightly concerns astronomers, but it need not worry us. It will take 50 million years.

Revised

The moon is now drifting away from the earth [about 2.5 cm a year.] [At a thousandth of a second every century,] this movement is lengthening our days. Forty-seven of our present days will someday make up a month, [if we don't eventually lose the moon altogether.] Such great planetary movement rightly concerns astronomers, but it need not worry us. It will take 50 million years.

Varied sentence beginnings

An English sentence often begins with its subject, which generally captures old information from a preceding sentence (see p. 27):

Canadian hip-hop artist K'naan was born in Mogadishu, Somalia, in 1978. He moved with his family to Toronto when he was thirteen.

However, an unbroken sequence of sentences beginning with the subject quickly becomes monotonous:

Monotonous

K'naan could not speak English when he arrived in Toronto. He learned to rap phonetically by listening to records. Canadian promoter Sol Guy invited K'naan to perform at the United Nations in 1999. K'naan had experienced the civil war in Somalia as well as urban violence in Toronto, and he has consistently performed on behalf of human rights. He has received many awards for his humanitarian work, his music, and his spoken words.

Revised

K'naan could not speak English when he arrived in Toronto. By listening to records, however, he learned to rap phonetically. In 1999, Canadian promoter Sol Guy invited K'naan to perform at the United Nations. Having experienced the civil war in Somalia as well as urban violence in Toronto, K'naan has consistently performed on behalf of human rights. In recognition, he has received many awards for his humanitarian work, his music, and his spoken words.

The underlined expressions represent the most common choices for varying sentence beginnings:

- Adverb modifiers, such as *In 1999* (modifies the verb *invited*).
- Adjective modifiers, such as *Having experienced the civil war in Somalia* (modifies *K'naan*).
- Transitional expressions, such as *however*. (See *transitional expression*, p. 260, for a list.)

Varied word order

Occasionally, to achieve special emphasis, reverse the usual word order of a sentence.

K'naan's hit single, "Wavin' Flag: The Celebration Mix," was chosen as the official anthem for the 2010 FIFA World Cup in South Africa. Celebration and unity, he hopes, will result from the song. [Compare normal word order: *The song, he hopes, will result in celebration and unity.*]

8b Details

Relevant details such as facts and examples create the texture and life that keep readers alert and help them grasp your meaning. For instance,

Flat

Built in Montreal harbour, the former Expo '67 site is a popular place for sports and also features other attractions.

Detailed

Built on a green archipelago of natural and artificial islands in Montreal harbour, the former Expo '67 site is a popular place for walking, cycling, rowing, swimming, and ice skating, and also features international gardens, a casino, a theatre, and a museum.

9 Appropriate Words

English-speaking Canadians share a common language, but sometimes they speak it quite differently. Newfoundland English has a vocabulary, syntax, and pronunciation all its own. To a lesser extent, so does Quebec English, the English of the Ottawa Valley, and the English of the Prairies. Canadians who speak indigenous languages such as Cree, Mohawk, and Inuktitut may flavour their English with syntax and idiom borrowed from their languages. Canadians from many regional and ethnic backgrounds have enriched our common English language.

Nevertheless, most academic and business writing calls for **standard English**, usually defined as the English expected and used by educated English-speaking people. Therefore, in academic and business writing, use regional and ethnic dialect words and phrases cautiously, only when you are aiming for a particular effect with a particular audience. In all cases, avoid words and expressions that your readers might find confusing, hurtful, or insulting.

9a Nonstandard dialect

Like many countries, Canada includes several regional, social, and ethnic groups that have their own distinct **dialects**, or versions of English: standard English, Newfoundland English, West Indian English, and Ottawa Valley English are examples. English-speaking Quebecers frequently use words and expressions borrowed from French, giving their English a unique flavour.

If you normally speak a dialect version of English, be aware that in academic or business writing, where audiences usually expect standard English, your dialect words and expressions may be misunderstood or perceived as mistakes.

Edit your drafts to eliminate dialect expressions, especially those that dictionaries label "nonstandard," such as *this here school, that there building, them books, knowed, throwed, eh, didn't ought, hadn't ought, didn't never, could of, would of, should of, that house there, I think me, I done it, I seen it.*

Visit www.mycanadiancomplab.ca for
added help and exercises on usage and style.

9b Slang

Slang is the insider language used by a group, such as bloggers, musicians, and hockey players, to reflect common experiences and to make technical references efficient. For example, a blogger may write blogs, blawgs, dreamlogs, splogs, vlogs, slogs, linklogs, moblogs, or tumblelogs. If interrupted while tweeting on Twitter or microblogging on MSN, some bloggers type "TTYL" or "BRB." Many blogs are described as granular, and a few go viral in the blogosphere.

Though valuable within a group, slang is often too private or imprecise for academic or business writing.

9c Colloquial language

Colloquial language is the everyday spoken language, including expressions such as *go crazy*, *get along with*, *a lot*, *kids* (for *children*), and *stuff* (for possessions or other objects). Dictionaries label this language "informal" or "colloquial."

Colloquial language suits informal writing, and an occasional colloquial word can help you achieve a desired emphasis in otherwise formal writing. But most colloquial language is not precise enough for academic or career writing.

9d Technical words

All disciplines and professions rely on specialized language that allows the members to communicate precisely and efficiently with each other. Chemists, for instance, have their *phosphatides,* soccer players have their *offside rule*, and literary critics have their *subtexts.* Use the terms of a discipline or profession when you are writing within it.

When you are writing for a nonspecialist audience, however, avoid unnecessary technical terms and carefully define the terms you must use.

9e Indirect and pretentious writing

Small, plain, and direct words are usually preferable to big, showy, or evasive words. Take special care to avoid the following:

- **Euphemisms** are presumably inoffensive words that substitute for words deemed potentially offensive or too blunt, such as *passed away* for *died* or *misspeak* for *lie.* Use euphemisms only when you know that

blunt, truthful words would needlessly hurt or offend
members of your audience.

- **Double-talk** (at times called **doublespeak** or **weasel
  words**) is language intended to confuse or to be misunderstood: the *revenue enhancement* that is really
  a tax, the *biodegradable* bags that still last decades.
  Double-talk has no place in honest writing.
- **Pretentious writing** is fancy language that is more
  elaborate than its subject requires. Choose your words
  for their exactness and economy. The big, ornate word
  may be tempting, but pass it up. Your readers will be
  grateful.

Pretentious	Many institutions of higher education rec-ognize the need for youth at the thresh-old of maturity to confront the choice of life's endeavour and thus require students to select a field of concentration.
Revised	Many colleges and universities force stu-dents to make decisions about their careers by requiring them to select a major.

9f   Sexist and other biased language

Even when we do not mean it to, our language can
reflect and perpetuate hurtful prejudices toward groups
of people. Such biased language can be obvious—words
such as *nigger, honky, mick, kike, fag, dyke,* or *broad.*
But it can also be subtle, generalizing about groups in
ways that may be familiar but that are also inaccurate
or unfair.

Biased language reflects poorly on the user, not on
the person or persons whom it mischaracterizes or insults.
Unbiased language does not submit to false generalizations. It treats people respectfully as individuals and labels
groups as they wish to be labelled.

Stereotypes of race, ethnicity, and other characteristics

A **stereotype** characterizes and judges people simply
on the basis of their membership in a group: *Men are
uncommunicative. Women are emotional. Maritimers expect
welfare. Westerners are rednecks.*

In your writing, avoid statements about the traits
of whole groups that may be true of only some members. Be especially cautious about substituting such
statements for the evidence you should be providing
instead.

Stereotype	Elderly drivers should have their licences limited to daytime driving only. [Asserts that all elderly people are poor night drivers.]
Revised	Drivers with impaired night vision should have their licences limited to daytime driving only.

Some stereotypes have become part of the language, but they are still potentially offensive.

Stereotype	The administrators are too blind to see the need for a new gymnasium.
Revised	The administrators do not understand the need for a new gymnasium.

9f

Sexist language

Sexist language distinguishes needlessly between men and women in such matters as occupation, ability, behaviour, temperament, and maturity. It can wound or irritate readers, and it indicates the writer's thoughtlessness or unfairness. The following guidelines can help you eliminate sexist language from your writing:

- Avoid demeaning and patronizing language—for instance, identifying women and men differently or trivializing either gender.

Sexist	Dr. Keith Kim and Lydia Hawkins co-authored the article.
Revised	Dr. Keith Kim and Dr. Lydia Hawkins co-authored the article.
Revised	Keith Kim and Lydia Hawkins co-authored the article.
Sexist	Ladies are entering almost every occupation formerly filled by men.
Revised	Women are entering almost every occupation formerly filled by men.

- Avoid occupational or social stereotypes that assume a role or profession is exclusively male or female.

Sexist	The considerate doctor commends a nurse when she provides his patients with good care.
Revised	The considerate doctor commends a nurse who provides good care for patients.

- Avoid using *man* or words containing *man* to refer to all human beings. Some alternatives:

businessman	businessperson
chairman	chair, chairperson
craftsman	craftsperson, artisan
layman	layperson
mankind	humankind, humanity, human beings, people
manpower	personnel, human resources
policeman	police officer
salesman	salesperson, sales representative

9f

Sexist   <u>Man</u> has not reached the limits of social justice.

Revised   <u>Humankind</u> [or <u>Humanity</u>] has not reached the limits of social justice.

Sexist   The furniture consists of <u>manmade</u> materials.

Revised   The furniture consists of <u>synthetic</u> materials.

- Avoid using *he* to refer to both genders. (See also pp. 64–65.)

Sexist   The newborn <u>child</u> explores <u>his</u> world.

Revised   Newborn <u>children</u> explore <u>their</u> world. [Use the plural for the pronoun and the word it refers to.]

Revised   The newborn <u>child</u> explores <u>the</u> world. [Avoid the pronoun altogether.]

Revised   The newborn <u>child</u> explores <u>his or her</u> world. [Substitute male and female pronouns.]

Use the last option sparingly—only once in a group of sentences and only to stress the singular individual.

Inappropriate labels

Labels for groups of people can be shorthand stereotypes and can be discourteous when they ignore readers' preferences. Although sometimes dismissed as "political correctness," sensitivity in applying labels hurts no one and helps gain your readers' trust and respect.

Use labels only when relevant. If the information is not necessary, don't use it.

- Avoid labels that (intentionally or not) disparage the person or group you refer to. A person with emotional problems is not a *mental patient*. A person with cancer is not a *cancer victim*. A person using a wheelchair is not *wheelchair-bound*.

- Use names for racial, ethnic, and other groups that reflect the preferences of each group's members, or at least many of them. Examples of current preferences include *First Nations* (for Canadians descended from Aboriginal peoples), *Inuit* (rather than Eskimo), and *people with disabilities* (rather than *the handicapped*). But the acceptability of labels changes often. To learn how a group's members wish to be labelled, ask them directly, attend to usage in reputable periodicals, or check a recent dictionary.

10a

10 Exact Words

To write clearly and effectively, you will want to find the words that fit your meaning exactly and convey your attitude precisely.

10a The right word for your meaning

One key to helping readers understand you is to use words according to their established meanings.

- Become acquainted with a dictionary. Consult it whenever you are unsure of a word's meaning.
- Distinguish between similar-sounding words that have widely different meanings.

Inexact   Older people often suffer <u>infirmaries</u> [places for the sick].

Exact   Older people often suffer <u>infirmities</u> [disabilities].

Some words, called **homonyms,** sound exactly alike but differ in meaning: for example, *principal/-principle* or *rain/reign/rein.* (Many homonyms and near-homonyms are listed in the Glossary of Usage, p. 239.)

- Distinguish between words with related but distinct meanings.

Visit www.mycanadiancomplab.ca for added help and exercises on usage and style.

| Inexact | Television commercials <u>continuously</u> [unceasingly] interrupt programming. |
| Exact | Television commercials <u>continually</u> [regularly] interrupt programming. |

- Distinguish between words that have similar basic meanings but different emotional associations, or **connotations**.

It is a <u>daring</u> plan. [The plan is bold and courageous.]
It is a <u>reckless</u> plan. [The plan is thoughtless and risky.]

10c

Many dictionaries list and distinguish such **synonyms**, words with approximately, but often not exactly, the same meanings.

10b Concrete and specific words

Clear, exact writing balances abstract and general words, which outline ideas and objects, with concrete and specific words, which sharpen and solidify.

- **Abstract words** name qualities and ideas: *beautiful, management, culture, freedom, awesome.* **Concrete words** name things we can know by our five senses of sight, hearing, touch, taste, and smell: *sleek, humming, brick, bitter, musty.*
- **General words** name classes or groups of things, such as *buildings, weather,* or *birds,* and include all the varieties of the class. **Specific words** limit a general class, such as *buildings,* by naming one of its varieties, such as *skyscraper, Victorian courthouse,* or *hut.*

Abstract and general statements need development with concrete and specific details. For example,

| Vague | The size of his hands made his smallness real. [How big were his hands? How small was he?] |
| Exact | Not until I saw his delicate, doll-like hands did I realize that he stood a full head shorter than most other men. |

10c Idioms

Idioms are expressions in any language that do not fit the rules for meaning or grammar—for instance, *put up with, plug away at, make off with.*

Because they are not governed by rules, idioms usually cause particular difficulty for people learning to speak and write a new language. But even native speakers of English misuse some idioms involving prepositions,° such as *agree <u>on</u> a plan, agree <u>to</u> a proposal,* and *agree <u>with</u> a person* or *occupied <u>by</u> a person, occupied <u>in</u> study,* and *occupied <u>with</u> a thing.*

When in doubt about an idiom, consult your dictionary under the main word (*agree* and *occupy* in the examples). (See also p. 52 on verbs with particles and pp. 149–50 on signal phrases.)

10d Clichés

Clichés, or **trite expressions**, are phrases or metaphors so old and so often repeated that they have become stale. Examples include *better late than never, beyond the shadow of a doubt, face the music, green with envy, ladder of success, at the end of the day, point with pride, sneaking suspicion,* and *wise as an owl.*

Clichés may slide into your drafts. In editing, be wary of any expression you have heard or used before. Substitute fresh words of your own, or restate the idea in plain language.

PART III

Grammatical Sentences

PEARSON
mycanadiancomplab

Visit the **Resources** tab in MyCanadianCompLab and click on **Grammar** to access grammar, punctuation, and mechanics exercises that will help you improve your writing skills and get a better grade in your course.

Grammatical Sentences

This checklist focuses on the most common and potentially confusing grammatical errors. See the contents inside the back cover for a more detailed guide to this part.

Verbs

☑ Use the correct forms of irregular verbs such as *has broken* [not *has broke*]. (See pp. 47–48.)

☑ Use helping verbs where required, as in *she has been* [not *she been*]. (See pp. 48–50.)

☑ Match verbs to their subjects, as in *The list of items is* [not *are*] *long.* (See pp. 57–60.)

Pronouns

☑ Match pronouns to the words they refer to, as in *Each of the women had her* [not *their*] *say.* (See pp. 63–65.)

☑ Make pronouns refer clearly to the words they substitute for, avoiding uncertainties such as *Jill thanked Tracy when she* [Jill or Tracy?] *arrived.* (See pp. 65–67.)

☑ Use pronouns consistently, avoiding shifts such as *When one enters university, you meet new ideas.* (See p. 67.)

Modifiers

☑ Place modifiers close to the words they describe, as in *Trash cans without lids invite animals* [not *Trash cans invite animals without lids*]. (See pp. 72–73.)

☑ Make each modifier clearly modify another word in the sentence, as in *Jogging, she pulled a muscle* [not *Jogging, a muscle was pulled*]. (See p. 74.)

Sentence faults

☑ Make every sentence complete, with its own subject and verb, and be sure none is a freestanding subordinate clause— for instance, *But first she called the police* [not *But first called the police*]; *New stores open weekly* [not *New stores weekly*]; and *The new cow calved after the others did* [not *The new cow calved. After the others did*]. (See pp. 75–77.)

☑ Within sentences, link main clauses with a comma and a coordinating conjunction (*Cars jam the roadways, and they contribute to smog*), with a semicolon (*Many parents did not attend; they did not want to get involved*), or with a semicolon and a conjunctive adverb (*The snow fell heavily; however, it soon melted*). (See pp. 77–79.)

PARTS OF SPEECH

Traditionally, English grammarians divided words into categories that explained how those words functioned in an English sentence. These categories are called **parts of speech**. A word can serve as more than one part of speech depending on its form and its place in a sentence.

The strike [noun] ended the game.

Why did he strike [verb] the bell?

That dress looks striking on you [adjective].

Below is a sentence with parts of speech labelled. Each part of speech is defined in the Glossary of Terms on pages 249–61.

11a

definite article	adverb	adjective	noun (subject)	adverb	verb	indefinite article
The	stylishly	dressed	server	carefully	handed	a

adjective	noun (direct object)	preposition	proper noun (indirect object)
brimming	glass	to	Carl.

VERBS

11 Verb Forms

Verb forms may give you trouble when the verb is irregular, when you omit certain endings, or when you need to use helping verbs.

11a Sing/sang/sung and other irregular verbs

Most verbs are **regular**: their past-tense form° and past participle° end in -*d* or -*ed*:

Today the birds migrate. [Plain form° of verb.]

Yesterday the birds migrated. [Past-tense form.]

In the past the birds have migrated. [Past participle.]

Visit www.mycanadiancomplab.ca for added help and exercises on basic grammar.

About two hundred **irregular verbs** in English create their past-tense form and past participle in some way besides adding *-d* or *-ed*.

> Today the birds <u>fly</u>. They <u>begin</u> migration. [Plain form.]
>
> Yesterday the birds <u>flew</u>. They <u>began</u> migration. [Past-tense form.]
>
> In the past the birds have <u>flown</u>. They have <u>begun</u> migration. [Past participle.]

You can find a verb's forms by looking up the plain form in a dictionary. For a regular verb, the dictionary will give the *-d* or *-ed* form. For an irregular verb, the dictionary will give the past-tense form and then the past participle. If the dictionary gives only one irregular form after the plain form, then the past-tense form and past participle are the same (*think, thought, thought*).

11b

11b Helping verbs

Helping verbs combine with some verb forms to indicate time and other kinds of meanings, as in *can run, might suppose, will open, was sleeping, had been eaten*. The main verb° in these phrases is the one that carries the main meaning (*run, suppose, open, sleeping, eaten*).

Required helping verbs

Standard English requires helping verbs in certain situations:

- The main verb ends in *-ing:*

  Archaeologists <u>are</u> conducting fieldwork all over the world. [Not *Archaeologists conducting. . . .*]

- The main verb is *been* or *be:*

  Many <u>have</u> been fortunate in their discoveries. [Not *Many been. . . .*]

  Some <u>could</u> be real-life Indiana Joneses. [Not *Some be. . . .*]

- The main verb is a past participle,° such as *talked, begun,* or *thrown:*

  The researchers <u>have</u> given interviews on TV. [Not *The researchers given. . . .*]

In these examples, omitting the helping verb would create an incomplete sentence, or sentence fragment (p. 75).

Combinations of helping and main verbs ESL

Helping verbs and main verbs combine in specific ways.

Note The main verb in a verb phrase (the one carrying the main meaning) does not change to show a change in subject or time: *she has <u>sung</u>, you had <u>sung</u>.* Only the helping verb may change, as in these examples.

Form of *be* + present participle

Create the progressive tenses° with *be, am, is, are, was, were,* or *been* followed by the main verb's present participle° (ending in *-ing*).

11b

| Faulty | She <u>is work</u> on a new book. |
| Revised | She <u>is working</u> on a new book. |

| Faulty | She <u>has been work</u> on it for several months. |
| Revised | She <u>has been working</u> on it for several months. |

Note Verbs that express mental states or activities rather than physical actions do not usually appear in the progressive tenses. These verbs include *adore, appear, believe, belong, have, hear, know, like, love, need, see, seem, taste, think, understand,* and *want.*

| Faulty | She <u>is wanting</u> to understand contemporary ethics. |
| Revised | She <u>wants</u> to understand contemporary ethics. |

Form of *be* + past participle

Create the passive voice° with *be, am, is, are, was, were, being,* or *been* followed by the main verb's past participle° (usually ending in *-d* or *-ed* or, for irregular verbs, in *-t* or *-n*).

| Faulty | Her last book <u>was complete</u> in four months. |
| Revised | Her last book <u>was completed</u> in four months. |

| Faulty | It <u>was bring</u> to the premier's attention. |
| Revised | It <u>was brought</u> to the premier's attention. |

Note Only transitive verbs° may form the passive voice.

| Faulty | A philosophy conference <u>was occurred</u> that week. [*Occur* is not a transitive verb.] |
| Revised | A philosophy conference <u>occurred</u> that week. |

Form of have + past participle

To create one of the perfect tenses,° use the main verb's past participle preceded by a form of *have,* such as *has, had, have been,* or *will have had.*

Faulty   Some students <u>have complain</u> about the lab.
Revised   Some students <u>have complained</u> about the lab.

Faulty   Money <u>has</u> not <u>been spend</u> on the lab in years.
Revised   Money <u>has</u> not <u>been spent</u> on the lab in years.

Form of *do* + plain form

Three forms of *do* serve as helping verbs with the plain form° of the main verb: *do, does, did.*

Faulty   Safety concerns <u>do exists</u>.
Revised   Safety concerns <u>do exist</u>.

Faulty   <u>Didn't</u> the lab <u>closed</u> briefly last year?
Revised   <u>Didn't</u> the lab <u>close</u> briefly last year?

Modal + plain form

Most **modal** helping verbs combine with the plain form of the main verb to convey ability, possibility, necessity, and other meanings. The modals include *be able to, be supposed to, can, could, had better, have to, may, might, must, ought to, shall, should, used to, will,* and *would.*

Faulty   The lab equipment <u>may causes</u> injury.
Revised   The lab equipment <u>may cause</u> injury.

Faulty   The school <u>ought to replaced</u> it.
Revised   The school <u>ought to replace</u> it.

Note   When a modal combines with another helping verb, the main verb generally changes from the plain form to a past participle:

Faulty   The equipment <u>could have fail</u>.
Revised   The equipment <u>could have failed</u>.

11c   Verb + gerund or infinitive ESL

A **gerund** is the *-ing* form of a verb used as a noun (<u>*Smoking kills*</u>). An **infinitive** is the plain form° of the verb plus *to* (*Try <u>to quit</u>*). Some verbs are followed by gerunds, some by infinitives, and some by either. And sometimes the use of a gerund or infinitive with the same verb changes the meaning of the verb.

Either gerund or infinitive

A gerund or an infinitive may follow these verbs with no significant difference in meaning: *begin, can't bear, can't stand, continue, hate, like, love, prefer, start.*

The pump began <u>working</u>. The pump began <u>to work</u>.

Meaning change with gerund or infinitive

With four verbs—*forget, remember, stop,* and *try*—a gerund has quite a different meaning from an infinitive.

The engineer stopped <u>watching</u> the pump. [She no longer watched.]

The engineer stopped <u>to watch</u> the pump. [She stopped in order to watch.]

11c

Gerund, not infinitive

Do not use an infinitive after these verbs: *admit, adore, appreciate, avoid, consider, deny, detest, discuss, dislike, enjoy, escape, finish, imagine, keep, mind, miss, practise, put off, quit, recall, recommend, resent, resist, risk, suggest, tolerate, understand.*

Faulty   She suggested <u>to check</u> the pump.

Revised   She suggested <u>checking</u> the pump.

Infinitive, not gerund

Do not use a gerund after these verbs: *agree, allow, ask, assent, beg, claim, decide, expect, have, hesitate, hope, manage, mean, offer, plan, pretend, promise, refuse, say, wait, want, wish.*

Faulty   She decided <u>checking</u> the pump.

Revised   She decided <u>to check</u> the pump.

Noun or pronoun + infinitive

Some verbs may be followed by an infinitive alone or by a noun° or pronoun° and an infinitive: *ask, beg, choose, dare, expect, help, need, promise, want, wish, would like.* A noun or pronoun changes the meaning.

She expected <u>to watch</u>.

She expected <u>her workers</u> <u>to watch</u>.

Some verbs *must* be followed by a noun or pronoun before an infinitive: *advise, allow, cause, challenge, command, convince, encourage, forbid, force, hire, instruct, order, permit, persuade, remind, require, teach, tell, warn.*

She instructed <u>her workers to watch</u>.

When these verbs are used in the passive voice,° they still require infinitives, not gerunds:

Faulty   He's allowed <u>crossing</u> the street.

Revised   He's allowed <u>to cross</u> the street.

Do not use *to* before the infinitive when it comes after one of the following verbs and a noun or pronoun: *feel, have, hear, let, make* ("force"), *see, watch.*

She let her workers <u>learn</u> by observation.

11d Verb + particle ESL

11d

Some verbs consist of two words: the verb itself and a **particle,** a preposition° or adverb° that affects the meaning of the verb, as in <u>*Look up*</u> *the answer* (research the answer) or <u>*Look over*</u> *the answer* (check the answer). Many of these two-word verbs, also called idioms, are defined in dictionaries. (For more on idioms, see pp. 43–44.)

Some two-word verbs may be separated in a sentence; others may not.

Inseparable two-word verbs

Verbs and particles that may not be separated by any other words include the following: *catch on, get along, give in, go out, grow up, keep on, look into, run into, run out of, speak up, stay away, take care of.*

Faulty   Children <u>grow</u> quickly up.

Revised   Children <u>grow up</u> quickly.

Separable two-word verbs

Most two-word verbs that take direct objects° may be separated by the object.

Parents <u>help out</u> their children.

Parents <u>help</u> their children <u>out</u>.

If the direct object is a pronoun,° the pronoun *must* separate the verb from the particle.

Faulty   Parents <u>help out</u> them.

Revised   Parents <u>help</u> them <u>out</u>.

The separable two-word verbs include the following: *call off, call up, fill out, fill up, give away, give back, hand in, help out, look over, look up, pick up, point out, put away, put back, put off, take out, take over, try on, try out, turn down.*

12 Verb Tenses

The **tense** of a verb expresses the time its action occurred. Definitions and examples of the verb tenses appear on pages 259–60. The following are the most common trouble spots.

12a Uses of the present tense (*sing*)

Most academic and business writing uses the past tense° (*the rebellion occurred*), but the present tense has several distinctive uses:

Action occurring now
We <u>define</u> the problem differently.

Habitual or recurring action
Banks regularly <u>undergo</u> audits.

A general truth
The earth <u>is</u> round.

Discussion of literature, film, and so on
Huckleberry Finn <u>has</u> adventures we all envy.

Future time
Funding <u>ends</u> in less than a year.

12b Uses of the perfect tenses (*have/had/ will have sung*)

The perfect tenses° generally indicate an action completed before another specific time or action. The present perfect tense° also indicates action begun in the past and continued into the present.

present perfect
The dancer <u>has performed</u> here only once.

past perfect
The dancer <u>had trained</u> in Asia before his performance here ten years ago.

future perfect
He <u>will have danced</u> here again by next month.

Visit www.mycanadiancomplab.ca for
added help and exercises on basic grammar.

12c Consistency in tense

Within a sentence, the tenses of verbs and verb forms need not be identical as long as they reflect actual changes in time: *Our children will enjoy the trees we planted that summer after we bought the house.* But needless shifts in tense will confuse or distract readers.

12d

Inconsistent	After weeks of preparation, the Canadian Corps attacked the German trenches at Vimy Ridge during Easter 1917. The Canadian troops, who fight together for the first time at Vimy, lose over ten thousand men in the battle.
Revised	fter weeks of preparation, the Canadian Corps attacked the German trenches at Vimy Ridge during Easter 1917. The Canadian troops, who fought together for the first time at Vimy, lost over ten thousand men in the battle.

12d Sequence of tenses

When the tenses in a sentence are in **sequence,** the verbs in the main clause° and the subordinate clause° relate appropriately for meaning. Problems with tense sequence often occur with the past tense and past perfect tense.°

Faulty	Researchers ^{past}tried to review the study, but many of the original participants ^{past}died.
Revised	Researchers ^{past}tried to review the study, but many of the original participants ^{past perfect}had died. [The deaths had occurred before the review.]
Faulty	Because other participants ^{past}refused interviews, the review ^{past perfect}had been terminated.
Revised	Because other participants ^{past}refused interviews, the review ^{past}was terminated. [The refusal occurred before the termination.]

Other tense-sequence problems occur with the distinctive verb forms of **conditional sentences,** in which a subordinate clause begins with *if, when,* or *unless* and the main clause states the result.

Faulty	If voters ^{present}have more confidence, they ^{would + verb}would vote more often.

Revised   If voters <u>had</u> more confidence, they <u>would vote</u>
past   would + verb
more often.

See below for more on verbs in conditional sentences.

13   Verb Mood

The **mood** of a verb indicates whether a sentence is a
statement or a question (*The theatre <u>needs</u> help. <u>Can</u> you
<u>help</u> the theatre?*), a command (*<u>Help</u> the theatre*), or a sug-
gestion, desire, or other nonfactual expression (*I wish I
<u>were</u> an actor*).

13a

13a   Subjunctive mood: *I wish I were*

The **subjunctive mood** expresses a suggestion,
requirement, or desire, or it states a condition that is contrary to fact (that is, imaginary or hypothetical).

- Suggestion or requirement with the verb *ask, insist,
  urge, require, recommend,* or *suggest:* use the verb's
  plain form° with all subjects.

  Rules require that every donation <u>be</u> mailed.

- Desire or present condition contrary to fact: use the
  verb's past-tense form°; for *be,* use the past-tense form
  were.

  If the theatre <u>were</u> in better shape and <u>had</u> more money,
  its future would be guaranteed.

  I wish I <u>were</u> able to donate money.

- Past condition contrary to fact: use the verb's past
  perfect form° (*had* + past participle).

  The theatre would be better funded if it <u>had been</u> better
  managed.

Note   In a sentence expressing a condition contrary
to fact, (1) use *have,* not *of,* after *would* or *could* in the
main clause; and (2) do not use *would* or *could* in the subordinate clause:

Faulty   People <u>would of</u> helped if they <u>would have</u>
known.

Revised   People <u>would have</u> helped if they <u>had</u>
known.

Visit **www.mycanadiancomplab.ca** for
added help and exercises on basic grammar.

13b | Consistency in mood

Shifts in mood within a sentence or among related sentences can be confusing. Such shifts occur most frequently in directions.

Inconsistent   <u>Dissolve</u> the crystals in the liquid. Then <u>you should heat</u> the solution to 120°C. [The first sentence is a command, the second a statement.]

Revised   <u>Dissolve</u> the crystals in the liquid. Then <u>heat</u> the solution to 120°C. [Consistent commands.]

14 Verb Voice

The **voice** of a verb tells whether the subject° of the sentence performs the action (**active voice**) or is acted upon (**passive voice**).

Active voice   Commercial services <u>expand</u> participation on the Internet.

Passive voice   Participation on the Internet <u>is expanded</u> by commercial services.

14a | Active voice vs. passive voice

The active voice always names the actor in a sentence (whoever performs the verb's action), whereas the passive voice puts the actor in a phrase after the verb or even omits the actor altogether. Thus, the active voice is usually more clear, emphatic, and concise than the passive voice.

Weak passive   Initially, the <u>Internet was used</u> for research by scholars, and its <u>expansion</u> to the general public <u>was criticized</u> by some.

Strong active   Initially, <u>scholars used</u> the Internet for research, and <u>some criticized</u> its expansion to the general public.

The passive voice is useful in two situations: when the actor is unknown and when the actor is unimportant or less important than the object of the action.

Visit www.mycanadiancomplab.ca for
added help and exercises on basic grammar.

The Internet was established in 1969 by the US Department of Defense. The network has now been extended both nationally and internationally. [In the first sentence the writer wishes to stress the Internet. In the second sentence the actor is unknown or too complicated to name.]

After the solution had been cooled to 10°C, the acid was added. [The person who cooled and added, perhaps the writer, is less important than the actions. Passive sentences are common in scientific writing.]

Some writers use the passive voice because they mistakenly believe that it sounds elegant. Unless you intend to emphasize the *object of the action* over the *actor*, avoid the passive voice.

15a

14b Consistency in voice

A shift in voice (and subject) within or between sentences can be awkward or even confusing.

| Inconsistent | Commercial services provide fairly inexpensive Internet access, and navigation is made easy by them. |
| Revised | Commercial services provide fairly inexpensive Internet access, and they make navigation easy. |

15 Agreement of Subject and Verb

A subject° and its verb° should agree in number°—singular with singular, plural with plural.

Cape Breton artists excel at traditional Celtic music.
subject   verb

Ashley MacIsaac is a superb fiddler.
subject   verb

15a -s ending for noun or verb, but not both

An -*s* or -*es* ending does opposite things to nouns and verbs: it usually makes a noun *plural*, but it always makes a present-tense verb *singular*. Thus if the subject noun is plural, it will probably end in -*s* or -*es* and the verb will not. If the subject is singular, it will not end in -*s* and the verb will.

Visit www.mycanadiancomplab.ca for
added help and exercises on basic grammar.

Singular noun	Plural noun
The <u>boy</u> plays.	The <u>boys</u> <u>play</u>.
The <u>bird</u> soars.	The <u>birds</u> <u>soar</u>.
The <u>street</u> is busy.	The <u>streets</u> <u>are</u> busy.
The <u>town</u> has a traffic problem.	The <u>towns</u> <u>have</u> a traffic problem.
The new <u>light</u> does not [or doesn't] help.	The new <u>lights</u> <u>do</u> not [or <u>don't</u>] help.

ESL Most noncount nouns—those that do not form plurals—take singular verbs: *That <u>information</u> <u>is</u> helpful.* (See pp. 71–72 for more on noncount nouns.)

15 d

15b   Words between subject and verb

An academic <u>calendar</u> of courses and requirements often <u>baffles</u> [not <u>baffle</u>] students.

The <u>requirements</u> stated in the calendar <u>are</u> [not <u>is</u>] unclear.

Phrases beginning with *as well as, together with, along with,* and *in addition to* do not change the number of the subject.

The <u>president</u>, as well as the deans, <u>has</u> [not <u>have</u>] agreed to revise the calendar.

15c   Subjects with *and*

<u>Frost and Roethke</u> <u>were</u> American poets who died in the same year.

Note When *each* or *every* precedes the compound subject, the verb is usually singular.

<u>Each</u> man, woman, and child <u>has</u> a right to be heard.

15d   Subjects with *or* or *nor*

When parts of a subject are joined by *or* or *nor*, the verb agrees with the nearer part.

Either the painter or the <u>carpenter</u> <u>knows</u> the cost.

The cabinets or the <u>bookcases</u> <u>are</u> too costly.

When one part of the subject is singular and the other is plural, the sentence will be awkward unless you put the plural part second.

Awkward   Neither the owners nor the <u>builder</u> <u>agrees</u>.

Improved   Neither the builder nor the <u>owners</u> <u>agree</u>.

15e   *Everyone* and other indefinite pronouns

Indefinite pronouns° include *anybody, anyone, each, everybody, everyone, neither, no one, one,* and *somebody.* Most are singular in meaning and take singular verbs.

Something smells.   Neither is right.

A few indefinite pronouns such as *all, any, none,* and *some* may take a singular or plural verb depending on whether the word they refer to is singular or plural.

All of the money is reserved for emergencies.

All of the funds are reserved for emergencies.

15h

15f   *Team* and other collective nouns

A collective noun° such as *team* or *family* takes a singular verb when the group acts as a unit.

The group agrees that action is necessary.

But when the group's members act separately, use a plural verb.

The old group have gone their separate ways.

15g   *Who, which,* and *that*

When used as subjects, *who, which,* and *that* refer to another word in the sentence. The verb agrees with this other word.

Mayor Garber ought to listen to the people who work for her.

Bardini is the only aide who has her ear.

Bardini is one of the aides who work unpaid. [Of the aides who work unpaid, Bardini is one.]

Bardini is the only one of the aides who knows the community. [Of the aides, only one, Bardini, knows the community.]

15h   *News* and other singular nouns ending in *-s*

Singular nouns° ending in *-s* include *athletics, economics, mathematics, measles, mumps, news, physics, politics,* and *statistics.*

After so long a wait, the news has to be good.

Statistics is required of psychology majors.

These words take plural verbs when they describe individual items rather than whole bodies of activity or knowledge.

The statistics prove him wrong.

15i Inverted word order

Is voting a right or a privilege?

Are a right and a privilege the same thing?

There are differences between them.

15j *Is, are,* and other linking verbs

Make a linking verb° agree with its subject, usually the first element in the sentence, not with other words referring to the subject.

The child's sole support is her court-appointed guardians.

Her court-appointed guardians are the child's sole support.

PRONOUNS

16 Pronoun Forms

A noun° or pronoun° changes form to show the reader how it functions in a sentence. These forms—called **cases**—are **subjective** (such as *I, she, they, man*), **objective** (such as *me, her, them, man*), and **possessive** (such as *my, her, their, man's*). A list of the case forms appears on pages 249–50.

Visit www.mycanadiancomplab.ca for
added help and exercises on basic grammar.

16a   Compound subjects and objects: *she* and *I* vs. *her* and *me*

Subjects° and objects° consisting of two or more nouns and pronouns have the same case forms as they would if one pronoun stood alone.

compound subject
<u>She and Ming</u> discussed the proposal.

compound object
The proposal disappointed <u>her and him</u>.

To test for the correct form, try one pronoun alone in the sentence. The case form that sounds correct is probably correct for all parts of the compound.

The prize went to [<u>he, him</u>] and [<u>I, me</u>].

The prize went to <u>him</u>.

The prize went to <u>him and me</u>.

16c

16b   Subject complements: *it was she*

Both a subject and a subject complement° appear in the same form—the subjective case.

subject
complement
The one who cares most is <u>she</u>.

If this construction sounds stilted to you, use the more natural order: <u>*She*</u> *is the one who cares most.*

16c   *Who* vs. *whom*

The choice between *who* and *whom* depends on the use of the word.

Questions

At the beginning of a question use *who* for a subject and *whom* for an object.

subject
<u>Who</u> wrote the policy?   object
<u>Whom</u> does it affect?

Test for the correct form by answering the question with the form of *he* or *she* that sounds correct. Then use the same form in the question.

[<u>Who, Whom</u>] does one ask?

One asks <u>her</u>.

<u>Whom</u> does one ask?

Subordinate clauses

In subordinate clauses° use *who* and *whoever* for all subjects, *whom* and *whomever* for all objects.

subject ⟶
Give old clothes to whoever needs them.

object ⟵
I don't know whom the mayor appointed.

Test for the correct form by rewriting the subordinate clause as a sentence. Replace *who* or *whom* with the form of *he* or *she* that sounds correct. Then use the same form in the original subordinate clause.

Few people know [who, whom] they should ask.

They should ask her.

Few people know whom they should ask.

Note Don't let expressions such as *I think* and *she says* confuse you when they come between the subject *who* and its verb.

subject ⟶
He is the one who I think is best qualified.

16d   Other constructions

We or *us* with a noun

The choice of *we* or *us* before a noun depends on the use of the noun.

object of preposition ⟶
Freezing weather is welcomed by us skaters.

subject ⟶
We skaters welcome freezing weather.

Pronoun in an appositive

An **appositive** is a word or word group that renames a noun or pronoun. Within an appositive the form of a pronoun depends on the function of the word the appositive renames.

object of verb ⟶
The class elected two representatives, Samir and me.

subject ⟶
Two representatives, Samir and I, were elected.

Pronoun after *than* or *as*

After *than* or *as* in a comparison, the form of a pronoun indicates what words may have been omitted. A subjective pronoun must be the subject of the omitted verb:

subject
Some critics like Glass more than she [does].

An objective pronoun must be the object of the omitted verb:

object
Some critics like Glass more than [they like] her.

Subject and object of an infinitive

An **infinitive** is the plain form° of the verb plus *to* (*to swim*). Both its object and its subject are in the objective form.

subject of
infinitive
The school asked him to speak.

object of
infinitive
Students chose to invite him.

Form before a gerund

17a

A **gerund** is the *-ing* form of a verb used as a noun (*a runner's* breathing). Generally, use the possessive form of a pronoun or noun immediately before a gerund.

The coach disapproved of their lifting weights.

The coach's disapproving was a surprise.

17 Agreement of Pronoun and Antecedent

The word a pronoun refers to is its **antecedent**.

antecedent   pronoun
Homeowners fret over their tax bills.

For clarity, a pronoun should agree with its antecedent in person° (first, second, third), number° (singular, plural), and gender° (masculine, feminine, neuter).

17a   Antecedents with *and*

The dean and my adviser have offered their help.

Note When *each* or *every* precedes the compound antecedent, the pronoun is singular.

Every girl and woman took her seat.

Visit www.mycanadiancomplab.ca for
added help and exercises on sentence grammar.

17b   Antecedents with *or* or *nor*

When parts of an antecedent are joined by *or* or *nor*, the pronoun agrees with the nearer part.

Tenants or owners must present their grievances.

Either the tenant or the owner will have her way.

When one subject is plural and the other singular, put the plural subject second to avoid awkwardness.

Neither the owner nor the tenants have made their case.

17c   *Everyone, person,* and other indefinite words

Indefinite words do not refer to any specific person or thing. They include indefinite pronouns° (such as *anyone, everybody, everything, no one, somebody*) and generic nouns° (such as *person, individual, child, student*).

Most indefinite words are singular in meaning. Although they are often mistakenly treated like plurals and referred to with plural pronouns, in fact they require singular pronouns.

Everyone on the women's team now has her own locker.

Each of the men still has his own locker.

Tradition has called for *he* to refer to indefinite pronouns and other indefinite words (*child, adult, individual, person*), even when both masculine and feminine genders are intended. But increasingly this so-called generic (or generalized) *he* is considered inaccurate or unfair because it excludes females. To avoid it, try one of the following techniques.

Generic *he*   Nobody in the class had the credits he needed.

- Substitute *he or she.*

Revised   Nobody in the class had the credits he or she needed.

To avoid awkwardness, don't use *he or she* more than once in several sentences.

- Recast the sentence using a plural antecedent and pronoun.

Revised   All the students in the class lacked the credits they needed.

- Rewrite the sentence to avoid the pronoun.

    Revised   Nobody in the class had the <u>necessary credits</u>.

17d   *Team* and other collective nouns

Use a singular pronoun with *team, family, group,* or another collective noun° when referring to the group as a unit.

The committee voted to disband <u>itself</u>.

When referring to the individual members of the group, use a plural pronoun.

The old group have gone <u>their</u> separate ways.

18a

18 Reference of Pronoun to Antecedent

If a pronoun° does not refer clearly to the word it substitutes for (its antecedent°), readers will have difficulty grasping the pronoun's meaning.

18a   Single antecedent

When either of two nouns can be a pronoun's antecedent, the reference will not be clear.

    Confusing   Emily Dickinson is sometimes compared with Jane Austen, but <u>she</u> was quite different.

Revise such a sentence in one of two ways:

- Replace the pronoun with the appropriate noun.

    Clear   Emily Dickinson is sometimes compared with Jane Austen, but <u>Dickinson</u> [or <u>Austen</u>] was quite different.

- Avoid repetition by rewriting the sentence. If you use the pronoun, make sure it has only one possible antecedent.

    Clear   Despite occasional comparison, Emily Dickinson and Jane Austen were quite different.

Visit www.mycanadiancomplab.ca for added help and exercises on sentence grammar.

Clear   Though sometimes compared with her, Emily Dickinson was quite different from Jane Austen.

18b   Close antecedent

A clause° beginning *who, which,* or *that* should generally fall immediately after the word it refers to.

Confusing   Jody found a dress in the attic that her aunt had worn.

Clear   In the attic Jody found a dress that her aunt had worn.

18c   Specific antecedent

A pronoun should refer to a specific noun° or other pronoun.

Vague *this, that, which,* or *it*

This, that, which, or *it* should refer to a specific noun, not to a whole word group expressing an idea or situation.

Confusing   Lord Selkirk's attempt to establish the Red River Colony was opposed by the fur traders of the North West Company and their Metis allies, who attacked the colony. This led Selkirk to fight both on the battlefield and in the courts.

Clear   Lord Selkirk's attempt to establish the Red River Colony was opposed by the fur traders of the North West Company and their Metis allies, who attacked the colony. This opposition led Selkirk to fight both on the battlefield and in the courts.

Implied nouns

A pronoun cannot refer clearly to a noun that is merely implied by some other word or phrase, such as *news* in *newspaper* or *happiness* in *happy.*

Confusing   Cohen's report brought her a lawsuit.

Clear   Cohen was sued over her report.

Confusing   Her reports on psychological development generally go unnoticed outside it.

18c

Clear   Her reports on psychological development generally go unnoticed outside the field.

Indefinite *it, they,* or *you*

It and *they* should have definite antecedents.

Confusing   In the average television drama they present a false picture of life.

Clear   The average television drama presents a false picture of life.

You should clearly mean "you, the reader," and the context must support such a meaning.

Inappropriate   In the fourteenth century you had to struggle simply to survive.

Revised   In the fourteenth century one [or a person or people] had to struggle to survive.

18d   Consistency in pronouns

Within a sentence or a group of related sentences, pronouns should be consistent. You may shift pronouns unconsciously when you start with *one* and soon find it too stiff.

Inconsistent   One will find when reading that your concentration improves with practice, so that you comprehend more in less time.

Revised   You will find when reading that your concentration improves with practice, so that you comprehend more in less time.

Inconsistent pronouns also occur when singular shifts to plural: *Everyone who reads regularly will improve his or her* [not *their*] *speed.* See pages 63–65.

MODIFIERS

19 Adjectives and Adverbs

Adjectives modify nouns° (*good child*) and pronouns° (*special someone*). **Adverbs** modify verbs° (*see well*), adjectives (*very happy*), other adverbs (*not very*), and

19

Visit www.mycanadiancomplab.ca for added help and exercises on sentence grammar.

whole word groups (*Otherwise, the room was empty*). The only way to tell if a modifier should be an adjective or an adverb is to determine its function in the sentence.

19a   Adjective vs. adverb

Use only adverbs, not adjectives, to modify verbs, adverbs, or other adjectives.

> Not   They took each other <u>serious</u>. They related <u>good</u>.

> But   They took each other <u>seriously</u>. They related <u>well</u>.

19b   Adjective with linking verb: *felt bad*

A modifier after a verb should be an adverb only if it describes the verb. If the modifier follows a linking verb and describes the subject, it should be an adjective. In the first example below, the linking verb° *felt* connects the subject and an adjective describing the subject.

> The sailors felt <u>bad</u>.
> linking   adjective
> verb

> Some sailors fare <u>badly</u> in rough weather.
> verb   adverb

Good and *well* are frequently confused after verbs.

> Decker trained <u>well</u>. [Adverb.]

> She felt <u>well</u>. Her prospects were <u>good</u>. [Adjectives.]

19c   Comparison of adjectives and adverbs

Comparison° allows adjectives and adverbs to show degrees of quality or amount by changing form: *red, redder, reddest; awful, more awful, most awful; quickly, less quickly, least quickly*. A dictionary will list the *-er* and *-est* endings if they can be used. Otherwise, use *more* and *most* or *less* and *least*.

Some modifiers are irregular, changing their spelling for comparison: for example, *good, better, best; many, more, most; badly, worse, worst*.

Comparisons of two or more than two

Use the *-er* form, *more*, or *less* when comparing two items. Use the *-est* form, *most*, or *least* when comparing three or more items.

> Of the two tests, the litmus is <u>better</u>.
> Of all six tests, the litmus is <u>best</u>.

Double comparisons

A double comparison combines the *-er* or *-est* ending with the word *more* or *most*. The extra words "more" and "most" are redundant.

> Jacques was the <u>wisest</u> [not <u>most wisest</u>] person in town. He was <u>smarter</u> [not <u>more smarter</u>] than anyone else.

The adjective *unique* never takes an intensifier or modifier:

> His inventions were <u>unique</u> [not <u>very unique</u> or <u>quite unique</u>].

Complete comparisons

A comparison should be complete.

▪ The comparison should state a relation fully enough to ensure clarity.

Unclear	Car makers worry about their industry more than environmentalists.
Clear	Car makers worry about their industry more than environmentalists <u>do</u>.
Clear	Car makers worry about their industry more than <u>they worry about</u> environmentalists.

▪ The items being compared should in fact be comparable.

Illogical	The cost of an electric car is greater than a gasoline-powered car. [Illogically compares a cost and a car.]
Revised	The cost of an electric car is greater than <u>the cost of</u> [or <u>that of</u>] a gasoline-powered car.

19d

19d   Double negatives

In a **double negative** two negative words cancel each other out. Some double negatives are intentional, as *She was <u>not unhappy</u>* indicates with understatement that she was indeed (fairly) happy. But most double negatives say the opposite of what is intended: *Jenny did <u>not</u> feel <u>nothing</u>* asserts that Jenny felt other than nothing, or in other words, she felt something.

Faulty	The CCRA <u>cannot hardly</u> audit all tax returns. <u>None</u> of its audits <u>never</u> touch many cheaters.
Revised	The CCRA <u>cannot</u> audit all tax returns. Its audits <u>never</u> touch many cheaters.

19e   Present and past participles as adjectives ESL

Both present participles° and past participles° may serve as adjectives: *a burning house, a burned house*. As in the examples, the two participles usually differ in the time they indicate.

But some present and past participles—those derived from verbs expressing feeling—can have altogether different meanings. The present participle refers to something that causes the feeling: *That was a frightening storm*. The past participle refers to something that experiences the feeling: *They quieted the frightened horses*. Similar pairs include the following:

annoying/annoyed	exhausting/exhausted
boring/bored	interesting/interested
confusing/confused	pleasing/pleased
exciting/excited	satisfying/satisfied
surprising/surprised	troubling/troubled
tiring/tired	worrying/worried

19f   Articles: *a, an, the* ESL

Articles° usually trouble native English speakers only in the choice of *a* versus *an: a* for words beginning with consonant sounds (*a bridge*), *an* for words beginning with vowel sounds, including silent *h*'s (*an apple, an hour*).

For non-native speakers, *a, an,* and *the* can be difficult because many other languages use such words quite differently or not at all. In English, their uses depend on their context and the kinds of nouns they precede.

Singular count nouns

A **count noun** names something countable and can form a plural: *glass/glasses, mountain/mountains, child/children, woman/women*.

- *A* or *an* precedes a singular count noun when your reader does not already know its identity, usually because you have not mentioned it before.

  A scientist in our chemistry department developed a process to strengthen metals. [*Scientist* and *process* are being introduced for the first time.]

- *The* precedes a singular count noun that has a specific identity for your reader, usually because (1) you have mentioned it before, (2) you identify it immediately before or after you state it, (3) it is unique (the only one in existence), or (4) it refers to an institution or facility that is shared by the community.

A scientist in our chemistry department developed a process to strengthen metals. The scientist patented the process. [*Scientist* and *process* were identified before.]

The most productive laboratory is the research centre in the chemistry department. [*Most productive* identifies *laboratory*. *In the chemistry department* identifies *research centre*. And *chemistry department* is a shared facility.]

The sun rises in the east. [*Sun* and *east* are unique.]

Some men and women aspire to the priesthood. [*Priesthood* is a shared institution.]

Plural count nouns

A or *an* never precedes a plural noun. *The* does not precede a plural noun that names a general category. *The* does precede a plural noun that names specific representatives of a category.

Men and women are different. [*Men* and *women* name general categories.]

The women formed a team. [*Women* refers to specific people.]

Noncount nouns

A **noncount noun** names something that is not usually considered countable in English, and so it does not form a plural. Examples include the following:

Abstractions: confidence, democracy, education, knowledge, evidence, health, information, intelligence, peace, luxury, equality, pollution, research, success, supervision, truth, wealth, work

Food and drink: bread, flour, meat, milk, salt, water, wine

Emotions: anger, courage, happiness, hate, love, respect, satisfaction

Natural conditions and substances: air, blood, dirt, gasoline, gold, hair, heat, ice, oil, oxygen, rain, smoke, wood

Groups: clergy, clothing, equipment, furniture, garbage, jewellery, junk, legislation, mail, military, money, police

Fields of study: accounting, architecture, biology, business, chemistry, engineering, literature, psychology, science

A or *an* never precedes a noncount noun. *The* does precede a noncount noun that names specific representatives of a general category.

Vegetation suffers from drought. [*Vegetation* names a general category.]

The vegetation in the park withered or died. [*Vegetation* refers to specific plants.]

Note Many nouns are sometimes count nouns and sometimes noncount nouns.

The library has a room for readers. [*Room* is a count noun meaning "walled area."]

The library has room for reading. [*Room* is a noncount noun meaning "space."]

Proper nouns

20a

A **proper noun** names a particular person, place, or thing and begins with a capital letter: *February, Joe Allen*. *A* or *an* never precedes a proper noun. *The* does occasionally, as with oceans (*the* Pacific), regions (*the* Middle East), rivers (*the* Fraser), some countries (*the* United States), and some universities (*the* University of Toronto).

Ian lives in Fredericton, where he attends the University of New Brunswick.

20 Misplaced and Dangling Modifiers

For clarity, modifiers generally must fall close to the words they modify.

20a Misplaced modifiers

A **misplaced modifier** falls in the wrong place in a sentence. It may be awkward, confusing, or even unintentionally funny.

Clear placement

Confusing   He served steak to the men on paper plates.

Revised   He served the men steak on paper plates.

Visit www.mycanadiancomplab.ca for
added help and exercises on sentence grammar.

| Confusing | Many dogs are killed by automobiles and trucks roaming unleashed. |
| Revised | Many dogs roaming unleashed are killed by automobiles and trucks. |

Only and other limiting modifiers

Limiting modifiers include *almost, even, exactly, hardly, just, merely, nearly, only, scarcely,* and *simply.* They should fall immediately before the word or word group they modify.

Unclear	They only saw each other during meals.
Revised	They saw only each other during meals.
Revised	They saw each other only during meals.

20a

Infinitives and other grammatical units

Some grammatical units should generally not be split by long modifiers. For example, a long adverb° between subject° and verb° can be awkward and confusing.

	subject ——————— adverb ————————
Awkward	The Canucks, after losing the first game,
	verb
	went on to win the series.
	———— adverb ———— subject
Revised	After losing the the first game, the Canucks
	verb
	went on to win the series.

A **split infinitive**—a modifier placed between *to* and the verb—can be especially awkward and will annoy many readers.

	infinitive
Awkward	Farmers expected temperatures to not rise.
Revised	Farmers expected temperatures not to rise.

A split infinitive may sometimes be unavoidable without rewriting, though it may still bother some readers.

| infinitive |

Several industries expect to more than triple their use of robots.

Order of adjectives ESL

English follows distinctive rules for arranging two or three adjectives before a noun. (A string of more than three adjectives before a noun is rare.) See the chart on page 74.

Determiner	Opinion	Size or shape	Colour	Origin	Material	Noun used as adjective	Noun
many						state	**laws**
	lovely		green	Thai			**birds**
a		square			wooden		**table**
all						business	**reports**
the			blue		litmus		**paper**

20b Dangling modifiers

A **dangling modifier** does not sensibly modify anything in its sentence.

Dangling   Passing the building, the vandalism became visible.

Like most dangling modifiers, this one introduces a sentence, contains a verb form (*passing*), and implies but does not name a subject (whoever is passing). Readers assume that this implied subject is the same as the subject of the sentence (*vandalism*). When it is not, the modifier "dangles" unconnected to the rest of the sentence.

Revise dangling modifiers to achieve the emphasis you want.

- Rewrite the dangling modifier as a complete clause with its own stated subject and verb. Readers can accept different subjects when they are both stated.

  Dangling   Passing the building, the vandalism became visible.

  Revised   As we passed the building, the vandalism became visible.

- Change the subject of the sentence to a word the modifier properly describes.

  Dangling   Trying to understand the causes, vandalism has been extensively studied.

  Revised   Trying to understand the causes, researchers have extensively studied vandalism.

SENTENCE FAULTS

21 Sentence Fragments

A **sentence fragment** is part of a sentence that is set off as if it were a whole sentence by an initial capital letter and a final period or other end punctuation. Although writers occasionally use fragments deliberately and effectively, readers perceive most fragments as serious errors in standard English. Use the tests below to ensure that you have linked or separated your ideas both appropriately for your meaning and correctly, without creating sentence fragments.

21a

ESL Some languages other than English allow the omission of the subject° or the verb.° Except in commands (*Close the door*), English always requires you to state the subject and verb.

21a Tests for fragments

A word group punctuated as a sentence should pass *all three* of the following tests. If it does not, it is a fragment and needs to be revised.

Test 1: Find the verb.

Some sentence fragments lack any verb form°:

Fragment	Uncountable numbers of sites on the web.
Revised	Uncountable numbers of sites <u>make up</u> the web.

The verb in a complete sentence must be able to change form as on the left of the following chart. A verb form that cannot change this way (as on the right) cannot serve as a sentence verb.

	Complete sentences	Sentence fragments
Singular	The network <u>grows</u>.	The network <u>growing</u>.
Plural	Networks <u>grow</u>.	Networks <u>growing</u>.
Present	The network <u>grows</u>.	
Past	The network <u>grew</u>.	The network <u>growing</u>.
Future	The network <u>will grow</u>.	

Visit www.mycanadiancomplab.ca for
added help and exercises on sentence grammar.

(See also p. 48 on the use of helping verbs° to prevent sentence fragments.)

Test 2: Find the subject.

The subject of the sentence will usually come before the verb. If there is no subject, the word group is probably a fragment.

Fragment	And has enormous popular appeal.
Revised	The web has enormous popular appeal.

Note   Commands, in which the subject *you* is understood, are not sentence fragments: [*You*] Use *the web*.

21b

Test 3: Make sure the clause is not subordinate.

A **subordinate clause** begins with either a subordinating conjunction° (such as *because, if, when*) or a relative pronoun° (*who, which, that*). Subordinate clauses serve as parts of sentences, not as whole sentences. They do not express complete thoughts.

Fragment	The Internet was greatly improved by web technology. Which allows users to move easily between sites.
Revised	The Internet was greatly improved by web technology, which allows users to move easily between sites. [The subordinate clause joins a main clause in a complete sentence.]
Revised	The Internet was greatly improved by web technology. It allows users to move easily between sites. [Substituting *It* for *Which* makes the subordinate clause into a complete sentence.]

Note   Questions beginning *who, whom,* or *which* are not sentence fragments: *Who rattled the cage?*

21b   Revision of fragments

Correct sentence fragments in one of the two ways shown in the revised examples above, depending on the importance of the information in the fragment:

- Combine the fragment with the appropriate main clause. The information in the fragment will then be subordinated to that in the main clause.

Fragment	The web is easy to use. Loaded with links and graphics.
Revised	The web, loaded with links and graphics, is easy to use.

- Rewrite the fragment as a complete sentence. The information in the fragment will then have the same importance as that in other complete sentences.

| Fragment | The Internet was a true innovation. <u>Because no expansive computer network existed before it.</u> |
| Revised | The Internet was a true innovation. No expansive computer network existed before it. [Deleting *Because* makes the fragment (a subordinate or dependent clause) into a complete sentence.] |

22 Comma Splices and Fused Sentences

22a

When you combine two complete sentences (main clauses°) in one sentence, you need to give readers a clear signal that one clause is ending and the other beginning. In a **comma splice** two main clauses are joined (or spliced) only by a comma, which is usually too weak to signal the link between main clauses.

| Comma splice | The ship was huge, its mast stood twenty-four metres high. |

In a **fused sentence** (or **run-on sentence**) the clauses are not separated at all.

| Fused sentence | The ship was huge its mast stood twenty-four metres high. |

22a Main clauses without *and, but, or, nor, for, so, yet*

Two main clauses in a sentence are usually separated with a comma and a coordinating conjunction° such as *and* or *but*. These signals tell readers to expect another main clause. When one or both signals are missing, the sentence may be confusing and may require rereading. Revise it in one of the following ways:

- **Insert a coordinating conjunction** when the ideas in the main clauses are closely related and equally important.

Visit www.mycanadiancomplab.ca for added help and exercises on sentence grammar.

| Comma splice | Some laboratory-grown foods taste good, they are nutritious. |
| Revised | Some laboratory-grown foods taste good, <u>and</u> they are nutritious. |

In a fused sentence insert a comma and a coordinating conjunction.

| Fused sentence | Chemists have made much progress they still have a way to go. |
| Revised | Chemists have made much progress<u>,</u> <u>but</u> they still have a way to go. |

- **Insert a semicolon between clauses** if the relation between the ideas is very close and obvious without a conjunction.

| Comma splice | Good taste is rare in laboratory-grown vegetables, they are usually bland. |
| Revised | Good taste is rare in laboratory-grown vegetables<u>;</u> they are usually bland. |

- **Make the clauses into separate sentences** when the ideas expressed are only loosely related.

| Comma splice | Chemistry has contributed to our understanding of foods, many foods, such as wheat and beans, can be produced in the laboratory. |
| Revised | Chemistry has contributed to our understanding of foods<u>.</u> Many foods, such as wheat and beans, can be produced in the laboratory. |

- **Subordinate one clause to the other** when one idea is less important than the other. The subordinate clause will modify something in the main clause.

| Comma splice | The vitamins are adequate, the flavour and colour are deficient. |
| Revised | <u>Even though</u> the vitamins are adequate, the flavour and colour are deficient. |

22b   Main clauses related by *however, for example,* and so on

Two kinds of words can describe how one main clause relates to another: conjunctive adverbs,° such as *however, instead, meanwhile,* and *thus*; and other transitional expressions,° such as *even so, for example, in fact,* and *of course.* Two main clauses related by all conjunctive adverbs and most transitional expressions must be separated by a period or by a semicolon. The connecting word or phrase is also generally set off by a comma or commas.

Comma splice	Most Canadians refuse to give up unhealthful habits, consequently our medical costs are higher than necessary.
Revised	Most Canadians refuse to give up unhealthful habits. Consequently, our medical costs are higher than necessary.
Revised	Most Canadians refuse to give up unhealthful habits; consequently, our medical costs are higher than necessary.

To test whether a word or phrase is a conjunctive adverb or transitional expression, try moving it around in its clause. Conjunctive adverbs and transitional expressions can move, whereas coordinating conjunctions (such as *and* or *because*) cannot.

22b

> Most Canadians refuse to give up unhealthful habits; our medical costs, consequently, are higher than necessary.

PART IV

Punctuation

PEARSON
mycanadiancomplab

Visit the **Resources** tab in MyCanadianCompLab and click on **Grammar** to access grammar, punctuation, and mechanics exercises that will help you improve your writing skills and get a better grade in your course.

Punctuation

This checklist focuses on the most troublesome punctuation marks and uses, showing correctly punctuated sentences with brief explanations. For the other marks and other uses covered in this part, see the contents inside the back cover.

Comma

☑ Subways are convenient**,** but they are costly to build.
Subways are convenient <u>but</u> costly.
[With *and, but,* etc., only between main clauses. See opposite.]

☑ <u>Because of their cost</u>**,** new subways are rarely built.
[With an introductory element. See opposite.]

☑ Light rail**,** <u>which is less costly</u>**,** is often more feasible.
Those <u>who favour mass transit</u> often propose light rail.
[With a nonessential element, not with an essential element. See p. 84.]

☑ In a few older cities, commuters can choose from <u>subways</u>**,** <u>buses</u>**,** <u>light rail</u>**,** and railroads.
[Separating items in a series. See p. 86.]

Semicolon

☑ She chose carpentry**;** she wanted manual work.
She had a law degree**;** <u>however</u>, she became a carpenter.
[Between main clauses not joined by *and, but,* etc., and those joined by *however, for example,* etc. See p. 88.]

Colon

☑ The school has one goal**:** to train businesspeople.
[With a main clause to introduce information. See p. 90.]

Apostrophe

☑ Bill <u>Smith**'**s</u> dog saved the life of the <u>Smiths**'**</u> grandchild.
[Showing possession: with -'s for singular nouns; with -' alone for plural nouns ending in -s. See pp. 91–92.]

☑ <u>It s</u> (Its) [for <u>The dog**'**s</u>] bark warned the family.
<u>It**'**s</u> [for <u>It is</u>] an intelligent dog.
[Not with possessive pronouns, only with contractions. See p. 92.]

23   The Comma

The comma helps to separate sentence elements and to prevent misreading. Its main uses (and misuses) appear below.

23a   Comma with *and, but, or, nor, for, so, yet*

Between main clauses

Use a comma before *and, but, or, nor, for, so,* and *yet* (the coordinating conjunctions°) when they link main clauses.°

> Banks offer many services **,** <u>but</u> they could do more.

> Many banks offer investment advice **,** <u>and</u> they may help small businesses establish credit.

Note   The comma goes before, not after, the coordinating conjunction.

Not between words, phrases, or subordinate clauses

Generally, do not use a comma before *and, but, or,* and *nor* when they link pairs of words, phrases,° or subordinate clauses°—that is, elements other than main clauses.

> Not   One bank <u>established</u> special accounts for older depositors**, and** <u>counselled</u> them on investments.

> But   One bank <u>established</u> special accounts for older depositors <u>**and** counselled</u> them on investments.

23b   Comma with introductory elements

Use a comma after most elements that begin sentences and are distinct from the main clause.

> <u>When a new century nears</u> **,** futurists multiply.

> <u>Fortunately</u> **,** some news is good.

You may omit the comma after a short introductory element if there's no risk that the reader will run the introductory element and main clause together: *By 2020 we may have reduced pollution.*

Visit www.mycanadiancomplab.ca for
added help and exercises on punctuation.

Note The subject° of a sentence is not an introductory element but a part of the main clause. Thus, do not use a comma to separate the subject and its verb.

Not   Some <u>pessimists, may</u> be disappointed.

But   Some <u>pessimists may</u> be disappointed.

23c   Comma or commas with interrupting and concluding elements

Use a comma or commas to set off information that could be deleted without altering the basic meaning of the sentence.

Note When such optional information falls in the middle of the sentence, be sure to use one comma *before* and one *after* it.

23c

Around nonessential elements

A **nonessential** (or **nonrestrictive**) **element** adds information about a word in the sentence. It is "nonrestrictive" because omitting the element from the sentence would remove incidental details but would not affect the sentence's basic meaning.

Nonessential modifiers

Hai Nguyen, <u>who emigrated from Vietnam</u>, lives in Edmonton.

His company, <u>which is ten years old</u>, studies air and water pollution.

Nguyen's family lives in Vancouver and Winnipeg, <u>even though he lives in Edmonton.</u>

Nonessential appositives

Appositives are words or word groups that rename nouns.

Hai Nguyen's work, <u>advanced research into air pollution</u>, keeps him in Edmonton.

His wife, <u>Tina Nguyen</u>, reports for a newspaper in Winnipeg.

The information between commas in these sentences is not required to identify the subject.

Not around essential elements

Do not use commas to set off **essential** (or **restrictive**) **elements,** modifiers and appositives that contain information essential to the meaning of the sentence. Omitting the underlined element from any sentence below would alter the meaning substantially, leaving the sentence unclear or too general.

Essential modifiers

People who join recycling programs rarely complain about the extra work.

The programs that succeed are often staffed by volunteers.

Most people recycle because they believe they have a responsibility to the earth.

Essential appositives

The label "Recycle" on products becomes a command.

The activist Susan Bower urges recycling.

The book *Efficient Recycling* provides helpful tips.

Around absolute phrases

An **absolute phrase** consists usually of the *-ing* form of a verb plus a subject for the verb. The phrase modifies the whole main clause of the sentence.

23c

Many students, their debts mounting, worry about student loans.

Around transitional or parenthetical expressions

A transitional expression,° such as *however, for example,* and *of course,* forms a link between ideas. It is nonessential and is usually set off with a comma or commas.

Some students, in fact, graduate owing thousands.

A parenthetical expression° provides supplementary information not essential for meaning—for instance, *fortunately, to be frank,* and *published in 1990.* It can be enclosed in parentheses (see p. 98) or, with more emphasis, in commas.

Most students, fortunately, are able to repay their loans.

Note Do not add a comma after a coordinating conjunction° (*and, but,* and so on) or a subordinating conjunction° (*although, because,* and so on). To distinguish between these words and transitional or parenthetical expressions, try moving the word or expression around in its clause. Transitional or parenthetical expressions can be moved; coordinating and subordinating conjunctions cannot.

Around phrases of contrast

Students should focus on education, not work.

Around *yes* and *no*

Provinces should recognize that, yes, education is expensive.

Around words of direct address

Heed this lesson, readers.

23d Commas with series

Between series items

Use commas to separate the items in lists or series.

The names Belial, Beelzebub, and Lucifer sound ominous.

The comma before the last item in a series (before *and*) is optional unless its absence causes ambiguity, but it is never wrong and it is usually clearer.

Not around series

Do not use a comma *before* or *after* a series.

Not   The skills of, agriculture, herding, and hunting, sustained the First Nations.

But   The skills of agriculture, herding, and hunting sustained the First Nations.

23e Comma with adjectives

Between equal adjectives

Use a comma between two or more adjectives° when each one modifies the same word equally. As a test, such adjectives could be joined by *and*.

The book had a worn, cracked binding.

Not between unequal adjectives

Do not use a comma between adjectives when one forms a unit with the modified word. As a test, the two adjectives could not sensibly be joined by *and*.

The house overflowed with ornate electric fixtures.

Among the junk in the attic was one lovely vase.

23f Commas with dates, addresses, place names, numbers

When they appear within sentences, elements punctuated with commas are also ended with commas.

Dates

On July 1, 1967, Canada celebrated its centennial. [Note that commas appear before *and* after the year.]

The Canadian Expeditionary Force reached France in February 1915. [No comma is needed between a month or season and a year.]

Addresses and place names

Use the address 49 Front Street, St. John's, Newfoundland and Labrador A1E 2Y2, for all correspondence. [No comma is needed between the name of the province and the postal code.]

Numbers

23g

In scientific usage, metric numbers require spaces instead of commas, but in non-technical usage, some writers continue to use commas. (See also p. 115.)

When completed, the Trans Canada Trail will consist of over 17 000 km of linked recreational trails running from St. John's, NL, to Victoria, BC.

Our local organizing committee raised nearly $10 000 for our portion of the trail.

One anonymous donor contributed $2,000,000 to the project.

Note In Quebec, it is common to use a comma instead of a decimal point:

My new running shoes cost 134,95$.

23g Commas with quotations

A comma or commas usually separate a quotation from a signal phrase, such as *she said* or *he replied,* that identifies the source.

Marshall McLuhan said, "The medium is the message."

"Knowledge is power," wrote Francis Bacon.

"You don't need a weatherman," sings Bob Dylan, "to know which way the wind blows."

Do not use a comma when the signal phrase interrupts the quotation between main clauses.° Instead, follow the signal phrase with a semicolon or period.

"That part of my life was over," she wrote; "his words had sealed it shut."

"That part of my life was over," she wrote. "His words had sealed it shut."

24 The Semicolon

The semicolon separates equal and balanced sentence elements, usually main clauses.°

24a

24a Semicolon between main clauses not joined by *and, but, or, nor,* etc.

Between main clauses

Use a semicolon between main clauses° that are not connected by *and, but, or, nor, for, so,* or *yet* (the coordinating conjunctions°).

Increased taxes are only one way to pay for programs; cost cutting also frees up money.

Not between main clauses and subordinate elements

Do not use a semicolon between a main clause and a subordinate element, such as a subordinate clause° or a phrase.°

Not According to African authorities; Pygmies today number only about thirty-five thousand.

But According to African authorities, Pygmies today number only about thirty-five thousand.

Visit www.mycanadiancomplab.ca for added help and exercises on punctuation.

Not	Anthropologists have campaigned; <u>for the protec-tion of the Pygmies' habitat.</u>
But	Anthropologists have campaigned <u>for the protec-tion of the Pygmies' habitat.</u>

24b Semicolon with *however, for example, and so on*

Use a semicolon between main clauses° that are related by two kinds of words: conjunctive adverbs,° such as *however, indeed, therefore,* and *thus;* and other transitional expressions° such as *after all, for example, in fact,* and *of course.*

> Blue jeans have become fashionable all over the world**;** <u>however,</u> Americans still wear more jeans than anyone else.

A conjunctive adverb or transitional expression may move around within its clause, so the semicolon will not always come just before the adverb or expression. The adverb or expression itself is usually set off with a comma or commas.

> Blue jeans have become fashionable all over the world**;** Americans**,** <u>however,</u> still wear more jeans than anyone else.

24c

24c Semicolons with series

Between series items

Use semicolons (rather than commas) to separate items in a series when the items contain commas.

> The custody case involved <u>Amy Dalton, the child</u>**;** <u>Ellen and Mark Dalton, the parents</u>**;** and <u>Ruth and Hal Blum, the grandparents.</u>

Not before a series

Do not use a semicolon to introduce a series. (Use a colon or a dash instead.)

Not	Teachers have heard all sorts of reasons why students do poorly; <u>psychological problems, family illness, too much work, too little time.</u>
But	Teachers have heard all sorts of reasons why students do poorly<u>:</u> <u>psychological problems, family illness, too much work, too little time.</u>

25 The Colon

The colon is mainly a mark of introduction, but it has a few other conventional uses as well.

25a Colon for introduction

At end of main clause

The colon ends a main clause° and introduces a word, phrase, list, quotation, or complete sentence that explains the first clause:

> The first warm days of spring, followed by cool nights, send an unmistakable message: it's time to visit the sugar bush. [Introduces an explanation.]

> We look forward to a variety of maple products: syrup, toffee, fudge, maple butter, and maple sugar. [Introduces a series.]

> The sugaring-off meal provides an essential ingredient for the men and women who work in the sugar bush: calories to fuel hard labour. [Introduces an appositive.°]

> A farmer in the Beauce gives his helpers plenty of food: "We serve maple-glazed ham, eggs poached in maple syrup, and maple-baked beans. For dessert we offer sugar pie." [Introduces a long quotation.]

Not inside main clause

Do not use a colon inside a main clause, especially after *such as* or a verb.

> Not   The best-known maple product is: syrup. Outside of Canada, few people have tasted such maple delicacies as: toffee or *tire*.

> But   The best-known maple product is syrup. Outside of Canada, few people have tasted such maple delicacies as toffee or *tire*.

25b Colon with salutations of business letters, titles and subtitles, and divisions of time

Salutation of a business letter
Dear Ms. Burak**:**

Title and subtitle
*Anna Freud***:** *Her Life and Work*

Time
12**:**26   6**:**00

26 The Apostrophe

The apostrophe (') appears as part of a word to indicate possession, the omission of one or more letters, or (in a few cases) a plural number.

26a Apostrophe with possessives

The **possessive** form of a word indicates that it owns or is the source of another word: *the dog's hair, everyone's hope*. For nouns° and indefinite pronouns,° such as *everyone*, the possessive form always includes an apostrophe and often an -*s*.

Note The apostrophe or apostrophe-plus-*s* is an *addition*. Before this addition, always spell the name of the owner or owners without dropping or adding letters.

26a

Singular words: Add -'s.

Bill <u>Boughton's</u> skillful card tricks amaze children.

<u>Anyone's</u> eyes would widen.

The -'s ending for singular words usually pertains to singular words ending in -*s*.

<u>Francis's</u> work is highly regarded.

The <u>business's</u> customers filed suit.

Some writers, however, add only the apostrophe to singular words ending in -*s*, especially when the additional *s* would make the word difficult to pronounce (*Moses'*) or when the name sounds like a plural (*Rivers'*).

Plural words ending in -s: Add -' only.

<u>Workers'</u> incomes have fallen slightly over the past year.

Many students take several <u>years'</u> leave after high school.

The <u>Murphys'</u> son lives at home.

Plural words not ending in -s: Add -'s.

<u>Children's</u> educations are at stake.

We need to attract the <u>media's</u> attention.

Compound words: Add -'s only to the last word.

The <u>brother-in-law's</u> business failed.

Taxes are always <u>somebody else's</u> fault.

Visit www.mycanadiancomplab.ca for
added help and exercises on punctuation.

Two or more owners: Add -'s depending on possession.

> <u>Zimbale's</u> and <u>Mason's</u> comedy techniques are similar. [Each comedian has his own technique.]

> The child recovered despite <u>her mother and father's</u> neglect. [The mother and father were jointly neglectful.]

26b Misuses of the apostrophe

Not with plural nouns°

> Not The unleashed <u>dog's</u> belonged to the Jones'.
> But The unleashed <u>dog s</u> belonged to the <u>Jones e</u>s.

Not with singular verbs°

> Not The subway break's down less often now.
> But The subway break s down less often now.

Not with possessives of personal pronouns°

> Not The car is <u>her's</u>, not <u>their's</u>. It's colour is red.
> But The car is <u>her s</u>, not <u>their s</u>. It s colour is red.

Note Don't confuse possessive pronouns and contractions: *its, your, their,* and *whose* are possessives. *It's, you're, they're,* and *who's* are contractions. See below.

26c Apostrophe with contractions

A **contraction** replaces one or more letters, numbers, or words with an apostrophe.

it is	it's	cannot	can't
you are	you're	does not	doesn't
they are	they're	were not	weren't
who is	who's	class of 2012	class of '12

Note The contractions *it's, you're, they're,* and *who's* are easily confused with the possessive pronouns° *its, your, their,* and *whose.* To avoid misusing any of these words, search for all of them in your drafts. Then test for correctness:

- Do you intend the word to contain the sentence verb *is* or *are,* as in *It <u>is</u> a shame, They <u>are</u> to blame, You <u>are</u> right, Who <u>is</u> coming?* Then use an apostrophe: *it's, they're, you're, who's.*
- Do you intend the word to indicate possession, as in *Its tail was wagging, <u>Their</u> car broke down, <u>Your</u> eyes are blue, <u>Whose</u> book is that?* Then don't use an apostrophe.

26c

26d Apostrophe with plural abbreviations, dates, and words or characters named as words

You'll sometimes see apostrophes used to form the plurals of abbreviations (*BA's*), dates (*1900's*), and words or characters used as words (*but*'s). However, current style guides recommend against the apostrophe in these cases.

BAs   PhDs
1990s   2000s

The sentence has too many *but*s.
Two *3*s end the security code.

Note Italicize a word or character named as a word (see pp. 112–113), but not the added *-s*. If handwriting, underline to indicate italics.

27 Quotation Marks

Quotation marks—either double (" ") or single (' ')—mainly enclose direct quotations from speech and from writing.

This chapter treats the main uses of quotation marks. Additional issues with quotations are discussed elsewhere in this book:

- Punctuating *she said* and other signal phrases that introduce quotations (pp. 87–88).
- Using brackets and the ellipsis mark to indicate changes to quotations (pp. 98–101).
- Quoting sources versus paraphrasing or summarizing them (pp. 145–48).
- Integrating quotations into your text (pp. 148–53).
- Avoiding plagiarism when quoting (pp. 153–58).
- Formatting long prose quotations and poetry quotations in MLA style (pp. 182–83), APA style (pp. 197–98), or Chicago style (p. 211).

Note Always use quotation marks in pairs, one at the beginning of a quotation and one at the end.

Visit www.mycanadiancomplab.ca for added help and exercises on punctuation.

27a   Quotation marks with direct quotations

Double quotation marks

A **direct quotation** reports what someone said or wrote, in the exact words of the original.

"Life," said the psychoanalyst Karen Horney, "remains a very efficient therapist."

Note   Do not use quotation marks with an **indirect quotation,** which reports what someone said or wrote but not in the exact words of the original: *Karen Horney remarked that life is a good therapist.*

Single quotation marks

Use single quotation marks to enclose a quotation within a quotation.

"In formulating any philosophy," Woody Allen writes, "the first consideration must always be: What can we know? Descartes hinted at the problem when he wrote, 'My mind can never know my body, although it has become quite friendly with my leg.'"

Dialogue

When quoting a conversation, put the speeches in double quotation marks and begin a new paragraph for each speaker.

"What shall I call you? Your name?" Andrews whispered rapidly, as with a high squeak the latch of the door rose.
"Elizabeth," she said. "Elizabeth."
—Graham Greene, *The Man Within*

27b   Quotation marks with titles of works

Do not use quotation marks for the titles of your own papers. Within your text, however, use quotation marks to enclose the titles of works that are published or released within larger works (see below). Use underlining or italics for all other titles (see pp. 111–112).

Short story	Essay
"The Loons"	"Joey: A 'Mechanical Boy'"
Short poem	Song
"Her Kind"	"Suzanne"

Article in a periodical
"Does 'Scaring' Work?"

Page or document
on a website

"Reader's Page"
(on the site *Friends of
Prufrock*)

Episode of a television or
radio program
"Dieppe" (on *Canada at
War*)

Subdivision of a book
"The Mast Head"
(Chapter 35 of *Moby-Dick*)

Note APA and CSE styles do not use quotation marks
for titles within source citations. See pages 187 and 216.

27c Quotation marks with words used in a special sense

On movie sets movable "wild walls" make a one-walled
room seem four-walled on film.

Avoid using quotation marks to excuse slang or to
express irony—that is, to indicate that you are using a word
with a different or even opposite meaning than usual.

Not   Settlers "justified" their treatment of native people.
But   Settlers <u>attempted to justify</u> their treatment of
       native people.

Note Use underlining or italics to highlight words
you are defining. (See p. 112.)

27d Quotation marks with other punctuation

Commas and periods: Inside quotation marks

Jonathan Swift wrote a famous satire, "A Modest
Proposal," in 1729.

"Swift's 'A Modest Proposal,'" wrote one critic, "is so
outrageous that it cannot be believed."

Exception When a parenthetical source citation immediately follows a quotation, place any comma or period
after the citation:

One critic calls the essay "outrageous" (Olms 26).

Colons and semicolons: Outside quotation marks

A few years ago the slogan in elementary education was
"learning by playing"; now educators stress basic skills.

We all know the meaning of "basic skills": reading, writing, and arithmetic.

27d

Dashes, question marks, and exclamation points: Inside quotation marks only if part of the quotation

When a dash, exclamation point, or question mark is part of the quotation, place it *inside* quotation marks. Don't use any other punctuation, such as a period or comma.

"But must you—" Marcia hesitated, afraid of the answer.

"Go away!" I yelled.

Did you say, "Who is she?" [When both your sentence and the quotation would end in a question mark or exclamation point, use only the mark in the quotation.]

When a dash, question mark, or exclamation point applies only to the larger sentence, not to the quotation, place it *outside* quotation marks—again, with no other punctuation.

Betty Friedan's question in 1963—"Who knows what women can be?"—encouraged others to seek answers.

Who said, "Now cracks a noble heart"?

---

28 End Punctuation

End a sentence with one of three punctuation marks: a period, a question mark, or an exclamation point.

28a Period for most sentences and some abbreviations

Statement   Mild command
The airline went bankrupt. Think of the possibilities.

Indirect question°
The article asks how we can improve math education.
It asks what cost we are willing to pay.

Abbreviations
Use periods with abbreviations that end in small letters. Otherwise, omit periods from abbreviations.

Dr.	Mr., Mrs.	e.g.	Feb.	ft.
St.	Ms.	i.e.	p.	a.m., p.m.
PhD	BC, AD	USA	IBM	CRTC
BA	AM, PM	UBC	CBC	AIDS

Visit www.mycanadiancomplab.ca for
added help and exercises on punctuation.

Note When a sentence ends in an abbreviation with a period, don't add a second period: *My first class is at 8 a.m.*

28b   Question mark for direct questions°

What is the result?
What is the difference between those proposals?

28c   Exclamation point for strong statements and commands

No! We must not lose this election!
Stop the car!

Note Use exclamation points sparingly to avoid seeming overly dramatic.

29   Other Marks

The other marks of punctuation are the dash, parentheses, the ellipsis mark, brackets, and the slash.

29a   Dash or dashes: Shifts and interruptions

The dash (—) punctuates sentences, while the hyphen (-) punctuates words. Form a dash with two hyphens (--), with no extra space before, after, or between the hyphens. Or use the character called an em dash on your word processor.

Note Be sure to use a pair of dashes when a shift or interruption falls in the middle of a sentence.

Shift in tone or thought

The novel—if one can call it that—appeared in 1994.

Nonessential element

The qualities Monet painted—sunlight, shadows, deep colours—abounded near the rivers and gardens he used as subjects. [Commas may also set off nonessential elements. See p. 84.]

Introductory series

Shortness of breath, skin discolouration, persistent indigestion—all these may signify cancer.

Visit www.mycanadiancomplab.ca for
added help and exercises on punctuation.

Concluding series or explanation

The patient undergoes a battery of tests—CAT scan, ultrasound, and biopsy. [A colon may also set off a concluding series. See p. 90.]

29b   Parentheses: Nonessential elements

Parentheses always come in pairs, one before and one after the punctuated material.

Parenthetical expressions

Parentheses de-emphasize explanatory or supplemental words or phrases. (Commas emphasize these expressions more, and dashes still more.)

Frederick Banting (later Sir Frederick Banting) and Charles Best discovered insulin in 1923.

29c

Don't put a comma before an opening parenthesis. After a parenthetical expression, place any punctuation *outside* the closing parenthesis.

Not   Although he did not receive the Nobel Prize, Charles Best had worked very closely with Frederick Banting, (later Sir Frederick Banting.)

But   Although he did not receive the Nobel Prize, Charles Best had worked very closely with Frederick Banting (later Sir Frederick Banting).

If a complete sentence falls within parentheses, place the period *inside* the closing parenthesis.

Banting became a professor at the University of Toronto in 1923. (He was knighted in 1934.)

Labels for lists within text

Today Type 1 diabetes is managed effectively with (1) glucose monitors, (2) insulin pens, and (3) insulin pumps.

Do not use parentheses for such labels when you set a list off (that is, indent it) from your text.

29c   Ellipsis mark: Omissions from quotations

The ellipsis mark, consisting of three spaced periods (. . .), generally indicates an omission from a quotation. The following examples quote from, or refer to, this passage about environmentalism:

Original quotation

"At the heart of the environmentalist world view is the conviction that human physical and spiritual health depends on sustaining the planet in a relatively unaltered state. Earth is our home in the full, genetic sense, where humanity and its ancestors existed for all the millions of years of their evolution. Natural ecosystems— forests, coral reefs, marine blue waters—maintain the world exactly as we would wish it to be maintained. When we debase the global environment and extinguish the variety of life, we are dismantling a support system that is too complex to understand, let alone replace, in the foreseeable future." —Edward O. Wilson, "Is Humanity Suicidal?"

1. Omission of the middle of a sentence

Wilson observes, "Natural ecosystems . . . maintain the world exactly as we would wish it to be maintained."

2. Omission of the end of a sentence, without source citation

29c

Wilson writes, "Earth is our home. . . ." [The sentence period, close up to the last word, precedes the ellipsis mark.]

3. Omission of the end of a sentence, with source citation

Wilson writes, "Earth is our home . . ." (27). [The sentence period follows the source citation.]

4. Omission of parts of two or more sentences

Wilson writes, "At the heart of the environmentalist world view is the conviction that human physical and spiritual health depends on sustaining the planet . . . where humanity and its ancestors existed for all the millions of years of their evolution."

5. Omission of one or more sentences

As Wilson puts it, "At the heart of the environmentalist world view is the conviction that human physical and spiritual health depends on sustaining the planet in a relatively unaltered state. . . . When we debase the global environment and extinguish the variety of life, we are dismantling a support system that is too complex to understand, let alone replace, in the foreseeable future."

6. Omission from the middle of a sentence through the end of another sentence

"Earth is our home. . . . When we debase the global environment and extinguish the variety of life, we are dismantling a support system that is too complex to understand, let alone replace, in the foreseeable future."

a. Bracketed capital letter

"[H]uman physical and spiritual health," Wilson writes, "depends on sustaining the planet in a relatively unaltered state." [No ellipsis mark is needed because the brackets around the *H* indicate that the letter was not capitalized originally and thus that the beginning of the sentence has been omitted.]

b. Small letter

According to Wilson, "human physical and spiritual health depends on sustaining the planet in a relatively unaltered state." [No ellipsis mark is needed because the small *h* indicates that the beginning of the sentence has been omitted.]

29c

c. Capital letter from the original

Hami comments, ". . .Wilson argues eloquently for the environmentalist world view." [An ellipsis mark *is* needed because the quoted part of the sentence begins with a capital letter and it is not clear that the beginning of the original sentence has been omitted.]

Wilson describes the earth as "our home." [No ellipsis mark needed.]

Note these features of the examples:

- Use an ellipsis mark when it is not otherwise clear that you have left out material from the source, as when you omit one or more sentences (examples 5 and 6) or when the words you quote form a complete sentence that is different in the original (examples 1–4 and 7c).
- You don't need an ellipsis mark when it is obvious that you have omitted something, such as when capitalization indicates omission (examples 7a and 7b) or when a phrase clearly comes from a larger sentence (example 8).
- After a grammatically complete sentence, an ellipsis mark follows the sentence period (examples 2, 5, and 6) *except* when a parenthetical source citation follows the quotation (example 3). Then the sentence period falls after the citation.

If your quotation omits one or more lines of poetry or paragraphs of prose, show the omission with an entire line of ellipsis marks across the full width of the quotation.

29d Brackets: Changes in quotations

Though they have specialized uses in mathematical equations, brackets mainly indicate that you have altered a quotation to fit it into your sentence or added an editorial comment to the quotation.

"[T]hat Petro-Canada station [just outside Calgary] is one of the busiest in the nation," said a company spokesperson.

29e Slash: Options, breaks in poetry lines, and URLs

Option

Some teachers oppose pass/fail courses.

29e

Break in poetry lines run into your text

Many readers have sensed a reluctant turn away from death in Frost's lines "The woods are lovely, dark and deep, / But I have promises to keep."

URL

http://www.statcan.gc.ca/start-debut-eng.html

P A R T V

Spelling and Mechanics

PEARSON

mycanadiancomplab

Visit the **Resources** tab in MyCanadianCompLab and click on **Grammar** to access grammar, punctuation, and mechanics exercises that will help you improve your writing skills and get a better grade in your course.

Spelling and Mechanics

This checklist covers the main conventions of spelling and mechanics. For a detailed guide to this part, see the contents inside the back cover.

Spelling

☑ Proofread for correct spelling. Don't rely on your spelling checker. Consistently follow either Canadian or American conventions. (See pp. 105–9.)

Capital letters

☑ Use capital letters appropriately for proper nouns and adjectives and for the titles of works and persons. (See pp. 109–11.)

Italics or underlining

☑ Use italics primarily for the titles of works published separately from other works. Ensure that italics in source citations conform to your instructor's requirements. (See pp. 111–13.)

Abbreviations

☑ Use abbreviations appropriately for the discipline or field you are writing in. (See pp. 113–15.)

Numbers

☑ Express numbers in numerals or words appropriately for the discipline or field you are writing in. (See pp. 115–16.)

30 Spelling and the Hyphen

Spelling, including using the hyphen, is a skill you can acquire by paying attention to words and by developing three habits:

- Carefully proofread your writing.
- Cultivate a healthy suspicion of your spellings.
- Habitually check a dictionary when you doubt a spelling.

30a Spelling checkers

A spelling checker can help you find and track spelling errors in your papers. But its usefulness is limited, mainly because it can't spot the confusion of words with similar spellings, such as *their/they're/there*. A grammar and style checker may flag such words, but only the ones listed in its dictionary, and you still must select the correct spelling. Proofread your papers to catch spelling errors.

See page 14–15 for more on spelling checkers.

30b Spelling rules

30b

We often misspell syllables rather than whole words. The following rules focus on troublesome syllables.

ie and *ei*

Follow the familiar jingle: *i* before *e* except after *c* or when pronounced "ay" as in *neighbour* and *weigh*.

i before *e*	bel<u>ie</u>ve	th<u>ie</u>f
e before *i*	rec<u>ei</u>ve	c<u>ei</u>ling
ei pronounced "ay"	fr<u>ei</u>ght	v<u>ei</u>n

Exceptions Remember common exceptions with this sentence: *The w<u>ei</u>rd for<u>ei</u>gner n<u>ei</u>ther s<u>ei</u>zes l<u>ei</u>sure nor forf<u>ei</u>ts h<u>ei</u>ght.*

Silent final *e*

Drop a silent *e* when adding an ending that begins with a vowel. Keep the *e* if the ending begins with a consonant.

advise + able = advi<u>s</u>able   care + ful = car<u>e</u>ful

---

Visit www.mycanadiancomplab.ca for added help and exercises on mechanics.

Exceptions Keep the final *e* before a vowel to prevent confusion or mispronunciation: *dyeing, changeable.* Drop the *e* before a consonant when another vowel comes before the *e: argument, truly.*

Final *y*

When adding to a word ending in *y*, change *y* to *i* when it follows a consonant. Keep the *y* when it follows a vowel, precedes *-ing,* or ends a proper name.

beauty, beauties	day, days
worry, worried	study, studying
supply, supplier	Minsky, Minskys

Consonants

When adding an ending to a one-syllable word that ends in a consonant, double the consonant if it follows a single vowel. Otherwise, don't double the consonant.

slap, slapping	pair, paired

For words of more than one syllable, double the final consonant when it follows a single vowel (1) if the syllable ending with that consonant is stressed in the newly formed word, or (2) if the final consonant is *l*, even if that syllable is not stressed.

submit, submitted	despair, despairing
refer, referred	refer, reference
label, labelled	revel, revelled

Plurals

Most nouns form plurals by adding *s* to the singular form. Nouns ending in *s, sh, ch,* or *x* add *es* to the singular.

boy, boys	kiss, kisses
table, tables	lurch, lurches
Murphy, Murphys	tax, taxes

Nouns ending in a vowel plus *o* add *s*. Nouns ending in a consonant plus *o* add *es*.

ratio, ratios	hero, heroes

Form the plural of a compound noun by adding *s* to the main word in the compound. The main word may not necessarily fall at the end.

passersby	breakthroughs
fathers-in-law	city-states

Some English nouns that come from other languages form the plural according to their original language.

analysis, analyses
crisis, crises
criterion, criteria

medium, media
phenomenon, phenomena
cognoscente, cognoscenti

ESL Noncount nouns do not form plurals, either regularly (with an added *s*) or irregularly. Examples of noncount nouns include *equipment, information,* and *wealth.* See page 71–72.

30c   Canadian spelling

Canadian spelling used to follow British usage. Increasingly, however, Canadians adopt American usage. Although it is usually acceptable (and very Canadian) to mix British and American spellings within one document, it is never acceptable to follow specific rules inconsistently.

For example, if you spell *theatre* with an *re* according to British spelling conventions, you should not then spell *metre* with an *er*, as in *meter*, which is American. Similarly, use both *colour* and *labour*, or *color* and *labor*, but not *colour* and *labor*. Many words that end in *re* and *our* in British spelling end in *er* and *or* in American spelling.

Be consistent as well with words that double their final *l*, that end in *ce* or *se*, or that end in *que*. Thus, *marvellous*, *defence*, and *cheque* are British (generally the preferred Canadian usage), while *marvelous*, *defense*, and *check* are American.

Some other words for which Canadians generally follow British spelling include *catalogue* (not *catalog*), *pyjamas* (not *pajamas*), and *whisky* (not *whiskey*).

Decide on the appropriate usage for your audience and stick to it, either by consistently following one dictionary's preferences or by setting your word processor's spelling-checker preference. This book, for example, follows the preferences of the *Canadian Oxford Dictionary*.

30d

30d   The hyphen

Use the hyphen to form compound words and to divide words at the ends of lines.

Compound words

Compound words may be written as a single word (*breakthrough*), as two words (*decision makers*), or as a hyphenated word (*cross-reference*). Check a dictionary for the spelling of a compound word. Except as explained below, any compound not listed in the dictionary should be written as two words.

Sometimes a compound word comes from combining two or more words into a single adjective.° When such a compound adjective precedes a noun, a hyphen forms the words clearly into a unit.

> She is a <u>well-known</u> actor.
> Some <u>Spanish-speaking</u> students work as translators.
> Alice reads <u>eighteenth-century</u> novels.

When a compound adjective follows the noun, the hyphen is unnecessary.

> The actor is <u>well known</u>.
> Some students are <u>Spanish speaking</u>.
> Alice studies the <u>eighteenth century</u>.

The hyphen is also unnecessary in a compound modifier containing an *-ly* adverb, even before the noun: *clearly defined terms*.

Fractions and compound numbers

Hyphens join the parts of fractions: *three-fourths, one-half*. And the whole numbers *twenty-one* to *ninety-nine* are always hyphenated.

30d Prefixes and suffixes

Do not use hyphens with prefixes except as follows:

- With the prefixes *self-, all-,* and *ex-: self-control, all-inclusive, ex-student*.
- With a prefix before a capitalized word: *un-American*.
- With a capital letter before a word: *T-shirt*.
- To prevent misreading: *de-emphasize, re-create a story*.

The only suffix that regularly requires a hyphen is *-elect,* as in *president-elect*.

Word division at the end of a line

You can avoid occasional short lines in your documents by setting your word processor to divide words automatically at appropriate breaks. To divide words manually, follow these guidelines:

- Divide words only between syllables—for instance, *win-dows,* not *wi-ndows*. Check a dictionary for correct syllable breaks.
- Never divide a one-syllable word.
- Leave at least two letters on the first line and three on the second line. If a word cannot be divided to follow this rule (for instance, *a-bus-er*), don't divide it.

If you must break an electronic address or URL—for instance, in a source citation—do so only after a slash. (Some documentation styles have more detailed rules: see Part VI.) Do not hyphenate, because readers may perceive any added hyphen as part of the address.

Not   http://www./statcan.ca/english/Sub-
      jects/Cpi/cpi-en.htm

But   http://www.statcan.ca/english/Subjects/
      Cpi/cpi-en.htm

31 Capital Letters

As a rule, capitalize a word only when a dictionary or conventional use says you must. Consult one of the style guides listed on page 163–64 for special uses of capitals in the social, natural, and applied sciences.

31a First word of a sentence

Every writer should own a good dictionary.

31b

31b Proper nouns° and proper adjectives°

Proper nouns name specific persons, places, and things: *Shakespeare, Alberta, World War I.* Proper adjectives are formed from some proper nouns: *Shakespearean, Albertan.* Capitalize all proper nouns and proper adjectives but not the articles (*a, an, the*) that precede them.

Specific persons and things
Pierre Berton   Rideau Canal

Specific places and geographical regions
Halifax   the North, the Maritimes

But: north of the city, a maritime climate

Days of the week, months, holidays
Monday   Yom Kippur
May   Christmas

Visit www.mycanadiancomplab.ca for
added help and exercises on mechanics.

Historical events, documents, periods, movements

the Meech Lake Accord	the Renaissance
the 1837 Rebellion	the Fenians

Government offices or departments and institutions

House of Commons	Supreme Court
Canada Council	Centennial Collegiate High School

Political, social, athletic, and other organizations and their members

B'nai Brith	Liberal Party, Liberals
Rotary Club	Toronto Blue Jays
National Farmers Union	Montreal Symphony Orchestra

Races, nationalities, and their languages

First Nations	Germans
African-Canadian	Swahili
Caucasian	Ukrainian

But: blacks, whites

Religions, their followers, and terms for the sacred

Christianity, Christians	God
Catholicism, Catholics	Allah
Judaism, Orthodox Jew	the Bible (*but* biblical)
Islam, Muslims *or* Moslems	the Qur'an *or* Koran

Common nouns as parts of proper nouns

Main Street	Lake Superior
Spadina Avenue	Ford Motor Company
Stanley Park	Memorial University
Great Slave Lake	Prince Edward County
Pacific Ocean	Jacques Cartier Bridge

But: the lake, university course, the company, the bridge

31c   Titles and subtitles of works

Capitalize all the words in a title and subtitle *except* articles (*a, an, the*), the word *to* in infinitives,° and connecting words of fewer than five letters. Capitalize even these words when they are the first or last word in the title or when they fall after a colon or semicolon.

Voyage of the Iceberg	*Swann: A Literary Mystery*
"The Albanian Virgin"	*To the Lighthouse*
File Under Architecture	"Knowing Whom to Ask"

Note   Some academic disciplines require other treatments of titles within source citations, such as capitalizing different words or only the first words. See pages 171 (MLA style), 187 (APA style), and 216 (CSE style).

31d   Titles of persons

Title before name   Professor Jane Covington
Title after name   Jane Covington, a professor

31e   Online communication

Online messages written in all-capital letters or with no capitals are difficult to read, and those in all-capitals are often considered rude. Use capital letters according to the rules in 31a–31d in all your online communication.

32   Italics or Underlining

Italic type and underlining indicate the same thing: the word or words are being distinguished or emphasized.

Note Grammar and style checkers cannot recognize problems with italics or underlining. Check your work yourself to ensure that any highlighting is appropriate.

32a   Italics vs. underlining

Italic type is now almost universally preferred over underlining for word-processed or typeset business and academic writing. MLA style, for example, now assumes the use of italic type (rather than underlining, as previously) to indicate book titles in sources and to identify non-English words in texts. Underlining should be reserved for handwritten documents, unless your instructor or the style guide you are following specifies otherwise. In any case, do not mix the two methods: use either italics or underlining consistently throughout your document.

32b   Titles of works

Do not italicize the title of your own paper unless it contains an element (such as a book title) that requires highlighting.

Within your text, italicize the titles of works that are published, released, or produced separately from other works. Use quotation marks for all other titles (see pp. 94–95).

Visit www.mycanadiancomplab.ca for added help and exercises on mechanics.

Book	Long poem
War and Peace	*Paradise Lost*
Play	Periodical
Hamlet	*The Hamilton Spectator*
Website	Television or radio program
Friends of Prufrock	
Google	*Ideas*
Computer software	Movie
Microsoft Internet Explorer	*Men with Brooms*
Acrobat Reader	Pamphlet
Long musical work	*The Truth About Alcoholism*
The Beatles' *Revolver*	
But: Symphony in C	Published speech
Work of visual art	Lincoln's *Gettysburg Address*
Emily Carr's *Wood Interior*	

Exceptions Legal documents, the Bible, and titles of their parts are generally not italicized.

We studied the Book of Revelation in the Bible.

32c   Ships, aircraft, spacecraft, trains

Challenger	the *Skeena*	*Queen Elizabeth 2*
Apollo XI	the *Canadian*	*Spirit of St. Louis*

32d   Non-English words

Italicize a non-English expression that has not been absorbed into our language. A dictionary will say whether a word is still considered foreign to English.

The scientific name for the brown trout is *Salmo trutta*. [The Latin scientific names for plants and animals are always italicized.]

In Quebec, a convenience store is called a *dépanneur* by English and French alike.

32e   Words or characters named as words

Italicize words or characters (letters or numbers) that are referred to as themselves rather than used for their meanings. Such words include terms you are defining.

Some children pronounce *th*, as in *thought*, with an *f* sound.

The word *syzygy* refers to a straight line formed by three celestial bodies, as in the alignment of the earth, sun, and moon.

32f Electronic addresses

Electronic addresses in essays and bibliographies should not be underlined or printed in a different colour from your text. Ensure that you turn off the *Hyperlink* option in your word processor's automatic formatting feature.

32g Online alternatives

Electronic mail and other forms of online communication may not allow conventional highlighting such as italics or underlining for the purposes described above. The program may not be able to produce the highlighting or may reserve it for a special function. (On websites, for instance, underlining often indicates a link to another site.)

To distinguish book titles and other elements that usually require italics or underlining, type an underscore before and after the element: *Measurements coincide with those in _Joule's Handbook_*. You can also emphasize words with asterisks before and after: *I *will not* be able to attend.*

Don't use all-capital letters for emphasis; they yell too loudly. (See also 31e, p. 111.)

33 Abbreviations

The following guidelines on abbreviations pertain to the text of a non-technical document. For any special requirements of the discipline you are writing in, consult one of the style guides listed on pages 163–64. In all disciplines, writers increasingly omit periods from abbreviations that end in capital letters. (See p. 96.)

If a name or term (such as *operating room*) appears often in a piece of writing, then its abbreviation (*OR*) can cut down on extra words. Spell out the full term at its first appearance, give the abbreviation in parentheses, and use the abbreviation thereafter.

Visit www.mycanadiancomplab.ca for added help and exercises on mechanics.

33a Familiar abbreviations

Titles before names	Dr., Mr., Mrs., Ms., Rev., Gen.
Titles after names	MD, DDS, DVM, PhD, Sr., Jr.
Institutions	SFU, AGO, UNB, DFAIT
Organizations	CUPE, NDP, YMCA, IATA
Corporations	IBM, CBC, CN, GM
People, positions	JFK, FDR, ADM, CEO
Countries	USA, UK
Specific numbers	no. 36 *or* No. 36
Specific amounts	$7.41, $1 million, $36K
Specific times	11:26 AM, 8:04 a.m., 2:00 PM, 8:05 p.m.
Specific dates	44 BC, AD 1492, 44 BCE, 1492 CE

Note The abbreviation AD (*anno domini,* "in the year of the Lord") always precedes the date. Sometimes AD and BC ("before Christ") are replaced by CE ("common era") and BCE ("before the common era").

33b Latin abbreviations

33c

Generally, use the common Latin abbreviations (without italics) only in source citations and comments in parentheses.

i.e.	*id est:*	that is
cf.	*confer:*	compare
e.g.	*exempli gratia:*	for example
et al.	*et alii:*	and others
etc.	*et cetera:*	and so forth
NB	*nota bene:*	note well

He said he would be gone a fortnight (i.e., two weeks).
Bloom et al., editors, *Anthology of Light Verse.*

33c Words usually spelled out

Generally, spell out certain kinds of words in the text of academic, general, and business writing. (In technical writing, however, abbreviate units of measurement.)

Units of measurement
The cottage is sixteen kilometres from town.

Geographical names
Margaret Laurence was born in Manitoba.

Names of days, months, and holidays

The truce was signed on <u>Tuesday</u>, <u>April</u> 16, and was ratified by <u>Christmas</u>.

Names of people

<u>Robert</u> Frost wrote accessible poems.

Courses of instruction

The writer teaches <u>psychology</u> and <u>composition</u>.

And

The new rules affect Vancouver <u>and</u> environs. [Use the ampersand, *&*, only in the names of business firms: *Lee & Sons*.]

34 Numbers

This chapter addresses the use of numbers (numerals versus words) in the text of a nontechnical document. Usage does vary, so consult one of the style guides listed on pages 163–64 for the requirements of the discipline you are writing in.

34a Numerals, not words

34a

Numbers requiring three or more words		Addresses
366	36,500	118 Sixth Street Prince Rupert BC V87 3L7

Note: "Sixth" is the *name* of the street, but 118 is the house *number*.

Round numbers over a million		Decimals, percentages, and fractions
26 million	2.45 billion	22.5 3½ 48% (*or* 48 percent)

Exact amounts of money		
$3.5 million	$4.50	

		Scores and statistics
		a ratio of 8 to 1 21 to 7 a mean of 26

Days and years		
June 18, 1985	AD 12	
456 BC	12 CE	

		Pages, chapters, volumes, acts, scenes, lines
		Chapter 9, page 123 *Hamlet*, act 5, scene 3

The time of day		
9:00 AM	16:45	

Visit www.mycanadiancomplab.ca for added help and exercises on mechanics.

34b Words, not numerals

Numbers of one or two words

<u>sixty</u> days, <u>forty-two</u> laps, <u>one hundred</u> people

In business and technical writing, use words only for numbers under 10 (<u>10</u> *reasons,* <u>four</u> *laps*).

Beginnings of sentences

<u>Seventy-five</u> riders entered the race.

If a number beginning a sentence requires more than two words to spell out, reword the sentence so that the number falls later.

Faulty	<u>103</u> visitors returned.
Awkward	<u>One hundred and three</u> visitors returned.
Revised	Of the visitors, <u>103</u> returned.

34b

PART VI

Research and Documentation

PEARSON
mycanadiancomplab

Visit the **Composing** space in MyCanadianCompLab to research, draft, and revise your written work and assignments. You can view instructor, peer, and tutor comments on your work, pulling together all the feedback you will need to produce better writing samples and get a better grade in your course.

Research and Documentation

This checklist covers the main considerations in using and documenting sources. For a detailed guide to this part, see the contents inside the back cover.

Developing a research strategy

☑ Formulate a question about your subject that can guide your research. (See opposite.)

☑ Set goals for your sources: library vs. Internet, primary vs. secondary, and so on. (See p. 120.)

☑ Prepare a working bibliography to keep track of sources. (See p. 124.)

Finding sources

☑ Develop keywords that describe your subject for searches of electronic sources. (See p. 127.)

☑ Consult appropriate sources to answer your research question. (See p. 129.)

Evaluating and synthesizing sources

☑ Evaluate both print and online sources for their relevance and reliability. (See p. 138.)

☑ Synthesize sources to find their relationships and to support your own ideas. (See p. 144.)

Integrating sources into your text

☑ Summarize, paraphrase, or quote sources depending on the significance of the source's ideas or wording. (See p. 145.)

☑ Work source material smoothly and informatively into your own text. (See p. 148.)

Avoiding plagiarism and documenting sources

☑ Do not plagiarize, either deliberately or accidentally, by presenting the words or ideas of others as your own. (See p. 153.)

☑ Using the style guide appropriate for your discipline, document your sources and format your paper. (See pp. 163–64 for a list of style guides and Chapters 40 for MLA style, 41 for APA style, 42 for Chicago style, and 43 for CSE and IEEE styles.)

35 Developing a Research Strategy

Research writing gives you a chance to work like a detective solving a case. The mystery is the answer to a question you care about. The search for the answer leads you to consider what others think about your subject, to build on that information, and ultimately to become an expert in your own right.

35a Subject, question, and thesis

Seek a research subject that you care about and want to know more about. Beginning with such an interest and with your own views will motivate you and will make you a participant in a dialogue when you begin examining sources.

Asking a question about your subject can give direction to your research by focusing your thinking on a particular approach. To discover your question, consider what about your subject intrigues or perplexes you, what you'd like to know more about. (See the next page for suggestions on using your own knowledge.)

Try to narrow your research question so that you can answer it in the time and space you have available.

From	What factors are responsible for reducing the East Coast cod stocks?
To	Has climate change affected the East Coast cod stocks?
From	How does the Internet affect business?
To	How should the Internet be taxed?

35a

Since each question requires more than a yes or no answer, even your tentative responses will require you to think seriously about pros and cons, causes and effects.

As you read and write, your question will probably evolve to reflect your increasing knowledge of the subject. Eventually its answer will become the **thesis** of your paper, the main idea that all the paper's evidence supports. (See also pp. 3–4.)

Visit www.mycanadiancomplab.ca for
added help and exercises on research assignments.

35b   Goals for sources

Before you start looking for sources, consider what you already know about your subject and where you are likely to find information on it.

Your own knowledge

Discovering what you already know about your topic will guide you in discovering what you don't know and thus need to research. Take some time to spell out facts you have learned, opinions you have heard or read elsewhere, and, of course, your own opinions.

When you've explored your thoughts, make a list of questions for which you don't have answers, whether factual (*How do today's cod stocks compare to those of thirty years ago? What laws govern taxes in Internet commerce?*) or more open-ended (*What ecological factors could affect cod stocks? Who benefits from a tax-free Internet? Who doesn't benefit?*). These questions will give you clues about the sources you need to look for first.

Kinds of sources

For many research projects, you'll want to consult a mix of sources, as described below. You may start by seeking the outlines of your subject—the range and depth of opinions about it—in reference works and articles in popular periodicals or through a search of the web. Then, as you refine your views and your research question, you'll move on to more specialized sources such as scholarly books and periodicals and your own interviews or surveys. (See pp. 129–38 for more on each kind of source.)

35b

Library and Internet sources

The print and electronic sources available through your library—mainly reference works, periodicals, and books—have two big advantages over most of what you'll find on the Internet: they are catalogued and indexed for easy retrieval; and they are generally reliable, having been screened first by their publishers and then by the library's staff. In contrast, the Internet's retrieval systems are more difficult to use effectively, and web sources can be less reliable because many do not pass through any screening before being posted.

Most instructors expect research writers to consult library sources. But they'll accept online sources, too, if you have used them judiciously. Increasingly, libraries are relying on Internet resources such as databases and e-texts to supplement their print holdings. Thus, even with its disadvantages, the Internet can be a valuable resource for primary sources, scholarly work, current information, and diverse views. For guidelines on evaluating both print and online sources, see pages 138–44.

Primary and secondary sources

As much as possible, you should rely on **primary sources**. These are first-hand accounts, such as historical documents (letters, speeches, and so on), eyewitness reports, works of literature, government documents, reports on experiments or surveys conducted by the writer, and your own interviews, experiments, observations, or correspondence.

In contrast, **secondary sources** report and analyze information drawn from other sources, often primary ones: a reporter's summary of a controversial issue, a historian's account of a battle, a critic's reading of a poem, a psychologist's evaluation of several studies. Secondary sources may contain helpful summaries and interpretations that direct, support, and extend your own thinking. However, most research-writing assignments expect you to do more than simply summarize such sources.

Scholarly and popular sources

The scholarship of acknowledged experts is essential for depth, authority, and specificity. The general-interest views and information of popular sources can help you apply more scholarly approaches to daily life.

When looking for sources, gauge how scholarly or popular they are from bibliographic information:

35b

- *Check the publisher.* Is it a scholarly journal (such as *Canadian Journal of Public Health*) or a publisher of scholarly books (such as University of Toronto Press), or is it a popular magazine (such as *Maclean's*) or a publisher of popular books (such as Little, Brown)?
- *Check the author.* Does the author have relevant credentials or experience?
- *Check the title.* Is it technical, or does it use a general vocabulary?
- *Check the URL.* Addresses, or URLs, for Internet sources often include a "tail" that tells you something about the source: *.edu* means the source comes from a US educational institution, *.gov* from a US government body, *.org* from a non-profit organization, *.com* from a commercial organization such as a corporation. Remember, however, that while a site ending in *.edu* may originate in a university, it might also

be the personal web page of a biased or ill-informed individual. Even sites sponsored by governments or by non-profit organizations must be evaluated critically. Note that *.ca* indicates a Canadian source.

Older and newer sources

For most subjects, a combination of older, established sources (such as books) and current sources (such as newspaper articles or interviews) will provide both background and up-to-date information. Only historical subjects or very current subjects require an emphasis on one extreme or another. Note that many Internet search engines access only recent sources. (See Chapter 36e.)

Impartial and biased sources

Seek a range of viewpoints. Sources that attempt to be impartial can offer an overview of your subject and trustworthy facts. Sources with clear biases can offer a diversity of opinion. Of course, to discover bias, you may have to read the source carefully (see pp. 139–44); but even a bibliographical listing can be informative.

- *Check the author*. You may have heard of the author as a respected researcher (thus more likely to be objective) or as a leading proponent of a certain view (less likely to be objective).
- *Check the title*. It may reveal something about point of view. (Consider these contrasting titles: "Keep the Internet Tax-Free" and "Taxation of Internet Commerce: Issues and Questions.")

Note Internet sources must be approached with particular care. See pages 140–44.

Sources with helpful features

Depending on your topic and how far along your research is, you may want to look for sources with features such as illustrations (which can clarify important concepts), bibliographies (which can direct you to other sources), and indexes (which can help you develop keywords for electronic searches; see pp. 127–28).

35c Information gathering

All methods for gathering source information share the same requirements:

- *Keep accurate records of what sources say*. Accuracy helps prevent misrepresentation and plagiarism.

- *Keep accurate records of how to find sources.* These records are essential for retracing steps and for citing sources in the final paper. (See p. 124 on keeping a working bibliography.)
- *Interact with sources.* Reading sources critically leads to your understanding them, the relationships among them, and their support for your own ideas.

Each method of gathering information has advantages and disadvantages. On any given project, you may use all the methods.

- *Handwritten notes:* Even if you prefer to use a computer, voice-recorder, or photocopier, sometimes they are not available when you need to record information from a source. In that case, write your notes in a notebook or on file cards rather than on random scraps of paper. Be careful to copy accurately. To prevent accidental plagiarism, avoid using the same words as the source unless you are quoting, in which case place all quotations within large quotation marks. For each new item of information, use a fresh card or page, labelled with a subject heading and cross-referenced by author or title to the record of the source in your working bibliography. Indicate any page breaks when copying quotations so that if you use only a portion of the quotation, you will know which pages to cite.
- *Notes on a computer:* Typing notes on a computer is faster than handwriting. You can import the notes into your draft as you write, and you can use *Find* and *Search* commands to locate notes on the same topic from other sources. Computer notes, however, share the disadvantages of handwritten notes: the risks of introducing errors and of accidentally plagiarizing. As with handwritten notes, strive for accuracy, clearly identify quotations, and organize notes by subject headings rather than sources.
- *Photocopies and printouts:* Photocopying or printing out source material is helpful when you have limited access to the source material, but you are merely postponing the necessary task of understanding, criticizing, evaluating, and selecting what, if anything, you will use from the source. As well, you must remember to record the complete publication information about the source. Without the source information, you *may not* use the source.
- *Downloads:* Researching online and through databases, you can often download précis or full-text articles, web

pages, and other materials into your computer and then into your draft. Downloads, however, carry the same risks as photocopies and printouts: you must still interact with the source material, and you must remember to record publication information about the source. More dangerously, you run the risk of importing the source's words into your draft as though they were your own. Be scrupulous to avoid plagiarism.

Whichever method you follow, for each source consulted, add publication information about the source to your list or file of sources, which should be organized according to an appropriate documentation style (see Chapters 40–43). For each item of information, opinion, or quotation, record a separate note using a subject heading, and cross-reference each note to the source listed in your file of sources. (See below, 35d, Working annotated bibliography.) You can then sort and rearrange notes by subject as you build your arguments.

35d   Working annotated bibliography

Keep records of sources so that you can always locate them and can fully acknowledge them in your paper. Use the following lists to track different kinds of sources. The safest strategy is to build an accurate working bibliography as you go, following the citation rules of whichever style you are using. For online sources, you may need extra effort to uncover the required information (see below).

35d

Bibliographic information

For a book
Library call number
Name(s) of author(s), editor(s), translator(s), or others listed
Title and subtitle
Publication data: (1) place of publication; (2) publisher's name; (3) year of publication
Other important data, such as edition or volume number

For a periodical article
Name(s) of author(s)
Title and subtitle of article
Title of periodical
Publication data: (1) volume number and issue number (if any) in which the article appears; (2) date of issue; (3) page numbers on which the article appears

For electronic sources

Name(s) of author(s)
Title and subtitle
Publication data for books and articles (see above)
Date of release, online posting, or latest revision
Medium (online, CD-ROM, etc.)
Format of online source (website, web page, e-mail, etc.)
Date you consulted the source
Complete URL or electronic address (unless the source
   was obtained through a subscription service and has
   no permanent address)
DOI (digital object identifier) if available (see p. 192)
For sources obtained through a database: (1) name of
   database; (2) date of access; (3) electronic address of
   the database's home page

For other sources

Name(s) of author(s) or others listed, such as a government department or a recording artist
Title of the work
Format, such as unpublished letter or live performance
Publication or production data: (1) publisher's or producer's name; (2) date of publication, release, or
   production; (3) location of publication; (4) identifying
   numbers (if any)

Online sources

The following guidelines can help you find and record
the publication information for online sources.

35d

1. *Find the DOI (if available), or the source's URL, or
   address, in the web browser's* Address *or* Location *field
   near the top of the screen.* You may need to use this
   URL in acknowledging the source. With a source you
   find through a database, however, the URL may be
   unusable. See page 178 for what to do in that case.
2. *Use as the source title the title of the page you are consulting.* This information usually appears as a heading
   at the top of the page, but if not, it may also appear in
   the bar along the top of the browser window.
3. *Look for publication information at the bottom of each
   page.* Check here for (*a*) the name of the author or the
   sponsoring organization, (*b*) an address for reaching
   the sponsor or author directly, and (*c*) the date of
   publication or last revision.

If the page you are reading does not list publication
information, look for it on the site's home page. There may
be a link to the home page, or you can find it by editing the

URL in the *Address* or *Location* field: working backward, delete the end of the URL up to the preceding slash; then hit Enter. If that doesn't take you to the home page, delete the end of the remaining address up to the preceding slash and hit Enter. Editing the address in this way, you'll eventually reach the home page.

Annotations

Creating annotations for a working bibliography converts it from a simple list to a tool for assessing sources. When you discover a possible source, record not only its publication information but also the following:

- **What you know about the content of the source.** Periodical databases and book catalogues generally include abstracts, or summaries, of sources that can help with this part of the annotation.
- **How you think the source may be helpful in your research.** Does it offer expert opinion, statistics, maps, photographs, a range of views, a significant interpretation, rare documents, or some other special feature? Does it place your subject in a historical, social, cultural, or economic context?

Here are two sample entries:

Cook, Tim. *At the Sharp End: Canadians Fighting the Great War, 1914–1916.* Vol. 1. Toronto: Viking Canada, 2007. Detailed military history of the Canadian Expeditionary Force in France and Belgium, with historic photos and military maps. Detailed index and bibliography.

Macdonald, Lyn. *They Called it Passchendaele: The Story of the Third Battle of Ypres and of the Men Who Fought in It.* London: Michael Joseph, 1978. Uses letters and interviews with soldiers to tell the story of the battle in their words. Some very moving personal stories. No Canadian content. With photos and maps.

36

36 Finding Sources

Your library and a computer connected to the Internet give you access to a vast range of sources. This chapter

Visit www.mycanadiancomplab.ca for added help and exercises on research assignments.

explains the basics of an electronic search and introduces reference works, books, periodicals, the web, online-communication sources, government publications, and your own sources.

36a   Electronic searches

As you conduct research, the World Wide Web will be your gateway to ideas and information. Always begin your academic research on your library's website rather than with a search engine such as *Google*. Although a direct web search can be productive, you'll find a higher concentration of relevant and reliable sources (many of them not accessible by *Google*) through the library site, whose resources have passed through editors and librarians to ensure their value.

Probably the most important element in an electronic search is appropriate **keywords,** or **descriptors,** that name your subject for databases and web search engines. With a database, such as a periodical index, your keywords will help you find the subject headings used by the database to organize the sources you seek. With a web search engine, such as *Google,* your keywords must match terms used in source titles and texts. In either case, you may have to use trial and error to discover keywords that accurately describe your subject.

Most databases and search engines work with **Boolean operators,** terms or symbols that allow you to expand or limit your keywords and thus your search. The basic operators appear below, but resources do differ. The Help or Advanced Search information of each resource explains its system.

36a

- Use *AND* or + to narrow the search by including only sources that use all the given words. The keywords *Internet AND tax* request only the sources in the shaded area:

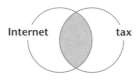

- Use *NOT* or – ("minus") to narrow the search by excluding irrelevant words. *Internet AND tax NOT access* excludes sources that use the word *access*.

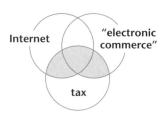

- Use *OR* to broaden the search by giving alternative keywords. *Internet OR (electronic commerce) AND tax* allows for sources that use *Internet* or *electronic commerce* (or both) along with *tax*.

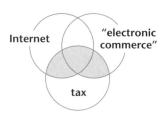

- Use double quotation marks to form search phrases. For instance, *"electronic commerce"* requests the exact phrase, not the separate words. (Some systems may use parentheses instead of quotation marks for this purpose.)
- Use *NEAR* to narrow the search by requiring the keywords to be close to each other—for instance, *Internet NEAR tax*. Depending on the resource you're using, the words could be directly next to each other or many words apart. Some resources use *WITHIN* so that you can specify the exact number of words apart—for instance, *Internet WITHIN 10 tax*.
- Use wild cards to permit different versions of the same word. In *child**, for instance, the wild card * indicates that sources may include *child, children, childcare, childhood, childish, childlike,* and *childproof.* If a wild card opens up your search too much (as with the example *child**), you may be better off using OR to limit the options: *child OR children.* (Some systems use ?, :, or + for a wild card instead of *.)
- Be sure to spell your keywords correctly. Some search tools will look for close matches or approximations, but correct spelling gives you the best chance of finding relevant sources.

36b Reference works

Reference works (often available online) include encyclopedias, dictionaries, digests, bibliographies, indexes, handbooks, atlases, and almanacs. Your research *must* go beyond these sources, but they can help you decide whether your subject really interests you, can help you develop your keywords for electronic searches, and can direct you to more detailed sources.

Note Always select the most specific reference work for your topic. For example, to learn about *The History of Emily Montague,* the first English novel written in Canada, use *The Oxford Companion to Canadian Literature* rather than *The Canadian Encyclopedia,* a general reference work about Canada.

You'll find many reference works through your library and directly on the web. The following lists give general web references for academic research.

All disciplines

Internet Public Library
   http://www.ipl.org
Library and Archives Canada
   http://collectionscanada.gc.ca
Library of Congress
   http://www.loc.gov
LSU Libraries Webliography
   http://www.lib.lsu.edu/weblio.html
McGill Library and Collections *http://www.mcgill.ca/library/library-findinfo/reference*
World Wide Web Virtual Library
   http://vlib.org

36b

Humanities

BUBL Humanities Resources
   http://bubl.ac.uk/link
EDSITEment
   http://edsitement.neh.gov
Voice of the Shuttle Humanities Gateway
   http://vos.ucsb.edu

Social sciences

Social Science Data on the Internet
   http://3stages.org/idata
Social Science Information Gateway
   http://www.intute.ac.uk/ (choose Social Sciences)
The WWW Virtual Library: Social and Behavioural
   Sciences *http://vlib.org/SocialSciences*

Natural and applied sciences

Google Web Directory Science Links
  http://directory.google.com/Top/Science
Internet Public Library and the Librarians' Internet Index
  http://www.ipl.org
Virtual Library: Science
  http://vlib.org/Science

Note The web-based encyclopedia *Wikipedia* (found at *http://www.wikipedia.org*) is one of the largest reference sites on the Internet. Like any encyclopedia, *Wikipedia* can provide background information for research on a topic; but unlike other encyclopedias, *Wikipedia* is a **wiki**, a kind of website that can be contributed to or edited by anyone. Older entries tend to be reliable because they have been reviewed and edited by experts, but recent entries may contain errors. Ask your instructor whether *Wikipedia* is an acceptable source before you use it. If you do use it, you must carefully evaluate any information you find, using the guidelines on pages 140–44.

36c Books

Depending on your subject, you may find some direction and information in so-called general or trade books, which include personal or popular views of culture, non-specialist explanations of scholarly work, and how-to guides. But usually the books you consult for academic research will be scholarly, intended for specialists, and will include detailed statements of theory or surveys of research.

36d

You can search your library's online catalogue by authors' names, titles, or keywords. Using the tips on pages 126–28, experiment with your own keywords until you locate a source that seems relevant to your subject. The book's detailed record will show subject headings that you can use to find similar books.

36d Periodicals

Periodicals include newspapers, academic journals, and magazines. Newspapers, the easiest to recognize, are useful for detailed accounts of past and current events. Journals and magazines can be harder to distinguish, but their differences are important. Most college and university instructors expect students' research to rely more on journals than on magazines.

Journals	Magazines
Examples: *American Anthropologist, Journal of Black Studies, Journal of Chemical Education*	Examples: *The New Yorker, Maclean's, Rolling Stone, The Walrus*
Articles are intended to advance knowledge in a particular field.	Articles are intended to express opinion, inform, or entertain.
Writers and readers are specialists in the field. Articles are vetted by other experts before publication.	Writers may or may not be specialists in their subjects. Readers are members of the general public or a subgroup with a particular interest.
Articles always include source citations.	Articles rarely include source citations.
Appearance is often bland, with black-only type, little or no decoration, and only illustrations that directly amplify the text, such as graphs.	Appearance varies but is generally lively, with colour, decoration (headings, sidebars, and other elements), and illustrations (drawings, photographs).
Issues may appear quarterly or less often.	Issues may appear weekly, biweekly, or monthly.
Issues may be paged separately (like a magazine) or may be paged sequentially throughout an annual volume, so that issue 3 (the third issue of the year) could open on page 327. (The method of pagination may affect source citations. See pp. 191 and 205.)	Issues are paged separately, each beginning on page 1.

36d

Periodical databases

Periodical databases index the articles in journals, magazines, and newspapers. Often these databases include abstracts, or summaries, of the articles, and they may offer the full text of the articles as well. Your library subscribes to many periodical databases and to services that offer multiple databases, such as the following:

> *EBSCOhost Academic Search.* A periodical index covering magazines and journals in the social sciences, sciences, arts, and humanities. Many articles are available in full text.

> *InfoTrac Expanded Academic ASAP.* The Gale Group's general periodical index covering the social sciences, sciences, arts, and humanities as well as national news periodicals. It includes full-text articles.
>
> *LexisNexis Academic.* An index of news and business, legal, and reference information, with full-text articles. *LexisNexis* includes international, national, and regional newspapers, newsmagazines, and legal and business publications.
>
> *19th Century Masterfile.* A periodical index for historical research prior to 1925.
>
> *ProQuest Research Library.* A periodical index covering the sciences, social sciences, arts, and humanities, including many full-text articles.
>
> *Wilson Databases.* A collection of indexes, often provided in a package, including *Business Periodicals Index, Education Index, General Science Index, Humanities Index, Readers' Guide to Periodical Literature,* and *Social Sciences Index.*

To decide which databases to consult, consider what you're looking for:

- **How broadly and deeply should you search?** Periodical databases vary widely in what they index. If your subject ranges across disciplines, then start with a broad database such as *EBSCOhost Academic Search*. If your subject focuses on a particular discipline, then start with a narrower database such as *Historical Abstracts* or *Computer Literature Index*.

- **Which databases most likely include the kinds of resources you need?** The websites of most libraries allow you to narrow a database search to a particular kind of periodical (such as newspapers or journals) or to a particular discipline. You can then discover each database's focus by checking the description of the database (sometimes labelled "Help" or "Guide") or the list of indexed resources (sometimes labelled "Publications" or "Index"). The description will also tell you the time period the database covers, so you'll know whether you also need to consult older print indexes at the library.

36d

Database searches

The screen shot on the next page shows partial results from a search of *EBSCOhost Academic Search*. Clicking on any of these items would lead to a more detailed record containing two important kinds of information: a list of the subject headings the database uses for the source, which you can use to refine your search;

and an **abstract,** or summary, of the article, which can tell you whether you want to pursue the article further. An abstract is not the article, however, and should not be used or cited as if it were.

Note   Many databases allow you to limit your search to so-called peer-reviewed or refereed journals—that is, scholarly journals whose articles have been reviewed before publication by experts in the field and then revised by the author. Limiting your search to peer-reviewed journals can help you navigate huge databases that might otherwise return scores of unusable articles.

36e

36e   The web

As an academic researcher, you enter the World Wide Web in two ways: through your library's website, and through public search engines such as *Yahoo!* and *Google.* The library entrance, covered in the preceding sections, is your main path to the books and periodicals that, for most subjects, should make up most of your sources. The public entrance, discussed here, can lead to a wealth of information and ideas, but it also has a number of disadvantages:

- *The web is a wide-open network.* Anyone with the right hardware and software can place information on the Internet, and even a carefully conceived search can turn up sources with widely varying reliability: journal articles, government documents, scholarly data, term papers written by high school students, sales pitches masked as objective reports, wild theories. You must be especially diligent about evaluating Internet sources (see p. 140).

- *The web changes constantly.* No search engine can keep up with the web's daily additions and deletions, and a source you find today may be different or gone tomorrow. Some sites are designed and labelled as archives: they do not change except with additions. But generally you should not put off consulting an online source that you think you may want to use.

- *The web provides limited information on the past.* Sources dating from before the 1980s, or even more recently, probably will not appear on the web.

- *The web is not all-inclusive.* Most books and many periodicals are available only via the library, not directly via the web.

Clearly, the web warrants cautious use. It should not be the only resource you work with.

Current search engines

The following lists include the currently most popular search engines. For a comprehensive and up-to-date guide to the latest search engines, consult *Search Engine Watch* at *http://searchenginewatch.com/links*.

36e

- **Several directories review sites:**

  BUBL Link (http://bubl.ac.uk/link)
  Internet Public Library and the Librarians' Internet Index (http://www.ipl.org/div/subject)
  Internet Scout Project (http://scout.wisc.edu/archives)

- **Two search engines are considered the most efficient and advanced:**

  AlltheWeb (http://www.alltheweb.com): One of the fastest and most comprehensive engines, *AlltheWeb* updates its database frequently so that it returns more of the web's most recent sites.

  Google (http://www.google.com): Also fast and comprehensive, *Google* ranks a site based not only on its content but also on the other sites that are linked to it, thus providing a measure of a site's usefulness.

- **A number of other engines can back up** *AlltheWeb* **and** *Google:*

    AltaVista (http://www.altavista.com)
    Ask Jeeves (http://www.ask.com)
    Dogpile (http://www.dogpile.com)
    Excite (http://www.excite.com)
    Lycos (http://www.lycos.com)
    MetaCrawler (http://www.metacrawler.com)
    *Yahoo! (http://www.yahoo.com) and Yahoo! Canada
        (http://ca.yahoo.com)*

Refining your search

Refining your keywords can narrow your search to maximize the number of relevant hits and minimize the irrelevant ones. For example, if you are researching the issue of dwindling East Coast cod stocks, you might start with a *Google* search using the keywords *cod AND Newfoundland*. But this search produces over a million hits—far too many to use, and a sure sign that the keywords need revising. A revised search using *"cod stocks" collapse AND causes AND Newfoundland* yields about five thousand hits—still too many, of course, but now including some useful, relevant sites on the first few screen pages.

36f   Online communication

Several online sources can put you directly in touch with experts and others whose ideas and information may inform your research. Because these sources, like websites, are unfiltered, you must always evaluate them carefully. (See p. 140.)

36f

- *Electronic mail* allows you to communicate with others who may be interested in your subject, such as a teacher at your school or an expert in another province. (See pp. 224–26 for more on e-mail.)
- *Discussion lists* (or listservs) use e-mail to connect subscribers who are interested in a common subject. Many have a scholarly or technical purpose. For an index of discussion lists, see *http://tile.net/lists*.
- *Newsgroups and web forums* are more open than discussion lists. For an index to web forums, see *http://www.delphiforums.com*. For a newsgroup index, see *http://groups.google.com*.
- *Web logs, or blogs,* are personal sites on which an author posts time-stamped comments, generally centring on

a common theme, in a format that allows readers to respond to the author and to each other. You can find directories of blogs and blog search engines at sites such as *http://www.bloglines.com, http://blogsearch.google.com,* and *http://www.blogsearchengine.com.*

- *Real-time, or synchronous, communication* allows you to participate in "live" conversation. For more on this resource, see *http://www.internet101.org/software/chatting.*

36g   Government publications

Government publications provide a vast array of data, public records, and other historical and contemporary information. For federal government publications, consult *http://publications.gc.ca.* The search engine will help you to locate government reports and publications on a wide variety of subjects. Select "Search by Date" to access the latest material. Many provinces also have websites with catalogues of government reports and publications. Use a search engine with the province's name as a keyword along with terms like "Queen's Printer" or "government publications." For example, a search on *Google* using the keywords "Manitoba government publications" results in *www.gov.mb.ca/queensprinter/,* the web page of Manitoba's Queen's Printer, which lists Manitoba's provincial statutory government publications along with links to other provinces' publications.

For US government publications, consult the *Monthly Catalog of US Government Publications,* available online. Many federal, state, and local government agencies post important publications—reports, legislation, press releases—on their own websites. You can find lists of sites for various federal agencies by using the keywords *United States federal government* with a search engine. In addition, several websites are useful resources, such as *http://www.fedstats.gov* (government statistics) and *http://infoplease.com/us.html* (links to information on federal, state, and local governments).

36h   Images, video, and audio

Images, video, and audio can be used as both primary and secondary sources in academic writing. A painting, an advertisement, or a video of a speech might be the subject of a paper and thus a primary source. A podcast of a radio interview or a college lecture might serve as a secondary source. Because many of these sources are unfiltered—

they can be posted by anyone—you must always evaluate them carefully. (See pp. 131–32.)

- **Images** such as charts, graphs, and photographs can be found in print or online. Online sources for images include public image databases, such as the Library of Congress's *American Memory (http://www. memory.loc.gov/ammem)* and the *New York Public Library Digital Gallery (http://www.digitalgallery.nypl. org)*; search engines such as *Google, Yahoo!*, and *AlltheWeb*; and subscription databases available through your library gateway.

- **Video files** capture performances, public presenta- tions and speeches, and news events, among other activities. They are available on the web and through your library on DVD. Online sources of video include the Library of Congress's *American Memory* (see above); *YouTube*, which encompasses commercials, historical footage, current events, and much more (*http://www.youtube.com*); and search engines such as *Google*.

- **Audio files** such as podcasts, webcasts, and CDs record radio programs, interviews, speeches, and music. They are available on the web and through your library. Online sources of audio include the Library of Congress's *American Memory* (see above) and podcasts at *http://www.podcast.com*.

36i Your own sources

Academic writing will often require you to conduct pri- mary research for information of your own. For instance, you may need to analyze a poem, conduct an experiment, survey a group of people, or interview an expert.

An interview can be especially helpful for a research project because it allows you to ask questions precisely geared to your subject. You can conduct an interview in person, over the telephone, or online using electronic mail or a form of synchronous communication (see pp. 135–36). A personal interview is preferable if you can arrange it, because you can hear the person's tone and see his or her expressions and gestures.

Here are a few guidelines for interviews:

- *Prepare a list of open-ended questions to ask*—perhaps ten or twelve for a one-hour interview. Do some research for these questions to discover background on the issues and your subject's published views on the issues.

- *Give your subject time to consider your questions.* Don't rush into silences with more questions.
- *Take care in interpreting answers,* especially if you are online and thus can't depend on facial expressions, gestures, and tone of voice to convey the subject's attitudes.
- *Keep thorough notes.* Take notes during an in-person or telephone interview, or record the interview if your subject agrees. For online interviews, save the discussion in a file of its own.
- *Verify quotations.* Before you quote your subject in your paper, check with him or her to ensure that the quotations are accurate.
- *Consult and adhere to the ethical policies* of your college or university.

37 Evaluating and Synthesizing Sources

Research writing is much more than finding sources and reporting their contents. The challenge and interest come from *selecting* appropriate sources and *interacting* with them through **critical reading**. To read critically, you analyze a text, identifying its main ideas, evidence, logic, bias, and other relevant elements; you evaluate its usefulness and quality; and you relate it to other texts and to your own ideas.

37a Evaluation of sources

For most projects you will seek the mix of sources described on pages 120–22. But not all the sources in your working bibliography will contribute to this mix. Some may prove irrelevant to your subject; others may prove unreliable.

In evaluating sources you need to consider how they come to you. The sources you find through the library, both print and online, have been previewed for you by their publishers and by the library's staff. They still require your critical reading, but you can have some confidence in the information they contain. With Internet

Visit www.mycanadiancomplab.ca for added help and exercises on research assignments.

sources, however, you can't assume similar previewing, so your critical reading must be especially rigorous.

Library sources

To evaluate sources you find through the library, look at dates, titles, summaries, introductions, headings, and author biographies. Try to answer the following questions about each source.

Evaluate relevance

- *Does the source devote some attention to your subject?* Check whether the source focuses on your subject or covers it marginally, and compare the source's coverage to that in other sources. Consult the index if there is one.
- *Is the source appropriately specialized for your needs?* Check the source's treatment of a topic you know something about, to ensure that it is neither too superficial nor too technical.
- *Is the source up to date enough for your subject?* Check the publication date. If your subject is current, your sources should be, too.

Evaluate reliability

- *Where does the source come from?* It matters whether you found the source through your library or directly on the Internet. (If the latter, see pp. 140–41.) Check whether a library source is popular or scholarly. Scholarly sources, such as refereed journals and university press books, are generally more thorough and more reliable.
- *Is the author an expert in the field?* The authors of scholarly publications tend to be experts. To verify expertise, check an author's credentials in a biography (if the source includes one), in a biographical reference, or by a keyword search of the web.
- *What is the author's bias?* Every author has a point of view that influences the selection and interpretation of evidence. How do the author's ideas relate to those in other sources? What areas does the author emphasize, ignore, or dismiss? When you're aware of sources' biases, you can attempt to balance them.
- *Is the source fair and reasonable?* Even a strongly biased work should present sound reasoning, adequate evidence, and a fair picture of opposing views— all in an objective, calm tone. The absence of any of these qualities should raise a warning flag.
- *Is the source well written?* A coherent organization and clear, error-free sentences indicate a careful author.

37a

Internet sources

To a great extent, the same critical reading that serves you with library sources will help you evaluate Internet sources that you reach directly. But websites and discussion-group postings can range from scholarly works to corporate promotions, from government-sponsored data to the self-published rantings of crackpots. You'll need to tell the difference.

To evaluate a website, add the following questions to those above for library sources. You can adapt these questions as well to discussion-group postings.

- *What does the URL lead you to expect about the site?* Are those expectations fulfilled? For the purposes of evaluation, the most important part of any URL is the domain name, which generally contains the name of the sponsoring organization (for example, *cbc.ca* is owned by the *Canadian Broadcasting Corporation*, and *cpha.ca* by the *Canadian Public Health Association*) and an abbreviation that may describe the type of organization. In URLs for US websites, common abbreviations are *.org* for non-profit organizations, *.edu* for educational institutions, *.gov* for government bodies, *.mil* for the military, and *.com* for commercial sites. Most institutional Canadian sites end in *.ca*. Remember that a site with *.edu* could belong to a biased or unqualified individual who works for an educational institution, a site with *.org* might belong to an organization that advocates specific policies, and a site with *.com* might contain reliable information even though the site exists for commercial, not educational, purposes.

- *Who is the author or sponsor?* How credible is the person or group responsible for the site? A reputable site will identify the sponsor or owner. If this information is lacking, do not use the source. You can further research an author or sponsoring organization's reliability through a database search of their names. Note that information posted to member-created sites like *Wikipedia* has not been vetted by experts. Such sites must be used with caution; they cannot replace professionally edited reference works.

- *What is the purpose of the site?* What does the site's author or sponsor intend to achieve? Is the purpose commercial and, if so, will that purpose distort the information and opinions provided? Does the site belong to an interest group with a particular viewpoint? Or is the site's purpose scholarly or educational?

37a

- *What does the context tell you?* What do you already know about the site's subject that can inform your evaluation? What kinds of support or other information do the site's links provide? If the site is linked to a relatively biased site, it may not be reliable.
- *What does the presentation tell you?* Is the site's design well thought out and effective? Is the writing clear and error free? Does it carry advertising that might compromise its impartiality?
- *How worthwhile is the content?* Are the site's claims well supported by evidence? Is the evidence from reliable scholarly sources rather than solely from popular journalism and personal websites?

A sample search

Let's apply some of these questions to websites that result from a *Google* search using the keywords *"cod stocks" collapse AND causes AND Newfoundland*.

The first site listed during a search conducted on June 25, 2010, is *http://archive.greenpeace.org/comms/cbio/cancod.html*, an archived site sponsored by the Greenpeace Foundation. The *.org* tail indicates that this site belongs to a non-profit, non-governmental organization.

This archive is linked to a newer site, *http://www.greenpeace.org/international*, whose "About Us" page states that "Greenpeace is an independent global campaigning organisation that acts to change attitudes and behaviour, to protect and conserve the environment and to promote peace . . . ." Clearly this site belongs to a private advocacy group whose purpose is to persuade people to act in support of its views and to donate to the organization.

37a

This newer site also features links to other sites, some of which contain scholarly essays that have been selected because they agree with Greenpeace's views. They do not necessarily represent the range of academic positions as articles on a more scholarly site might, so you must read the articles critically to see how fairly they present evidence and weigh competing claims.

Another site on that first *Google* screen is *http://www.emagazine.com/view/?507*, an e-magazine with a cover story on "How Factory Fishing Decimated Newfoundland Cod." This site's lively graphic identifies it as "THE ONLINE HOME OF *E* – THE ENVIRONMENTAL MAGAZINE." The "About Us" page states:

> Now in its 19th year, **E – The Environmental Magazine** is a bimonthly "clearinghouse" of information, news and resources for people concerned about the environment

who want to know "What can I do?" to make a difference. A 13-time Independent Press Awards winner and
nominee, **E** is chock full of everything environmental—
from recycling to rainforests, and from the global village
to our own backyards. . . .

Published by the **nonprofit (501-c-3) Earth Action
Network, Inc.**, **E** is independent of any membership
organization and has no agenda to promote except that
of our very diverse and dynamic movement as a whole.

In other words, it too is a non-profit advocacy site.
This site further claims:

E is featured and quoted widely by the press, and is
regularly syndicated by several national and international news agencies, including *The New York Times* syn-
dicate, and *AlterNet*. [I]n calendar year 2006, over 100
articles from **E's** pages were selected for republication
in other newspapers, magazines and online services. **E**
reprints and excerpts can be found in scores of books,
textbooks, teachers guides, research services, and online
in many forms, including extensively throughout the
library market.

These claims, if true, suggest that **E**'s approach to
journalism is respected and responsible. While not a
scholarly source, it popularizes material from some
scholarly sources, while its main purpose is to advocate
practical actions. Like the Greenpeace site, it probably
contains useful scholarly articles, but you must still read
those articles critically.

Lower on the first *Google* screen are links to two
academic sources available as PDFs—*Portable Document
Formats*. (Note that unlike the two "wiki" sites also listed
on the screen, whose information can be modified by
readers, PDFs cannot be altered.)

"The Political Ecology of Crisis and Institutional
Change: The Case of the Northern Cod" is written by two
university scholars at Rutgers State University in New
Jersey and was presented at an academic conference, both
indications that the writers have expertise and credibility.
On the other hand, the article is dated 1995, which suggests it may no longer be current.

The second PDF is an academic paper titled "Why
Do Fish Stocks Collapse? The Example of Cod in Atlantic
Canada." The authors are associated with the Department of Fisheries in St. John's, NL (government), and the
Department of Biology, Dalhousie University, Halifax, NS
(academic), and the article appeared in *Ecological Applications*, the journal of the Ecological Society of America,

37a

an academic organization. Unlike the Greenpeace and E articles, this article was written for fellow scientists and was evaluated by them before being accepted for publication, indicating that the science is trustworthy. It is copyrighted 1997, however, so may be slightly out of date.

Of the hundreds of other hits on *Google*, some will refer to further academic studies, some to other advocacy groups, many to journalistic sources both trustworthy and untrustworthy, and quite a few will be blogs expressing personal opinions, some of them well informed and well reasoned, others not. Approach each site critically to evaluate its authority and usefulness to your own research.

Other online sources

Blogs, online discussions, images, and video or audio files require the same critical scrutiny as websites do. Blogs, web forums, and newsgroups can be sources of in-depth information and informed opinion, but none have the authority of a scholarly publication. An e-mail discussion list may be more trustworthy if its subscribers are professionals in the field, but you may still find wrong or misleading data and skewed opinions. A podcast of a reputable radio program may provide an interview with a recognized expert, but another podcast may claim authority that it doesn't deserve. Video sources are similarly inconsistent: for instance, a *Google* or *YouTube* search using "Canadian minority parliaments" brings up the official website of the Parliament of Canada as well as media sites with editorials and commentaries strongly supporting or condemning the Conservative minority government elected in 2008, historic speeches by Tommy Douglas, and some Rick Mercer comic routines.

37a

Use the following questions for evaluating blogs, discussion groups, and multimedia:

- **Who is the author or creator?** How credible is that person? If the author/creator uses a screen name, write directly to him or her requesting full name and credentials. Do not use the source if he or she fails to respond.
- **What is the author's or creator's purpose?** What can you tell about *why* the author/creator is publishing this work? Look for cues in the work—claims, use (or not) of evidence, and the treatment of opposing views—to figure out how to position the source among your other sources.
- **What does the context reveal?** What do others' comments on the work indicate about the source's balance and reliability? Looking at the responses of

others will give you a sense of how the author/creator is regarded.

- **How worthwhile is the content?** Are the claims made by the author/creator supported by evidence from reliable sources? If you don't see supporting information, ask the author/creator for it. Then verify the sources with your own research: are they reputable?

- **How does the source compare with other sources?** Do the claims seem accurate and fair given what you've seen in sources you know to be reliable? Always consider blogs, messages, and multimedia in comparison to other sources so that you can distinguish singular, untested views from more mainstream views that have been subject to verification.

37b   Synthesis of sources

Evaluating sources moves you into the most significant part of research writing: forging relationships for your own purpose. This **synthesis** is an essential step in reading sources critically and in creating new knowledge.

Respond to sources

Write down what your sources make you think. Do you agree or disagree with the author? Do you find his or her views narrow, or do they open up new approaches for you? Is there anything in the source that you need to research further before you can understand it? Does the source prompt questions that you should keep in mind while reading other sources? Does the source refer to other sources that could be useful?

Connect sources

When you notice a link between sources, jot it down. Do two sources differ in their theories or their interpretations of facts? Does one source illuminate another—perhaps commenting or clarifying or supplying additional data? Do two or more sources report studies that support a theory you've read about or an idea of your own? Does an issue arise in more than one source, indicating that it is a key issue you will have to consider?

Heed your own insights

Apart from ideas prompted by your sources, you are sure to come up with independent thoughts: a conviction, a point of confusion that suddenly becomes clear, an exciting comparison, a question you haven't seen anyone else ask. These insights may occur at unexpected times, so it's good practice to keep a notebook handy to record them.

Use sources to support your own ideas

As your research proceeds, the responses, connections, and insights you form through synthesis will lead you to answer your starting research question with a statement of your thesis (see p. 119). They will also lead you to the main ideas supporting your thesis—conclusions you have drawn from your synthesis of sources, forming the main divisions of your paper. When drafting the paper, make sure each paragraph focuses on an idea of your own, with supporting source material sandwiched between your explanations of it. Then your paper will synthesize others' work into something wholly your own.

38 Integrating Sources into Your Text

The evidence of others' information and opinions should back up, not dominate, your own ideas. To synthesize sources, you must decide whether to summarize, paraphrase, or quote them (below); you must introduce and interpret the borrowed material (p. 148); and you must clearly mark the boundaries of borrowed material (p. 153).

Note Integrating sources into your text may involve several conventions discussed elsewhere:

- For the punctuation of signal phrases such as *he insists,* see page 87.
- For guidelines on when to run quotations into your text and when to display them separately from your text, see pages 182–83 (MLA style), 197–98 (APA style), and 211 (Chicago style).
- For the use of the ellipsis mark (. . .) to indicate omissions from quotations, see pages 98–101.
- For the use of brackets ([ ]) to indicate changes in or additions to quotations, see pages 101 and 148.

38a

38a Summary, paraphrase, and direct quotation

As you take notes from sources or work source material into your draft, you can summarize, paraphrase, quote, or combine methods. The choice should depend on why you are using a source.

Visit www.mycanadiancomplab.ca for
added help and exercises on research assignments.

Note Summaries, paraphrases, and quotations all require source citations. A summary or paraphrase without a source citation, or a quotation without quotation marks, is plagiarism. (See pp. 153–58 for more on plagiarism.)

Summary

When you **summarize,** you condense an extended idea or argument into a sentence or more in your own words. Summary is most useful when you want to record the gist of an author's idea without the background or supporting evidence. Here, for example, is a passage from a history of Canada's involvement in World War I, followed by a one-sentence summary.

Original Quotation

The wealthy young men who enjoyed their socially-admired role as officers in the militia were quick to offer their services, displaying the leadership that was expected of the English-speaking, moneyed class who resided in "the Square Mile." One of the most notable among them was twenty-six-year-old Guy Melfort Drummond. Young Drummond, an officer in the 5th Royal Highlanders, seemed to have a glittering future. Handsome and very tall (six foot four), fluently bilingual and a millionaire, Drummond was being groomed for a career high in Conservative party politics, and there were those who whispered that the post of prime minister was not unlikely for Drummond some day.

—DANIEL D. DANCOCKS, *Welcome to Flanders Fields*, (Toronto: McClelland & Stewart, 1988), 40.

Summary

Assuming the leadership roles expected of them, rich young men from the Montreal English-speaking establishment volunteered for war in 1914; Guy Drummond was a notable example.

Paraphrase

When you **paraphrase**, you follow much more closely the author's original presentation, but you still restate it in your own words. Paraphrase is most useful when you want to reconstruct an author's line of reasoning but don't feel the original words merit direct quotation. Here is a paraphrase of the final sentence in the passage quoted above:

Paraphrase

Tall, handsome, rich, and bilingual, Guy Drummond was thought by some to be a future Conservative prime minister.

38a

Follow these guidelines when paraphrasing:

- Read the material until you understand it.
- Restate the main ideas in your own words and sentence structures. Use phrases if complete sentences seem cumbersome.
- Be careful not to distort the author's meaning.

Your paraphrase may include brief, essential words or phrases from the original—in quotation marks, of course. For examples of poor and revised paraphrases, see pages 156–58.

ESL If English is your second language, you may have difficulty paraphrasing the ideas in sources because synonyms don't occur to you, or you don't see how to restructure sentences. Before attempting a paraphrase, read the original passage several times. Then, instead of "translating" line by line, try to state the gist of the passage without looking at it. Check your effort against the original to be sure you have captured the source author's meaning and emphasis without using his or her words and sentence structures. If you need a synonym for a word, look it up in a dictionary.

Direct quotation

If your purpose is to analyze a particular work, such as a short story or historical document, then you will use many direct quotations from the work. But otherwise you should quote from sources only in the following circumstances:

- *The author's original satisfies one of these requirements:*

  The language is unusually vivid, bold, or inventive.
  The quotation cannot be paraphrased without distortion or loss of meaning.
  The words themselves are at issue in your interpretation.
  The quotation represents and emphasizes the view of an important expert.
  The quotation is a graph, diagram, or table.

- *The quotation is as short as possible:*

  It includes only material relevant to your point.
  It is edited to eliminate superfluous words, examples, and other unneeded material.

38a

When taking a quotation from a source, copy the material *carefully*. Take down the author's exact wording, spelling, capitalization, and punctuation. Indicate any page breeaks in case you end up using only part of the quotation. Proofread every direct quotation *at least twice*, and be sure you have supplied big quotation marks so that later you won't confuse the direct quotation with a paraphrase or summary.

38b Introduction and interpretation of source material

Note Most examples in the following pages use the documentation style of the Modern Language Association (MLA) and also present-tense° verbs that are typical of much writing in the humanities. For specific variations in the academic disciplines, see pages 151–52.

Introduction

Work all quotations, paraphrases, and summaries smoothly into your own sentences, adding words as necessary to mesh structures.

> Awkward   One editor disagrees with this view and "a good reporter does not fail to separate opinions from facts" (Lyman 52).
>
> Revised   One editor disagrees with this view, <u>maintaining that</u> "a good reporter does not fail to separate opinions from facts" (Lyman 52).

To mesh your own and your source's words, you may sometimes need to make a substitution or addition to the quotation, signalling your change with brackets:

Words added

"The tabloids [of England] are a journalistic case study in bad reporting," claims Lyman (52).

Verb form changed

A bad reporter, Lyman implies, is one who "[fails] to separate opinions from facts" (52). [The bracketed verb replaces *fail* in the original.]

Capitalization changed

"[T]o separate opinions from facts" is a goal of good reporting (Lyman 52). [In the original, *to* is not capitalized.]

Noun supplied for pronoun

The reliability of a news organization "depends on [reporters'] trustworthiness," says Lyman (52). [The bracketed noun replaces *their* in the original.]

Interpretation

Even when it does not conflict with your own sentence structure, source material will be ineffective if you merely dump it in readers' laps without explaining how you intend it to be understood. In the following passage, we must figure out for ourselves that the writer's sentence and the quotation state opposite points of view.

> Dumped   Many news editors and reporters maintain that it is impossible to keep personal opinions from influencing the selection and presentation of facts. "True, news reporters, like everyone else, form impressions of what they see and hear. However, a good reporter does not fail to separate opinions from facts" (Lyman 52).

> Revised   Many news editors and reporters maintain that it is impossible to keep personal opinions from influencing the selection and presentation of facts. <u>Yet not all authorities agree with this view. One editor grants that</u> "news reporters, like everyone else, form impressions of what they see and hear." <u>But, he insists</u>, "a good reporter does not fail to separate opinions from facts" (Lyman 52).

Signal phrases

In the preceding revised passage, the words *One editor grants* and *he insists* are **signal phrases**: they tell readers who the source is and what to expect in the quotations. Signal phrases usually contain (1) the source author's name (or a substitute for it, such as *One editor* and *he*) and (2) a verb that indicates the source author's attitude or approach to what he or she says, as *grants* implies concession and *insists* implies argument.

Below are some verbs to use in signal phrases. For the appropriate tense° of such verbs (present,° as here, or past° or present perfect°) see pages 151–52.

38b

Author is neutral	Author infers or suggests	Author argues	Author is uneasy or disparaging
comments	analyzes	claims	belittles
describes	asks	contends	bemoans
explains	assesses	defends	complains
illustrates	believes	disagrees	condemns
mentions	concludes	holds	deplores
notes	considers	insists	deprecates
observes	finds	maintains	derides
points out	predicts		laments
records	proposes	Author agrees	warns
relates	reveals	accepts	
reports	shows	admits	
says	speculates	agrees	
sees	suggests	concedes	
thinks	supposes	concurs	
writes		grants	

Note that some signal verbs, such as *describes* and *assesses*, cannot be followed by *that*.

Vary your signal phrases to suit your interpretation of source material and also to keep readers' interest. A signal phrase may precede, interrupt, or follow the borrowed material:

Signal phrase precedes

<u>Lyman insists</u> that "a good reporter does not fail to separate opinions from facts" (52).

Signal phrase interrupts

"However," <u>Lyman insists,</u> "a good reporter does not fail to separate opinions from facts" (52).

Signal phrase follows

"[A] good reporter does not fail to separate opinions from facts," <u>Lyman insists</u> (52).

Background information

You can add information to source material to integrate it into your text and inform readers why you are using it. Often, you may want to provide the author's name in the text:

Author named

<u>Harold Lyman</u> grants that "news reporters, like everyone else, form impressions of what they see and hear." But, Lyman insists, "a good reporter does not fail to separate opinions from facts" (52).

38b

If the source title contributes information about the author or the context of the borrowed material, you can provide the title in the text:

Title given

Harold Lyman, <u>in his book *The Conscience of the Journalist*</u>, grants that "news reporters, like everyone else, form impressions of what they see and hear." But, Lyman insists, "a good reporter does not fail to separate opinions from facts" (52).

Finally, if the source author's background and experience reinforce or clarify the borrowed material, you can provide these credentials in the text:

Credentials given

Harold Lyman, <u>a newspaper editor for more than forty years</u>, grants that "news reporters, like everyone else, form impressions of what they see and hear." But, Lyman insists, "a good reporter does not fail to separate opinions from facts" (52).

You need not name the author, title, or credentials in your text when you are simply establishing facts or weaving together facts and opinions from varied sources to support a larger point. In the following passage, the information is more important than the source, so the author's name is confined to a parenthetical acknowledgment:

> The inexperienced Canadian troops at Saint-Julien, in their first major offensive of the Great War, achieved the only successful Allied attack of the Second Battle of Ypres (Dancocks 188).

Discipline styles for interpreting sources

The preceding guidelines for interpreting source material apply generally across academic disciplines, but there are differences in verb tenses and documentation style.

English and some other humanities

Writers in English, foreign languages, and related disciplines use MLA style for documenting sources (see Chapter 40) and generally use the present tense° of verbs in signal phrases. (See the list of signal-phrase verbs on p. 149.) In discussing sources other than works of literature, the present perfect tense° is also sometimes appropriate:

> Lyman <u>insists</u> . . . [present].
> Lyman <u>has insisted</u> . . . [present perfect].

38b

In discussing works of literature, use only the present tense to describe both the work of the author and the action in the work:

> Kate Chopin <u>builds</u> irony into every turn of "The Story of an Hour." For example, Mrs. Mallard, the central character, <u>finds</u> joy in the death of her husband, whom she <u>loves</u>, because she <u>anticipates</u> "the long procession of years that would belong to her absolutely" (23).

Avoid shifting tenses in writing about literature. You can, for instance, shorten quotations to avoid their past-tense verbs:

Shift   Her freedom <u>elevates</u> her, so that "she <u>carried</u> herself unwittingly like a goddess of victory" (24).

No shift   Her freedom <u>elevates</u> her, so that she <u>walks</u> "unwittingly like a goddess of victory" (24).

See pages 182–83 for MLA format with poetry quotations and long prose quotations.

History and other humanities

Writers in history, art history, philosophy, and related disciplines generally use the present tense or present perfect tense of verbs in signal phrases. (See the list of possible verbs on p. 149.)

> As Dancocks <u>has noted</u>, "The second Battle of Ypres was a relatively minor affair so far as the Great War was concerned.'"[6]

> Eksteins <u>claims</u>, "For the Germans, this was a war to change the world; for the British this was a war to preserve a world."[7]

> Eksteins <u>sees</u> the Christmas Truce of 1914 as the last European expression of traditional values such as honour, duty, and sportsmanship.[8]

The raised numbers after the quotations are part of the Chicago documentation style, used in history and other disciplines and discussed in Chapter 42.

See page 211 for the Chicago format with long prose quotations.

Social and natural sciences

Writers in the sciences generally use a verb's present tense just for reporting the results of a study (*The data suggest* . . .). Otherwise, they use a verb's past tense° or present perfect tense in a signal phrase, as when introducing an explanation, interpretation, or other commentary. (Thus, when you are writing for the sciences, generally convert the list of signal-phrase verbs on p. 149 from the present to the past or present perfect tense.)

38b

> In an exhaustive survey of the literature published between 1990 and 2000, Walker (2001) <u>found</u> "no proof, merely a weak correlation, linking place of residence and rate of illness" (p. 121).

> Lin (1999) <u>has suggested</u> that preschooling may significantly affect children's academic performance through high school (pp. 22–23).

These passages conform to the documentation style of the American Psychological Association (APA), discussed in Chapter 41. APA style or the similar CSE and IEEE styles (Chapter 43) are used in sociology, education, nursing, biology, and many other sciences.

For APA format with long prose quotations, see pages 197–98.

38c Clear boundaries for source material

Position source citations in your text to accomplish two goals: (1) make it clear exactly where your borrowing of source material begins and ends; (2) keep the citations as unobtrusive as possible. You can accomplish both goals by placing an in-text citation at the end of the sentence element containing the borrowed material. This sentence element may be a phrase or a clause, and it may begin, interrupt, or conclude the sentence.

> The inflation rate might climb as high as 30 percent (Kim 164), an increase that could threaten the small nation's stability.
>
> The inflation rate, which might climb as high as 30 percent (Kim 164), could threaten the small nation's stability.
>
> The small nation's stability could be threatened by its inflation rate, which, one source predicts, might climb as high as 30 percent (Kim 164).

In the last example the addition of *one source predicts* clarifies that Kim is responsible only for the inflation rate prediction, not for the statement about stability.

When your paraphrase or summary of a source runs longer than a sentence, clarify the boundaries by using the author's name in the first sentence and placing the parenthetical citation at the end of the last sentence.

> Juliette Kim studied the effects of acutely high inflation in several South American and African countries since World War II. She discovered that a major change in government accompanied or followed the inflationary period in 56 percent of cases (22–23).

39 Avoiding Plagiarism and Documenting Sources

The knowledge building that is the focus of academic writing rests on participants' integrity in using sources. This standard of integrity derives from the idea that the work of an author is his or her intellectual property: if you use that work, you must acknowledge the author's

Visit www.mycanadiancomplab.ca for added help and exercises on avoiding plagiarism.

ownership. At the same time, source acknowledgments tell readers what your own writing is based on, creating the trust that knowledge building requires.

Plagiarism (from a Latin word for "kidnapper") is the presentation of someone else's ideas or words as your own. Whether deliberate or accidental, plagiarism is a serious and often punishable offence.

- *Deliberate plagiarism* includes copying or download-ing a phrase or sentence from a source and passing it off as your own, summarizing someone else's ideas without acknowledging your debt, or buying a term paper and handing it in as your own.
- *Accidental plagiarism* includes forgetting to place quo-tation marks around another writer's words, omitting a source citation because you are not aware of the need for it, or carelessly copying a source when you mean to paraphrase.

ESL In some cultures, students may be encouraged to copy the words of scholars without acknowledgment in order to demonstrate their mastery of or respect for the scholars' work. In Canada, however, teachers value students' original thinking, so any use of another's words or ideas without a source citation is plagiarism and is unacceptable. When in doubt about the guidelines in this section, ask your instructor for advice.

39a   Plagiarism and the Internet

39a

The Internet has made it easier to plagiarize than ever before, but it has also made plagiarism easier to catch.

Even honest students risk accidental plagiarism by downloading sources and importing portions into their drafts. Dishonest students may take advantage of downloading to steal others' work. They may also use the term-paper businesses on the web, which offer both ready-made research and complete papers, usually for a fee. *Paying for research or a paper does not make it the buyer's work.* Anyone who submits someone else's work as his or her own is a plagiarist.

Students who plagiarize from the Internet both deprive themselves of an education in honest research and expose themselves to detection. Teachers can use search engines to locate specific phrases or sentences anywhere on the web, including among scholarly publications, all kinds of websites, and term-paper collections. They can search the term-paper sites as easily as students can, looking for similarities to papers they have received. Increasingly,

CHECKLIST FOR AVOIDING PLAGIARISM

Type of source

☑ Are you using (1) your own independent material, (2) common knowledge, or (3) someone else's independent material? *You must acknowledge someone else's material.*

Quotations

☑ Do all quotations exactly match their sources? Check them.
☑ Have you inserted quotation marks around quotations that are run into your text?
☑ Have you shown omissions with ellipsis marks and additions with brackets?
☑ Does every quotation have a source citation?

Paraphrases and summaries

☑ Have you used your own words and sentence structures for every paraphrase and summary? If not, use quotation marks around the original author's words.
☑ Does every paraphrase and summary have a source citation?

The web

☑ Have you obtained any necessary permission to use someone else's material on your website?

Source citations

☑ Have you acknowledged every use of someone else's material in the place where you use it?
☑ Does your list of works cited include all the sources you have used?

39b

teachers can use plagiarism-detection programs that compare students' work with other work anywhere on the Internet, seeking matches as short as a few words.

Some instructors suggest that their students use plagiarism-detection programs to verify that their own work does not include accidental plagiarism, at least not from the Internet.

39b   What *not* to acknowledge

Your independent material

You are not required to acknowledge your own observations, thoughts, compilations of facts, or experimental results, expressed in your own words and format.

Common knowledge

You need not acknowledge common knowledge: the standard information of a field of study as well as folk literature and commonsense observations.

If you do not know a subject well enough to determine whether a piece of information is common knowledge, make a record of the source. As you read more about the subject, the information may come up repeatedly without acknowledgment, in which case it is probably common knowledge. But if you are still in doubt when you finish your research, always acknowledge the source.

39c What *must* be acknowledged

You must always acknowledge other people's independent material—that is, any facts or ideas that are not common knowledge or your own. The source may be anything, including a book, an article, a movie, an interview, a microfilmed document, a web page, a computer program, a newsgroup posting, or an opinion expressed on the radio. You must acknowledge summaries or paraphrases of ideas or facts as well as quotations of the language and format in which ideas or facts appear: wording, sentence structures, arrangement, and special graphics (such as a diagram). You must acknowledge another's material no matter how you use it, how much of it you use, or how often you use it.

Note See pages 145–51 on integrating quotations into your own text without plagiarism. And see pages 158 and 162–64 on acknowledging sources.

39c

Copied language: Quotation marks
and a source citation

The following example baldly plagiarizes the original quotation from Jessica Mitford's *Kind and Usual Punishment*, page 9. Without quotation marks or a source citation, the example matches Mitford's wording (underlined) and closely parallels her sentence structure:

Original quotation
"The character and mentality of the keepers may be of more importance in understanding prisons than the character and mentality of the kept."

Plagiarism
But <u>the character</u> of prison officials (<u>the keepers</u>) is more <u>important in understanding prisons than the character</u> of prisoners (<u>the kept</u>).

To avoid plagiarism, the writer has two options: (1) paraphrase and cite the source (see the examples below and on p. 158) or (2) use Mitford's actual words *in quotation marks* and *with a source citation* (here, in MLA style):

Revision
(quotation)
> According to one critic of the penal system, "The character and mentality of the keepers may be of more importance in understanding prisons than the character and mentality of the kept" (<u>Mitford 9</u>).

Even with a source citation and with a different sentence structure, the next example is still plagiarism because it uses some of Mitford's words (underlined) without quotation marks:

Plagiarism
> According to one critic of the penal system, the psychology of <u>the kept</u> may say less about prisons than the psychology of <u>the keepers</u> (Mitford 9).

Revision
(quotation)
> According to one critic of the penal system, the psychology of "the kept" may say less about prisons than the psychology of "the keepers" (Mitford 9).

Paraphrase or summary: Your own words and a source citation

The example below changes Mitford's sentence structure, but it still uses her words (underlined) without quotation marks and without a source citation:

Plagiarism
> <u>In understanding prisons</u>, we should know more about the character and mentality of <u>the keepers</u> than <u>of the kept</u>.

39c

To avoid plagiarism, the writer can use quotation marks and cite the source (above) or *use his or her own words* and still *cite the source* (because the idea is Mitford's, not the writer's):

Revision
(paraphrase)
> <u>Mitford</u> holds that we may be able to learn more about prisons from the psychology of the prison officials than from that of the prisoners (<u>9</u>).

Revision
(paraphrase)
> We may understand prisons better if we focus on the personalities and attitudes of the prison workers rather than on those of the inmates (<u>Mitford 9</u>).

In the next example, the writer cites Mitford and does not use her words but still plagiarizes her sentence structure:

Plagiarism	One critic of the penal system maintains that <u>the psychology of prison officials may</u> be more informative about prisons than <u>the psychology of prisoners</u> (Mitford 9).
Revision (paraphrase)	One critic of the penal system maintains that we may be able to learn less from the psychology of prisoners than from the psychology of prison officials (Mitford 9).

39d Online sources

You should acknowledge online sources when you would any other source: whenever you use someone else's independent material in any form. But online sources may present additional challenges:

- *Record complete source information* as noted on pages 125–26 each time you consult the source. Online sources may change from one day to the next or even be removed entirely. Without the source information, you *may not* use the source.
- *Acknowledge linked sites.* If you use not only a website but also one or more of its linked sites, you must acknowledge those linked sites as well. The fact that one person has used a second person's work does not release you from the responsibility to acknowledge the second work.
- *Seek the author's permission* to use any ideas, information, or wording you obtain from e-mail correspondence or a discussion group.

39e

If you want to use material in something you publish online, such as your own website, seek permission from the copyright holder in addition to citing the source. Generally, you can find information about a site's copyright on the home page or at the bottom of other pages: look for a notice using the symbol ©. Most worthwhile sites also provide information for contacting the author or sponsor. (See p. 161 for an illustration.) If you don't find a copyright notice, you *cannot* assume that the work is unprotected by copyright. Only if the site explicitly says it is not copyrighted or is available for free use can you use it online without permission.

39e Documentation of sources

Every time you borrow the words, facts, or ideas of others, you must **document** the source—that is, supply a reference (or document) telling readers that you

(Text continues on p. 162)

A book (Title page)

39e

Copyright page (following the title page)

A journal article

Journal cover

Volume and/or issue number

SPRING 2005   VOLUME 23   NUMBER 1

Year of publication

Title of periodical

SOCIAL SCIENCE COMPUTER REVIEW

First page of article

Title of article

The Social Processes of Learning to Use Computers

Author

NEIL SELWYN
Cardiff School of Social Sciences

The ability to use a computer is assumed to be a cornerstone of effective citizenship in the Information Age, with a range of initiatives and educational provisions being introduced to encourage people to become competent with information technology (IT). Despite such provision, levels of computer use and competence have been found to vary widely throughout the general population, and we know little of how different ways of learning to use computers contribute to people's eventual use of IT. Based on data from in-depth interviews with 100 adults in the United Kingdom, this article examines the range and social stratification of formal and informal learning about computers that is taking place, suggesting that formal computer instruction orientated toward the general public may inadvertently widen the digital knowledge gap. In particular, the data highlight the importance of informal learning about IT and of encouraging such learning, especially in the home.

AUTHOR'S NOTE: This article is based on a project funded by the Economic and Social Research Council (R000239518). I would like to thank the other members of the Adults Learning@Home project (Stephen Gorard and John Furlong) as well as the individuals who took part in the in-depth interviews. Correspondence concerning this article may be addressed to Neil Selwyn, School of Social Sciences, Cardiff University, Glamorgan Building, King Edward VII Avenue, Cardiff CF10 3WT, UK; e-mail: selwynnc@cardiff.ac.uk.

Starting page number of article

122

39e

A short work from a website

Home page of site

39e

An article from a subscription service

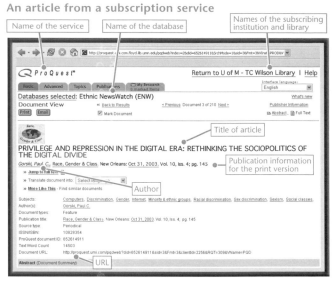

Image published with permission of ProQuest-CSA LLC. © 2007, ProQuest-CSA LLC; all rights reserved. Further reproduction is prohibited without permission.

borrowed the material and where you borrowed it from. This section shows where to find information for various kinds of sources and explains the similarities and differences in documentation among academic disciplines (see below and pp. 163–64).

Information for source citations

Documenting sources requires finding certain information in them, such as author, title, and publication facts. The samples on pages 159–61 and above show how to find this information for a book, a journal article, a short work from a website, and an article from a subscription service.

Documentation styles in the disciplines

Editors and teachers in most academic disciplines require special documentation formats (or styles) in their scholarly journals and in students' papers. All the styles use a citation in the text that serves two purposes: it signals that material is borrowed, and it refers readers to detailed information about the source so that they can locate both the source and the place in the source where the borrowed material appears. The detailed source information appears either in footnotes or at the end of the paper.

Aside from these essential similarities, the disciplines' documentation styles differ markedly in citation form, arrangement of source information, and other particulars. Each discipline's style reflects the needs of its practitioners for certain kinds of information presented in certain ways. For instance, the currency of a source is important in the social and natural sciences, where studies build on and correct each other; thus in-text citations in these disciplines usually include a source's date of publication. In the humanities, however, currency is less important, so in-text citations do not include date of publication.

The documentation formats of the disciplines are described in style guides, including those in the following list. This book presents the styles of the guides that are marked *.

Humanities

The Chicago Manual of Style. 16th ed. 2010. (See pp. 200–13.)

MLA Handbook for Writers of Research Papers. 7th ed. 2009. (See pp. 164–84.)

Social sciences

American Anthropological Association. *AAA Style Guide.* 2009. Available at http://www. aaanet.org/publications/style_ guide.pdf

American Political Science Association. *Style Manual for Political Science.* 2006.

*American Psychological Association. *Publication Manual of the American Psychological Association.* 6th ed. 2009. (See pp. 184–99.)

American Sociological Association. *ASA Style Guide.* 3rd ed. 2007.

Bluebook: A Uniform System of Citation (law). 18th ed. 2005.

39e

Sciences and mathematics

American Chemical Society. *ACS Style Guide: A Manual for Authors and Editors.* 2nd ed. 1997.

American Institute of Physics. *Style Manual for Guidance in the Preparation of Papers.* 4th ed. 1997.

American Medical Association Manual of Style. 10th ed. 2007.

Bates, Robert L., Rex Buchanan, and Marla Adkins-Heljeson, eds. *Geowriting: A Guide to Writing, Editing, and Printing in Earth Science.* 5th ed. 1995.

*Council of Science Editors. *Scientific Style and Format: The CSE Manual for Authors, Editors, and Publishers.*

7th ed. 2006. (CSE was formerly called the Council of Biology Editors.) (See pp. 214–21.)

*IEEE (formerly the Institute of Electrical and Electronics Engineers), www.ieee.org, has a number of specialized guides to standards and manuscript preparation available online, but students may find it easier to use the *Guide to IEEE Manuscript Preparation* available as a PDF file at *http://www.ecf.toronto.edu/~writing/handbook-docum1b.html*. (See pp. 221–22.)

Ask your instructor or supervisor which style you should use. If no style is required, use the guide from the preceding list that's most appropriate for the discipline in which you're writing. Do follow one system for citing sources—and one system only—so that you provide all the necessary information in a consistent format.

Note Various computer programs can help you format your source citations in the style of your choice. The programs prompt you for needed information (author's name, book title, and so on) and then format the information as required by the style. The programs remove some tedium from documenting sources, but they can't substitute for your own care and attention in giving your sources accurate and complete acknowledgment. Always ask your instructor if you may use this software.

MLA
40

40 MLA Documentation and Format

Widely used in English, foreign languages, and other humanities, the MLA documentation style originates with the Modern Language Association. It appears in *MLA Handbook for Writers of Research Papers*, 7th ed. (2009). The MLA's website, at *http://www.mla.org*, offers occasional updates and answers to frequently asked questions about MLA style.

In MLA style, brief parenthetical citations in the text (opposite) direct readers to a list of works cited at the end of the text (p. 169). This chapter also details the MLA format for papers (p. 181).

Visit www.mycanadiancomplab.ca for added help and exercises on citing sources.

40a	MLA parenthetical text citations

Citation formats

The in-text citations of sources must include just enough information for the reader to locate (1) the appropriate source in your list of works cited and (2) the place in the source where the borrowed material appears. Usually, you can meet both these requirements by providing the author's last name and the page(s) in the source on which the borrowed material appears.

Note Models 1 and 2 below show the two ways of writing in-text citations. In models 3–13, any citation with the author or title named in the text could be written instead with the author or title named in parentheses, and vice versa. The choice depends on how you want to introduce and interpret your sources (see pp. 148–52):

1. Author named in your text

Boyden describes how Elijah, after killing a German soldier, "pulls the man's hair back and removes his scalp . . ." (193).

2. Author not named in your text

After killing a German solidier, Elijah "pulls the man's hair back and removes his scalp . . ." (Boyden 193).

MLA PARENTHETICAL TEXT CITATIONS

MLA
40a

3. A work with two or three authors

"Most historians," Copp and McAndrew observe, "in their preoccupation with weapons, tactics, technology, and grand strategy . . . have ignored the vast human dimension of battle" (11).

Historians have tended to ignore the psychological impact of battle (Copp and McAndrew 11).

One text discusses the "ethical dilemmas in public relations practice" (Wilcox, Ault, and Agee 125).

4. A work with more than three authors

Give all authors' names, or give only the first author's name followed by "et al." (the abbreviation for the Latin *et alii*, meaning "and others"). Do the same in your list of works cited.

Lopez, Salt, Ming, and Reisen observe that it took the combined forces of the Americans, Europeans, and Japanese to break the rebel siege of Beijing in 1900 (362).

5. A work with numbered paragraphs or screens instead of pages

According to Palfrey, twins raised apart report similar feelings (pars. 6-7).

6. An entire work or a work with no page or other numbers

Richard Brown's *Voyage of the Iceberg* traces the history of the iceberg that struck *Titanic*.

Voyage of the Iceberg traces the history of the iceberg that struck *Titanic* (Brown).

7. A multivolume work

If you name more than one volume in your list of works cited, give the volume you're acknowledging in your text citation (here, volume 5).

After issuing the Emancipation Proclamation, Lincoln said, "What I did, I did after very full deliberations, and under a very heavy and solemn sense of responsibility" (5: 438).

If you name only one volume in your list of works cited, give only the page number in your text citation.

8. A work by an author of two or more cited works

Give the title of the particular work you're citing, shortening it in a parenthetical citation unless it's already brief. In the following example, *Fables* is short for the full title, *Fables of Identity*.

An author's "*profession* of personal sincerity" may itself be a literary convention (Frye, *Fables* 45).

9. An unsigned work

Use the title (or a brief version of it) in place of an author's name. This citation has no page number because the entire source is only a page.

"The Right to Die" notes that a death-row inmate may demand his own execution to achieve a fleeting notoriety.

10. A government publication or a work with a corporate author

One study found that teachers of secondary social studies are receiving more training in methods but less in the discipline itself (Lorenz Research 64).

11. A source referred to by another source

George Davino maintains that "even small children have vivid ideas about nuclear energy" (qtd. in Boyd 22).

12. A literary work

For novels that may be available in many editions, cite the page number, then add a semicolon followed by part, chapter, or other numbers.

Toward the end of James's novel, Maggie suddenly feels "the intimate, the immediate, the familiar, as she hadn't had them for so long" (535; pt. 6, ch. 41).

For verse plays and poems that are divided into parts, omit a page number. Instead, as in the next example, cite the part (act 3, scene 4) and line number(s) (147).

Later in *King Lear* Shakespeare has the disguised Edgar say, "The prince of darkness is a gentleman" (3.4.147).

13. The Bible

Abbreviate any book title longer than four letters, and then give chapter and verse(s).

According to the Bible, at Babel God "did . . . confound the language of all the earth" (Gen. 11.9).

Note that "the Bible" is not italicized, but see 40b, model 10.

14. An electronic source

Many electronic sources can be cited just as printed sources are. For a source with no named author, see model 9. For a source that uses paragraph or some other numbers instead of page numbers, see model 5. For a source with no numbering, just give the author's name, either in parentheses, as in model 6, or in the text:

Michael Tourville, for one, believes that Europe's single currency will strengthen the continent's large and technologically advanced companies.

15. Two or more works in the same citation

Two recent articles point out that a computer badly used can be less efficient than no computer at all (Gough and Hall 201; Richards 162).

Footnotes or endnotes in special circumstances

Footnotes or endnotes may supplement parenthetical citations when you cite several sources at once, when you comment on a source, or when you provide information that does not fit easily in the text. Signal a footnote or endnote in your text with a numeral raised above the appropriate line. Then write a note with the same numeral.

Text

The role of First Nations snipers in the Great War is well documented.[1]

Note

    1. For further studies of First Nations snipers in the Great War, see Cook 289; Dancocks 125; Scott 3: 285-328.

In a note, the numeral is indented one-half inch (1.25 cm) or five spaces and is followed by a period. If the note appears as a footnote, place it at the bottom of the page on which the citation appears, set it off from the text with quadruple spacing, and double-space the note itself. If the note appears as an endnote, place it in numerical order with the other endnotes on a page between the text and the list of works cited; double-space all the endnotes.

40b   MLA list of works cited

On a new page at the end of your paper, a list titled "Works Cited" includes all the sources you quoted, paraphrased, or summarized in your paper. The format of the list is described below and illustrated on page 184.

Arrangement Arrange your sources in alphabetical order by the last name of the author (the first author if there is more than one). If an author is not given in the source, alphabetize the source by the first main word of the title (excluding *A*, *An*, or *The*).

Spacing and indention Double-space all entries. Type the first line of each entry at the left margin, and indent all subsequent lines one-half inch (1.25 cm).

Authors List the author's name last-name first. If there are two or more authors, list all names after the first in normal order. Separate the names with commas, omitting titles like *Dr.* End with a period.

MLA WORKS-CITED MODELS

Nonperiodical print publications

1. A book with one author *171*
2. A book with two or three authors *171*
3. A book with more than three authors *171*
4. Two or more works by the same author(s) *172*
5. A book with an editor *172*
6. A book with an author and an editor *172*
7. A translation *172*
8. A book with a corporate author *172*
9. An anonymous book *172*
10. The Bible *172*
11. A later edition *172*
12. A republished book *172*
13. A book with a title in its title *172*
14. A work in more than one volume *173*
15. A work in a series *173*
16. Published proceedings of a conference *173*
17. An anthology *173*
18. A selection from an anthology or collection *173*
19. Two or more selections from the same anthology *173*
20. An introduction, preface, foreword, or afterword *174*
21. An article in a reference work *174*

Periodical print publications: Journals, magazines, newspapers

22. An article in a journal *174*
23. An article in a journal that numbers only issues, not volumes *174*

MLA
40b

Title Give full titles, including subtitles, separated by a colon, and capitalize all important words (see p. 110). For periodic titles, omit any initial *A, An,* or *The.* Italicize the titles of books and periodicals; place titles of periodical articles in quotation marks, and end with a period.

Publication Information Provide the publication information after the title. For books, give place of publication, then a colon, followed by the publisher's name, then a comma and the year of publication. (Shorten publishers' names—for instance, *Little* for Little, Brown and *Carleton UP* for Carleton University Press.) For periodical articles, give the volume and issue number, date, and page numbers. Following this information, give the medium of publication (*Print* or *Web*) or the medium of reception (*Television, DVD, Performance,* etc.).

Punctuation Separate the main parts of an entry with a period followed by one space.

Nonperiodical print publications

1. A book with one author

Boyden, Joseph. *Three Day Road*. Toronto: Viking Canada,
  2005. Print.

2. A book with two or three authors

Copp, Terry, and Bill McAndrew. *Battle Exhaustion: Soldiers
  and Psychiatrists in the Canadian Army, 1939-1945.*
  Kingston: McGill-Queen's UP, 1990. Print.

Wilcox, Dennis L., Phillip H. Ault, and Warren K. Agee.
  Public Relations: Strategies and Tactics. 4th ed. New
  York: Harper, 1999. Print.

MLA
40b

3. A book with more than three authors

Give all authors' names, or give only the first author's name followed by "et al." ("and others"). Do the same in your in-text citations of the source.

Lopez, Geraldo, Judith P. Salt, Anne Ming, and Henry
  Reisen. *China and the West*. Boston: Little, 1995. Print.

Lopez, Geraldo, et al. *China and the West*. Boston: Little,
  1995. Print.

4. Two or more works by the same author(s)

Frye, Northrop. *The Double Vision: Language and Meaning in Religion*. Toronto: U of Toronto P, 1991. Print.

---. *Fables of Identity: Studies in Poetic Mythology*. New York: Harcourt, 1963. Print.

5. A book with an editor

Sabor, Peter, ed. *The Cambridge Companion to Frances Burney*. Cambridge: CUP, 2007. Print.

6. A book with an author and an editor

Austen, Jane. *Emma*. Ed. Kristen Flieger Samuelian. Peterborough: Broadview, 2004. Print.

7. A translation

Marchessault, Jovette. *Mother of the Grass*. Trans. Yvonne M. Klein. Vancouver: Talon, 1989. Print.

8. A book with a corporate author

Lorenz Research, Inc. *Research in Social Studies Teaching*. Baltimore: Arrow, 2004. Print.

9. An anonymous book

The Dorling Kindersley World Reference Atlas. London: Dorling, 2005. Print.

MLA 40b

10. The Bible

The Bible. King James Version. Print.

The New English Bible. London: Oxford UP and Cambridge UP, 1970. Print.

11. A later edition

Bolinger, Dwight L. *Aspects of Language*. 3rd ed. New York: Harcourt, 1981. Print.

12. A republished book

James, Henry. *The Golden Bowl*. 1904. London: Penguin, 1966. Print.

13. A book with a title in its title

Eco, Umberto. *Postscript to* The Name of the Rose. Trans. William Weaver. New York: Harcourt, 1983. Print.

14. A work in more than one volume

Using two or more volumes:

Lincoln, Abraham. *The Collected Works of Abraham Lincoln.*
Ed. Roy P. Basler. 8 vols. New Brunswick: Rutgers UP,
1953. Print.

Using only one volume:

Lincoln, Abraham. *The Collected Works of Abraham Lincoln.*
Ed. Roy P. Basler. Vol. 5. New Brunswick: Rutgers UP,
1953. Print. 8 vols.

15. A work in a series

Bergman, Ingmar. *The Seventh Seal.* New York: Simon,
1995. Print. Mod. Film Scripts Ser. 12.

16. Published proceedings of a conference

*Watching Our Language: A Conference Sponsored by the
Program in Architecture and Design Criticism.* 6-8 May
2005. New York: Parsons School of Design, 2005. Print.

17. An anthology

Kennedy, X. J., and Dana Gioia, eds. *Literature: An
Introduction to Fiction, Poetry, and Drama.* 9th ed.
New York: Longman, 2005. Print.

18. A selection from an anthology or collection

Duer, Leslie. "Portraits, Effigies, and the Narrative
Impulse." *Literature and Ethics: Essays Presented to
A. E. Malloch.* Ed. Gary Wihl and David Williams.
Kingston: McGill-Queen's UP, 1988. 32-45. Print.

A reprinted scholarly article:

Reekmans, Tony. "Juvenal on Social Change." *Ancient
Society 2* (1971): 117-61. Rpt. in *Private Life in Rome.*
Ed. Helen West. Los Angeles: Coronado, 1981.
124-69. Print.

19. Two or more selections from the same anthology

Harrison, Keith. "Other Tricks." Thompson 97.

Shields, Carol. "The Journal." Thompson 91-94.

Thompson, Kent, ed. *Open Windows: Canadian Short
Stories.* Kingston: Quarry, 1988. Print.

20. An introduction, preface, foreword, or afterword

Samuelian, Kristin Flieger. Introduction. *Emma*. By Jane
Austen. Peterborough: Broadview, 2004. 9-46. Print.

21. An article in a reference work

Mark, Herman F. "Polymers." *The New Encyclopaedia
Britannica: Macropaedia*. 16th ed. 1997. Print.

"Reckon." *Merriam-Webster's Collegiate Dictionary*. 11th ed.
2003. Print.

Periodical print publications: Journals, magazines, newspapers

22. An article in a journal

McCarron, Kevin. "Skin and Self-Indictment: Prison Tatoos,
Race, and Heroin Addiction." *English Studies in
Canada* 34.1 (2008): 85-102. Print.

23. An article in a journal that numbers only issues, not
volumes

Omhovère, Claire. "Routes and Roots in a Selection of Stories
by Alistair MacLeod." *Canadian Literature* 189 (2006):
50-67. Print.

24. An article in a monthly or bimonthly magazine

Tilin, Andrew. "Selling the Dream." *Worth* Sept. 2001:
94-100. Print.

25. An article in a weekly or biweekly magazine

Hawaleshka, Danylo. "Killer Viruses." *Maclean's*
31 Mar. 2003: 50-51. Print.

26. An article in a daily newspaper

Lopez Pacheco, Alexandra. "Health Lessons Start at Home."
National Post 11 Aug. 2003, natl. ed.: SR6. Print.

27. An anonymous article

"The Right to Die." *Time* 11 Oct. 1996: 101. Print.

28. An editorial or letter to the editor

"Move Fast but Safely Back to Balanced Budgets." Editorial.
   The Gazette 9 Feb. 2010, Sports Final: A16. Print.

Dowding, Michael. Letter. *Economist* 5-11 Jan. 2005: 4.
   Print.

29. A review

Jeffries, Joel. "Psychosis." Rev. of *The Spectrum of Psychotic
   Disorders: Neurobiology, Etiology, and Pathogenesis*,
   ed. Daryl Fujii and Iqbal Ahmed. *Canadian Journal of
   Psychiatry* 55.1 (2010). 58. Print.

30. An abstract of a dissertation or article

Steciw, Steven K. "Alterations to the Pessac Project of Le
   Corbusier." Diss. U of Michigan, 1986. *DAI* 46 (1986):
   565C. Print.

Lever, Janet. "Sex Differences in the Games Children Play."
   Social Problems 23 (1996): 478-87. *Psychological
   Abstracts* 63 (1996): item 1431. Print.

Electronic sources

Electronic sources include those you find online
(either through the library website or directly over the
Internet) and those you find on CD-ROM. The following
list itemizes the possible elements of an online source,
in order of their appearance in a works-cited entry. No
source will include all of the elements.

MLA
40b

1. Name of author, editor, compiler, or translator
2. Title of a short work
3. Title of a book
4. Name of editor, compiler, or translator of the source
5. Publication information for any print version of the
   source
6. Title of the website
7. Name of site editor
8. Version number, if any, or volume/issue numbers for
   an online journal
9. Date of electronic publication, latest revision, or posting
10. Title of a database

11. Title of a discussion group
12. Inclusive page numbers, number of paragraphs, or other identifying numbers
13. Name of site sponsor
14. Medium of publication (*Web or CD-ROM*)
15. Date you consulted the source

Note Include a URL only if the reader is unlikely to locate the source without it (since readers now mostly locate sources by searching for titles and names) or if your professor requires it. Make the URL as complete as possible and include *http*; place it within angle brackets (</>) at the very end of the citation.

31. A source on a periodical CD-ROM database

Lewis, Peter H. "Many Updates Cause Profitable Confusion."

New York Times 21 Jan. 2004, natl. ed.: D1+. CD-ROM.

New York Times Ondisc. UMI-ProQuest. Web. Mar. 2010.

32. A source on a nonperiodical CD-ROM

Shelley, Mary Wollstonecraft. *Frankenstein. Classic Library*.

CD-ROM. Alameda: Andromeda, 1999. Web.

33. An online book

An entire book:

Austen, Jane. *Emma*. 1816. Ed. Ronald Blythe.

Harmondsworth: Penguin, 1972. *Oxford Text Archive*.

1998. Oxford U. Web. 15 Dec. 2009.

A part of a book:

Conrad, Joseph. "A Familiar Preface." *Modern Essays*.

Ed. Christopher Morley. New York: Harcourt, 1921.

Bartleby.com: Great Books Online. Ed. Steven van

Leeuwan. Nov. 2000. Web. 16 Apr. 2010.

34. An article in an online journal

Palfrey, Andrew. "Choice of Mates in Identical Twins."

Modern Psychology 4.1 (1996): 26-40. Web. 25 Feb. 2010.

35. An online abstract

Palfrey, Andrew. "Choice of Mates in Identical Twins."

Modern Psychology 4.1 (1996): 26-40. Abstract. Web.

25 June 2010.

36. An article in an online newspaper

Rusk, James. "Pearson Drug Ring Broken." Globe and Mail.

Globe and Mail. Web. 22 Aug. 2010.

37. An article in an online magazine

Lewis, Ricki. "The Return of Thalidomide." Scientist 22 Jan.

2001: 5. Web. 24 Jan. 2009.

38. An online review

Detwiler, Donald S., and Chu Shao-Kang. Rev. of Important

Documents of the Republic of China, ed. Tan Quon

Chin. Journal of Military History 56.4 (1992): 669-84.

Web. 16 Sept. 2010.

39. An entire site (scholarly project, professional site, personal site, etc.)

Corbett, John, ed. Scots Teaching and Research Network.

2 Feb. 2003. U of Glasgow. Web. 5 Mar. 2009.

Lederman, Leon. Topics in Modern Physics--Lederman.

10 Oct. 2004. Web. 12 Dec. 2009.

MLA
40b

40. A poem, essay, or other short work from an online site

Barbour, John. "The Brus." Scots Teaching and Research

Network. Ed. John Corbett. 2 Feb. 2003. U of Glasgow.

Web. 5 Mar. 2010.

41. The home page for a course

Alexander, Carole. Introduction to College English. Course

home page. Jan.-May 2010. English Department,

Marianopolis College. Web. 16 Apr. 2010. <http://

www2.marianopolis.edu/faculty/alexander.html>.

42. A work from an online database

Netchaeva, Irina. "E-Government and E-Democracy." *International Journal for Communication Studies* 64 (2002): 467-78. *Academic Search Elite.* Web. 20 Dec. 2009.

Your library subscribes to a number of online services that provide access to the full text of articles in periodicals, reference works, and other sources. For a database source you find online, follow the publication information with the name of the database you used in italics. End the entry with the date of your access.

43. A work from an online service to which you subscribe

"China—Dragon Kings." *The Encyclopedia Mythica.* America Online. Web. 6 Jan. 2010.

44. An online government publication

Canada. Health Canada. *It's Your Health.* "Avian Influenza (Bird Flu)." 18 Jan. 2006. Web. 6 May 2010.

45. An article in an online information database

Pull, Jack L. "Wu-ti." *Encyclopaedia Britannica Online.* Enclyclopaedia Britannica, 2004. Web. 23 Dec. 2010.

MLA 40b

46. An online image (artwork, advertisement, graph, etc.)

Hamilton, Calvin J. *Components of Comets.* Diagram. 2008. *Space Art.* Web. 20 Dec. 2009.

Absolut Vodka. Advertisement. *Vanity Fair* Jan. 2006. *Adflip.* Web. 18 Nov. 2006.

Keefe, Mike. "Suspicious Package." Cartoon. *Denver Post* 21 July 2006. *PoliticalCartoons.com.* Web. 6 Jan. 2007. <http://www.politicalcartoons.com>.

47. Electronic mail

Millon, Michele. "Re: Grief Therapy." Message to the author. 4 May 2010. E-mail.

48. A posting to an e-mail discussion list

Tourville, Michael. "European Currency Reform." Online posting. 6 Jan. 2004. International Finance Archive. Web. 12 Jan. 2010.

49. A posting to a newsgroup or web forum, or a blog entry

Cramer, Sherry. "Recent Investment Practices." Online post-

  ing. Usenet, *biz.investment.current*. 26 Mar. 2004.

  Web. 3 Apr. 2010 <news:biz.investment.current.2700>.

Daswani, Susheel. "Hollywood vs. Silicon Valley."

  Berkeley Intellectual Property Weblog. 16 Mar. 2006.

  Web. 22 Aug. 2009.

Franklin, Melanie. "The Creative Process." Online posting.

  New York Times Forum. 25 Jan. 2005. Web. 27 Jan.

  2010.

50. A podcast

"The House." *CBC Past Podcasts*. CBC Radio. 27 Mar. 2010.

  Web. 6 Apr. 2010.

51. A synchronous communication

Bruckman, Amy. McdiaMOO Symposium: "Virtual Worlds

  for Business?" 20 Jan. 2005. MediaMOO.

  Web. 26 Feb. 2005.

52. Computer software

Project Scheduler 9000. Ver. 5.1. Orlando: Scitor,

  2005. Web.

**MLA
40b**

Other sources

53. A government publication

Generally, begin with the issuing agency or the political jurisdiction (nation, province or state, municipality);
then the subgroup or agency; then the title; then the
author; then the identifying publication information. If
an individual author is specified, MLA style begins with
the author's name. Always provide sufficient detail for
your reader to locate the document. For detailed advice,
consult Diane L. Garner, Diane H. Smith, and Diane
L. Gapner, *The Complete Guide to Citing Government
Information Resources: A Manual for Writers and Librarians*, rev. ed. (American Library Association Government
Documents Round Table, 1993), or *http://www.library.
ubc.ca/govpubs/CitingGovernmentPublications.html*.

Canada. Library of Parliament. *The War Paintings in the*

  Senate Chamber. Ottawa: Library of Parliament, 2002.

  Print.

Kogawa, Joy. *Writing in Canada*. Canadian Heritage.
Ottawa: Canada Heritage, 1994. Print.

Canada. Parliament. House of Commons. *Debates*, 38th
Parliament, 1st session, vol. 140, 2004. Print.

United States. Cong. House. Committee on Ways and
Means. *Medicare Payment for Outpatient Physical and
Occupational Therapy Services*. 108th Cong., 1st sess.
Washington: GPO, 2003. Print.

Fauré, Gabriel. *Sonata for Violin and Piano No. 1 in A Major,
op. 1*. 1876. Van Nuys: Alfred, 1985. Print.

Thomson, Tom. *Snow in October*. 1916-17. Oil on canvas.
National Gallery of Canada, Ottawa.

If citing a published reproduction of a work of art, include
the source:

Thomson, Tom. *Snow in October*. 1916-17. Oil on canvas.
National Gallery of Canada, Ottawa. *The Group of
Seven and Tom Thomson: An Introduction*. By Anne
Newlands. Willowdale: Firefly, 1995. 31. Print.

**MLA
40b**

Schindler's List. Dir. Steven Spielberg. Perf. Liam Neeson
and Ben Kingsley. Universal, 1993. Film.

George Balanchine, chor. *Serenade*. Perf. San Francisco
Ballet. Dir. Hilary Bean. 1981. PBS Video, 1987.
Videocassette.

"I'm Sorry, I'm Lost." By Alan Ball. Dir. Jill Soloway. *Six
Feet Under*. HBO. 2 Sept. 2004. Television.

Billy Bishop Goes to War. By John Gray, with Eric Peterson.
Dir. Sarah Rodgers. Granville Island Stage, Vancouver.
10 Apr. 2010. Performance.

Lamon, Jeanne, cond. Tafelmusik Baroque Orch. Concert.
Trinity-St. Paul's Centre, Toronto. 17 Sept. 2003.
Performance.

58. A sound recording

Springsteen, Bruce. "Empty Sky." *The Rising*. Columbia,
2002. CD.

Brahms, Johannes. *Concerto No. 2 in B-flat, op. 83*.
Perf. Artur Rubinstein. Cond. Eugene Ormandy.
Philadelphia Orch. RCA, 1992. CD.

59. A published letter

Buttolph, Mrs. Laura E. Letter to Rev. and Mrs. C. C. Jones.
20 June 1857. In *The Children of Pride: A True Story
of Georgia and the Civil War*. Ed. Robert Manson
Myers. New Haven: Yale UP, 1972. 334. Print.

60. A personal letter

Packer, Ann E. Letter to the author. 15 June 2008. TS.

61. A lecture or address

Khouri, Katia. "Ownership Convergence." Symposium on
Canadian Journalism. City Hall, Cambridge. 16 Oct.
2002. Address.

MLA
40c

62. An interview

Graaf, Vera. Personal interview. 19 Dec. 2009.

Rumsfeld, Donald. Interview. *Frontline*. PBS. WGBH,
Boston. 13 Oct. 2004. Television.

63. A map or other illustration

Women in the Armed Forces. Map. *Women in the World: An
International Atlas*. By Joni Seager and Ann Olson.
New York: Touchstone, 2004. 44-45. Print.

40c MLA paper format

The document format recommended by the *MLA
Handbook* is fairly simple, with just a few elements. See
pages 183–84 for illustrations of the elements. See also

pages 15–21 for guidelines on type fonts, headings, lists, illustrations, and other features that are not specified in MLA style.

Margins Use minimum one-inch (2.5 cm) margins on all sides of every page.

Spacing and indentions Double-space throughout. Indent paragraphs one-half inch (1.25 cm). (See below and next page for indention of poetry and long prose quotations.)

Paging Begin numbering on the first page, and number consecutively through the end (including the list of works cited). Type Arabic numerals (1, 2, 3) in the upper right about one-half inch (1.25 cm) from the top. Place your last name one space before the page number in case the pages later become separated.

Identification and title In the upper left of the first page, give your name, your instructor's name, the course title, and the date—all double-spaced. Centre the title. Do not underline or italicize it, type it in all-capitals or boldface, or place it in quotation marks.

Poetry and long prose quotations Treat a single line of poetry like any other quotation, running it into your text and enclosing it in quotation marks. You may run in two or three lines of poetry as well, separating the lines with a slash:

> An example of Robert Frost's incisiveness is in two
> lines from "Death of the Hired Man": "Home is the place
> where, when you have to go there / They have to take
> you in" (119-20).

Always separate quotations of more than three lines of poetry from your text. Use double spacing and a one-inch (2.5 cm) indention. *Do not add quotation marks.*

> Emily Dickinson stripped ideas to their essence, as in this
> description of a snake as "A narrow Fellow in the Grass":
>> I more than once at Noon
>> Have passed, I thought, a Whip lash
>> Unbraiding in the Sun
>> When stopping to secure it
>> It wrinkled, and was gone – (12-16)

Also separate prose quotations of five or more typed lines. *Do not add quotation marks.*

> In his 1967 study of the lives of unemployed black
> men, Elliot Liebow observes that "unskilled" construc-

tion work requires more experience and skill than is generally assumed.

> A healthy, sturdy, active man of good
> intelligence requires from two to four
> weeks to break in on a construction job. . . .
> It frequently happens that his foreman
> or the craftsman he services is not willing
> to wait that long for him to get into condi-
> tion or to learn at a glance the difference in
> size between a rough 2 x 8 and a finished
> 2 x 10. (62)

40d   Sample pages in MLA style

First page

Second page

MLA
40d

Works cited

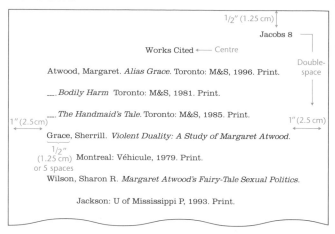

¹/₂″ (1.25 cm)

Jacobs 8

Works Cited ←—— Centre

Double-space

Atwood, Margaret. *Alias Grace.* Toronto: M&S, 1996. Print.

___.*Bodily Harm* Toronto: M&S, 1981. Print.

___.*The Handmaid's Tale.* Toronto: M&S, 1985. Print.

1″ (2.5cm)

1″ (2.5 cm)

Grace, Sherrill. *Violent Duality: A Study of Margaret Atwood.*

¹/₂″
(1.25 cm)   Montreal: Véhicule, 1979. Print.
or 5 spaces

Wilson, Sharon R. *Margaret Atwood's Fairy-Tale Sexual Politics.*

Jackson: U of Mississippi P, 1993. Print.

---

41 APA Documentation and Format

The documentation style of the American Psychological Association is used in psychology and some other social sciences and is very similar to the styles in sociology, economics, and other disciplines. The following examples show the APA style from the *Publication Manual of the American Psychological Association*, 6th ed. (2010).

**APA
41a**

Note The APA provides occasional updates of its style and answers to frequently asked questions at *http://www.apastyle.org/learn/faqs/index.aspx*.

41a APA parenthetical text citations

Citation formats

In APA style, parenthetical citations in the text refer to a list of sources at the end of the text. The basic parenthetical citation contains the author's last name and the date of publication. If you name the author in your text, then the citation includes just the date. Unless none is available, the APA also requires a page or other identifying number for a direct quotation and recommends an identifying number for a paraphrase.

> Visit www.mycanadiancomplab.ca for added help and an exercise on citing sources.

APA PARENTHETICAL TEXT CITATIONS

1. Author not named in your text

One critic of Milgram's experiments insisted that the subjects "should have been fully informed of the possible effects on them" (Baumrind, 1968, p. 34).

2. Author named in your text

Baumrind (1968) insisted that the subjects in Milgram's study "should have been fully informed of the possible effects on them" (p. 34).

3. A work with two authors

Pepinsky and DeStefano (1997) demonstrated that a teacher's language often reveals hidden biases.

One study (Pepinsky & DeStefano, 1997) demonstrated hidden biases in a teacher's language.

4. A work with three to five authors

First reference:
Pepinsky, Dunn, Rentl, and Corson (1999) further demonstrated the biases evident in gestures.

Later references:
In the work of Pepinsky et al. (1999), the loaded gestures included head shakes and eye contact.

APA
41a

5. A work with six or more authors

One study (Rutter et al., 1996) attempted to explain these geographical differences in adolescent experience.

6. A work with a group author

An earlier prediction was even more somber (Lorenz Research, 2003).

Use this model for works that list an agency, institution, corporation, or other group as the author.

7. A work with no author or an anonymous work

One article ("Right to Die," 1996) noted that a death-row inmate may crave notoriety.

For a work that lists "anonymous" as the author, use this word in the citation: (Anonymous, 1999).

8. One of two or more works by the same author(s) published in the same year

At about age seven, most children begin to use appropriate gestures to reinforce their stories (Gardner, 1973a).

(See the reference for this source on p. 190.)

9. Two or more works by different authors

Two studies (Herskowitz, 1994; Marconi & Hamblen, 1999) found that periodic safety instruction can dramatically reduce employees' accidents.

10. An indirect source

Supporting data appear in a study by Wong (as cited in Marconi & Hamblen, 1999).

11. An electronic source

Cite electronic sources like printed sources, usually with the author's last name and the publication date. When quoting or paraphrasing electronic sources that number paragraphs instead of pages, provide the paragraph number preceded by "para."

Ferguson and Hawkins (2005) did not anticipate the "evident hostility" of participants (para. 6).

If the source does not have numbering of any kind, provide just the author's name and the date.

Footnotes for supplementary content

When you need to explain something in your text—for instance, commenting on a source or providing data that don't fit into the relevant paragraph—you may place the supplementary information in a footnote. Follow the instructions for footnotes in the Chicago style (pp. 200–01). Be careful not to overuse such notes: they can be more distracting than helpful.

41b APA reference list

In APA style, the in-text parenthetical citations refer to the list of sources at the end of the text. In this list, titled "References," you include full publication information on every source cited in your paper. The reference list falls at the end of the paper, numbered in sequence with the preceding pages. For an illustration of the following elements and their spacing, see page 199.

Arrangement Arrange sources alphabetically by the author's last name or, if there is no author, by the first main word of the title.

Spacing Double-space all entries.

Indention Begin each entry at the left margin, and indent the second and subsequent lines one-half inch (1.25 cm) or five to seven spaces.

Authors For works with up to seven authors, list all authors with last name first, separating names and parts of names with commas. Use initials for first and middle names. Use an ampersand (&) before the last author's name. See model 3 on page 189 for treatment of eight or more authors.

Publication date Place the publication date in parentheses after the author's or authors' names, followed by a period. Generally, this date is the year only, though for some sources (such as magazine and newspaper articles) it includes month and sometimes day as well.

Title In the title of a book or article, capitalize only the first word of the title, the first word of the subtitle, and proper nouns°; all other words begin with small letters. In the title of a journal, capitalize all significant words. Italicize the titles of books and journals, along with any comma following. Do not italicize or use quotation marks around the titles of articles.

APA
41b

APA
41b

City of publication   For print sources, such as books or government publications, that are not periodicals, give the city of publication followed by the province or state, using two-letter postal abbreviations (e.g., ON, BC, NY, MA). Follow the province or state with a colon. (You may omit the province or state if the publisher is a university whose name includes the name of the province or state, such as "University of Alberta.")

Publisher's name   For nonperiodical print sources, give the publisher's name after the place of publication and a colon. Use shortened names for many publishers (such as "Morrow" for William Morrow), and omit "Co.," "Inc.," and "Publishers." However, give full names for associations, corporations, and university presses, and do not omit "Books" or "Press" from a publisher's name.

Page numbers   Use the abbreviation "p." or "pp." before page numbers in books and in newspapers, but *not* in other periodicals. For inclusive page numbers, include all figures: "667–668."

Punctuation   Separate the parts of the reference (author, date, title, and publication information) with a period and one space. Do not use a final period in references to electronic sources, which conclude with an electronic address (see pp. 192–94).

Books

1. A book with one author

Rodriguez, R. (1982). *A hunger of memory: The education of Richard Rodriguez.* Boston, MA: Godine.

2. A book with two to seven authors

Nesselroade, J. R., & Baltes, P. B. (1999). *Longitudinal research in the study of behavioral development.* New York, NY: Academic Press.

3. A book with eight or more authors

Wimple, P. B., Van Eijk, M., Potts, C. A., Hayes, J., Obergau, W. R., Zimmer, S., . . . Harris, N. R. (2001). *Case studies in moral decision making among adolescents.* San Francisco: Jossey-Bass.

Give the first six authors' names, followed by an ellipsis mark, and end with the last author's name. Do not include an ampersand.

APA
41b

4. A book with an editor

Dohrenwend, B. S., & Dohrenwend, B. P. (Eds.). (1999).

> *Stressful life events: Their nature and effects.*
> New York, NY: Wiley.

5. A book with a translator

Trajan, P. D. (1927). *Psychology of animals.* (H. Simone,

> Trans.). Washington, DC: Halperin.

6. A book with a group author

Lorenz Research, Inc. (2005). *Research in social studies*

> *teaching.* Baltimore, MD: Arrow Books.

7. A book with no author or an anonymous book

Merriam-Webster's collegiate dictionary (11th ed.). (2003).

> Springfield, MA: Merriam-Webster.

For a work whose author is actually given as "Anony-mous," use this word in place of the author's name and alphabetize it as if it were a name.

8. Two or more works by the same author(s)
published in the same year

Gardner, H. (1973a). *The arts and human development.* New

> York, NY: Wiley.

Gardner, H. (1973b). *The quest for mind: Piaget, Lévi-Strauss,*

> *and the structuralist movement.* New York, NY: Knopf.

9. A later edition

Bolinger, D. L. (1975). *Aspects of language* (2nd ed.). New

> York: Harcourt.

10. A work in more than one volume

Reference to a single volume:

Lincoln, A. (1953). *The collected works of Abraham Lincoln*

> (R. P. Basler, Ed.). (Vol. 5). New Brunswick, NJ:
> Rutgers University Press.

APA
41b

Reference to all volumes:

Lincoln, A. (1953). *The collected works of Abraham Lincoln* (R. P. Basler, Ed.). (Vols. 1–8). New Brunswick, NJ: Rutgers University Press.

11. An article or chapter in an edited book

Paykel, E. S. (1999). Life stress and psychiatric disorder: Applications of the clinical approach. In B. S. Dohrenwend & B. P. Dohrenwend (Eds.), *Stressful life events: Their nature and effects* (pp. 239–264). New York, NY: Wiley.

Periodicals: Journals, magazines, newspapers

12. An article in a journal with continuous pagination throughout the annual volume

Emery, R. E. (2003). Marital turmoil: Interpersonal conflict and the children of divorce. *Psychological Bulletin, 92,* 310–330.

13. An article in a journal that pages issues separately

Dacey, J. (1998). Management participation in corporate buy-outs. *Management Perspectives, 7*(4), 20–31.

14. An abstract of a journal article

Emery, R. E. (2003). Marital turmoil: Interpersonal conflict and the children of discord and divorce. *Psychological Bulletin, 92,* 310–330. Abstract obtained from *Psychological Abstracts,* 1992, *69,* Item 1320.

15. An article in a magazine

Hawaleshka, D. (2003, March 31). Killer viruses. *Maclean's,* 50–51.

16. An article in a newspaper

Lopez Pacheco, A. (2003, August 11). Health lessons start at home. *National Post,* p. SR6.

APA
41b

17. An unsigned article

The right to die. (1996, October 11). *Time*, 101.

18. A review

Dinnage, R. (1987, November 29). Against the master and his

men [Review of the book *A mind of her own: The life of*

Karen Horney, by S. Quinn]. *The New York Times Book*

Review, 10–11.

Electronic sources

In general, the APA's electronic-source references begin as those for print references do: author(s), date, title, and source. Some online material is now identified by the DOI System, which assigns a unique number to an article no matter what site it appears on. The DOI (digital object identifier) usually appears on the first page of an electronic journal article, or on a database "landing page" for an article. In the reference list, the DOI appears at the end of the entry in the format doi:xx.xxxxxxxxxx.

If no DOI is assigned, give the URL preceded by the words *Retrieved from*; for example, Retrieved from *http://sites.unc.edu/daniel/social_constructionism* (in APA style, angle brackets are not used and no period follows a URL at the end of the reference). Note that the models here do not show retrieval dates, which APA now requires only if the source (such as a report on medical research or a wiki) is likely to change significantly over time.

APA
41b

When you need to divide a URL from one line to the next, APA style calls for breaking before most punctuation (the exception is http://). Do not hyphenate a URL.

Try to locate all the information required by a model, referring to pages 125–26 for help. However, if you search for and still cannot find some information, then give what you can find. If a source has no publication date, use "n.d." (for *no date*) in place of a publication date (see model 28, p. 194).

19. A journal article published online and in print, with DOI

Seo, D. C., & Jiang, N. Associations between smoking

and extreme dieting among adolescents. *Journal*

of Youth and Adolescence, *38*, 1364–1373. doi:10.1007

/s10964-009-9421-0

20. An online journal article without DOI

Findlay, L. C., & Coplan, R. J. (2008). Come out and play:
 Shyness in childhood and the benefits of organized
 sports participation. *Canadian Journal of
 Behavioural Science, 40,* 153–161. Retrieved from
 http://www.cpa.ca/publications/cpajournals/#cjbs

21. A journal article from an electronic database

Wilkins, J. M. (1999). The myths of the only child. *Psychology Update, 11*(1), 16–23. Retrieved from database.www3
 .interscience.wiley.com/journal/30170/home

22. An abstract from an electronic database

Wilkins, J. M. (1999). The myths of the only child. *Psychology Update, 11*(1), 16–23. Abstract retrieved from
 ProQuest Direct database.

23. An article in an online newspaper

Johnston, J. C. (2007, March 29). Income gap is widening,
 data show. *The New York Times.* Retrieved from http://
 www.nytimes.com

24. An entire website (text citation)

The APA's website provides answers to frequently asked
questions about style (http://www.apa.org).

Cite an entire website (rather than a specific page or
document) by giving the electronic address in your text.

25. An independent document on the web

Anderson, D. (2009, May 1). *Social constructionism and
 MOOs.* Retrieved from http://sites.unc.edu/~daniel
 /social_constructionism

26. A document from the website of a university
or government agency

McConnell, L. M., Koenig, B. A., Greely, H. T., & Raffin,
 T. A. (2004, August 17). *Genetic testing and Alzheimers
 disease: Has the time come?* Retrieved from Stanford
 University, Project in Genomics, Ethics, and Society
 website: http://scbe.stanford.edu/pges

27. An online government report

Canada. Health Canada. It's Your Health. (2006, January
     18). *Avian Influenza (bird flu)*. Retrieved from http://
     www.hc-sc.ca/iyh-vsv/diseases-maladies
     /avian-aviare_e.html

28. A multipage online document

Elston, C. (n.d.). *Multiple intelligences*. Retrieved from http://
     education.com/teachspace/intelligences

29. A part of an online document

Elston, C. (n.d.). Logical/math intelligence. In *Multiple
     intelligences*. Retrieved from http://education.com
     /teachspace/intelligences/logical.jsp

30. A retrievable online posting

Tourville, M. (2005, January 6). European currency reform
     [Electronic mailing list message]. Retrieved from http://
     www.liasu.edu/finance-dl/46732

Include postings to discussion lists and newsgroups in
your list of references *only* if they are retrievable by others. The source above is archived (as the reference makes
plain) and thus retrievable at the address given.

APA
41b

31. Electronic mail or a nonretrievable online posting
(text citation)

At least one member of the research team has expressed res-
ervations about the design of the study (L. Kogod, personal
communication, February 6, 2009).

Personal electronic mail and other online postings that
are not retrievable by others should be cited only in your
text, as in the example above.

32. Computer software

Project scheduler 9000 [Computer software]. (2005).
     Orlando, FL: Scitor.

Other sources

33. A report

Gerald, K. (1998). *Micro-moral problems in obstetric care*
     (Report No. NP-71). St. Louis, MO: Catholic Hospital
     Association.

Jolson, M. K. (1991). *Music education for preschoolers*
(Report No. TC-622). New York, NY: Teachers College,
Columbia University. (ERIC Document Reproduction
Service No. ED 264 488)

34. A government publication

See "A government publication," pages 179–80.

Canada. Library of Parliament. (2002). *The war paintings in
the Senate Chamber.* Ottawa, ON: Author.

Kogawa, Joy. (1994). *Writing in Canada.* Ottawa, ON:
Canadian Heritage.

U.S. House. Committee on Ways and Means. (2003).
*Medicare payment for outpatient physical and
occupational therapy services.* 108th Cong., 1st Sess.
Washington, DC: Government Printing Office.

35. A doctoral dissertation

A dissertation abstracted in *DAI* and obtained from UMI:

Steciw, S. K. (1986). Alterations to the Pessac project of
Le Corbusier. *Dissertation Abstracts International, 46,*
565C. (UMI No. 6216202)

A dissertation abstracted in *DAI* and obtained from the
university:

Chang, J. K. (2000). Therapeutic intervention in treatment
of injuries to the hand and wrist (Doctoral dissertation, University of Michigan). *Dissertation Abstracts
International, 50,* 162.

An unpublished dissertation:

Delaune, M. L. (2001). *Child care in single-mother and single-
father families: Differences in time, activity, and stress*
(Unpublished doctoral dissertation). University of
California, Davis.

36. A published interview

Brisick, W. C. (1998, July 1). [Interview with Ishmael Reed].
Publishers Weekly, 41–42.

For an interview you conduct yourself, use an in-text parenthetical citation, as shown in model 31 (previous page)
for a nonretrievable online posting.

**APA
41b**

37. A motion picture

Spielberg, S. (Director). (1993). *Schindler's list* [Motion
    picture]. United States: Viacom.

American Psychological Association (Producer). (2001).
    Ethnocultural psychotherapy [Motion picture].
    (Available from the American Psychological
    Association, 750 First Street, NE, Washington, DC
    20002-4242, or online from http://www.apa org
    /videos/4310240.html)

38. A musical recording

Springsteen, B. (2002). Empty sky. On *The rising* [CD]. New
    York, NY: Columbia.

39. A television series or episode

Taylor, C., Cleveland, R., & Andries, L. (Producers). (2004).
    Six feet under [Television series]. New York, NY: HBO.

Cleveland, R. (writer), & Engler, M. (Director). (2004). Dillon
    Michael Cooper [Television series episode]. In C. Taylor,
    R. Cleveland, & L. Andries (Producers), *Six feet under*.
    New York, NY: HBO.

APA
41c

41c   APA paper format

The APA *Publication Manual* distinguishes between
documents intended for publication (which will be set
in type) and those submitted by students (which are the
final copy). The guidelines below apply to most under-
graduate papers. Check with your instructor for any
modifications to this format.

For illustrations of the following elements, see pages
198–99. And see pages 15–21 for guidelines on type fonts,
lists, tables and figures, and other elements of document
design.

Margins Use one-inch (2.5 cm) margins on the top,
bottom, and right side. Add another half-inch (1.25 cm)
on the left to accommodate a binder.

Spacing and indentions Double-space your text and
references. (See the next page for spacing of displayed
quotations.) Indent paragraphs and displayed quotations
one-half inch (1.25 cm) or five to seven spaces.

Paging Begin numbering on the title page, and number consecutively through the end (including the reference list). Type Arabic numerals (1, 2, 3) in the upper right, about one-half inch (1.25 cm) from the top.

Place a shortened version of your title five spaces to the left of the page number.

Title page Include the full title, your name, the course title, the instructor's name, and the date. Type the title on the top half of the page, followed by the identifying information, all centred horizontally and double-spaced. Include a shortened form of the title along with the page number at the top of this and all other pages.

Abstract Summarize (in a maximum of 120 words) your subject, research method, findings, and conclusions. Put the abstract on a page by itself.

Body Begin with a restatement of the paper's title and then an introduction (not labelled). The introduction concisely presents the problem you researched, your research method, the relevant background (such as related studies), and the purpose of your research.

The "Method" section provides a detailed discussion of how you conducted your research, including a description of the research subjects, any materials or tools you used (such as questionnaires), and the procedure you followed.

The "Results" section summarizes the data you collected, explains how you analyzed them, and presents them in detail, often in tables, graphs, or charts.

The "Discussion" section interprets the data and presents your conclusions. (When the discussion is brief, you may combine it with the previous section under the heading "Results and Discussion.")

APA 41c

Headings Label the "Method," "Results," and "Discussion" sections with centred first-level headings, and use second- and third-level headings as needed. Double-space all headings.

First-Level Heading

Second-Level Heading

Third-level heading. Run this heading into the text paragraph.

Long quotations Run into your text all quotations of forty words or less, and enclose them in quotation marks. For quotations of more than forty words, set them off from your text by indenting all lines one-half inch (1.25 cm) or five to seven spaces, double-spacing above and below. For student papers, the APA allows single-spacing of displayed quotations:

> Echoing the opinions of other Europeans at the time, Freud (1961) had a poor view of Americans:
>
>> The Americans are really too bad. . . . Competition is much more pungent with them, not succeeding means civil death to every one, and they have no private resources apart from their profession, no hobby, games, love or other interests of a cultured person. And success means money. (p. 86)

Do not use quotation marks around a quotation displayed in this way.

41d Sample pages in APA style

Title page

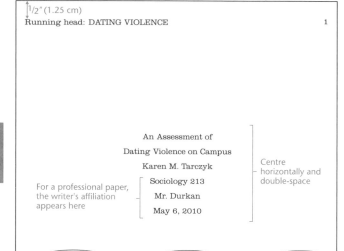

1/2" (1.25 cm)
Running head: DATING VIOLENCE   1

An Assessment of
Dating Violence on Campus
Karen M. Tarczyk
Sociology 213
Mr. Durkan
May 6, 2010

For a professional paper, the writer's affiliation appears here

Centre horizontally and double-space

Abstract

1/2" (1.25 cm)
DATING VIOLENCE   2
No indention
                        Abstract ⟵ Centre

Little research has examined the patterns of abuse and
violence occurring within couples during courtship. With a
questionnaire administered to a sample of university students,
the extent and nature of such abuse and violence were in-
vestigated. The results, interpretations, and implications for

1 1/2" (3.75 cm)

Double-space

1" (2.5 cm)

APA
41d

First page of body

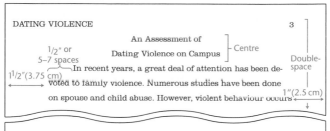

DATING VIOLENCE   3

An Assessment of
Dating Violence on Campus — Centre

1/2″ or 5–7 spaces

In recent years, a great deal of attention has been de-
voted to family violence. Numerous studies have been done
on spouse and child abuse. However, violent behaviour occurs

1 1/2″ (3.75 cm)

Double-space

1″(2.5 cm)

premarital violence was a problem of "abusive relationships"
as well as "abusive individuals" (p. 90).

1″(2.5 cm)

Later page of body

DATING VIOLENCE   4

All the studies indicate a problem that is being neglected.
My objective was to gather data on the extent and nature of premarital violence and to discuss possible interpretations.

Method → Double-space

Sample

I conducted a survey of 200 students (134 females,
66 males) at a large East Coast urban university. The sample
consisted of students enrolled in an introductory sociology course.

APA 41d

References

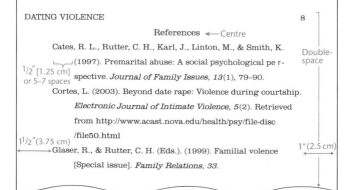

DATING VIOLENCE   8

References ← Centre

Cates, R. L., Rutter, C. H., Karl, J., Linton, M., & Smith, K.
(1997). Premarital abuse: A social psychological pe r-
spective. *Journal of Family Issues, 13*(1), 79–90.

Cortes, L. (2003). Beyond date rape: Violence during courtship.
Electronic Journal of Intimate Violence, 5(2). Retrieved
from http://www.acast.nova.edu/health/psy/file-disc
/file50.html

Glaser, R., & Rutter, C. H. (Eds.). (1999). Familial volence
[Special issue]. *Family Relations, 33.*

1/2″ [1.25 cm] or 5–7 spaces

1 1/2″ (3.75 cm)

Double-space

1″(2.5 cm)

42 Chicago Documentation and Format

Writers in history, art history, philosophy, and other humanities use the note style of documentation from *The Chicago Manual of Style*, 16th ed. (2010), or the student reference adapted from the fourteenth edition, *A Manual for Writers of Term Papers, Theses, and Dissertations*, by Kate L. Turabian, 6th ed., revised by John Grossman and Alice Bennett (1996). *The Chicago Manual* has a website that answers frequently asked questions about its style: *http://www.chicagomanualofstyle.org/CMS_FAQ/qatopics.html*.

This chapter explains the Chicago note style (below) and Chicago paper format (p. 211).

42a Chicago notes and list of works cited

In the Chicago note style, a raised numeral in the text refers the reader to source information in endnotes or footnotes. Generally, the first citation of each source contains all the information readers need to find the source, but when there is a works-cited list, which provides much the same information, a shortened note form can be used for the first and subsequent notes (see p. 210). Ask your instructor whether you should use footnotes or endnotes and whether you should include a list of works cited.

The examples below illustrate the essentials of a note and a works-cited entry. (See p. 213 for additional illustrations.)

Note

> 6. Martin Gilbert, *Atlas of British History* (New York: Dorset, 1988), 96.

Works-cited entry

> Gilbert, Martin. *Atlas of British History*. New York: Dorset, 1988.

Notes and works-cited entries share certain features:

- Single-space each note or entry, and double-space between them.
- Italicize or underline the titles of books and periodicals (ask your instructor for his or her preference).
- Enclose in quotation marks the titles of parts of books or articles in periodicals.

- Give publishers' names in full or in a moderately abbreviated form, omitting "Inc.," "Co.," and so on.
- Do not use "p." or "pp." before page numbers unless required for clarity.
- For anything other than a traditional print product, name the medium.

Notes and works-cited entries also differ in important ways.

Notes	Works-cited entries
Start with a number that corresponds to the note number in the text.	Do not begin with a number.
Indent the first line five spaces.	Indent the second and subsequent lines five spaces.
Give the author's name in normal order.	Begin with the author's last name.
Use commas between elements such as author's name and title.	Use periods between elements, followed by one space.
Enclose publication information in parentheses, with no preceding punctuation.	Precede the publication information with a period, and don't use parentheses.
Include the specific page number(s) you borrowed from, omitting "p." or "pp."	Omit page numbers except for parts of books or articles in periodicals.

Chic 42b

Many word-processing programs automatically position footnotes at the bottom of appropriate pages. Some automatically number notes and even renumber them if you add or delete one or more.

42b   Chicago models

In the following models for common sources, notes and works-cited entries appear together for easy reference. In your papers, be sure to use the numbered note form for notes and the unnumbered works-cited form for works-cited entries.

Books

1. A book with one, two, or three authors

1. Joseph Boyden, *Three Day Road* (Toronto: Viking Canada, 2005), 134.

Boyden, Joseph. *Three Day Road*. Toronto: Viking Canada, 2005.

1. Dennis L. Wilcox, Phillip H. Ault, and Warren K. Agee, *Public Relations: Strategies and Tactics,* 4th ed. (New York: HarperCollins, 1995), 182.

Wilcox, Dennis L., Phillip H. Ault, and Warren K. Agee. *Public Relations: Strategies and Tactics.* 4th ed. New York: HarperCollins, 1995.

2. A book with more than three authors

2. Geraldo Lopez et al., *China and the West* (Boston: Little, Brown, 2000), 461.

Lopez, Geraldo, Judith P. Salt, Anne Ming, and Henry Reisen. *China and the West.* Boston: Little, Brown, 2000.

CHICAGO NOTES AND WORKS-CITED MODELS

Books

Chic
42b

Periodicals: Journals, magazines, newspapers

Electronic sources

3. A book with an editor in place of an author

3. Hendrick Ruitenbeek, ed., *Freud as We Knew Him* (Detroit: Wayne State University Press, 1973), 64.

Ruitenbeek, Hendrick, ed. *Freud as We Knew Him*. Detroit: Wayne State University Press, 1973.

4. A book with an author and an editor

4. Frances Burney, *Evelina, or, The History of a Young Woman's Entrance into the World,* Norton Critical Edition, ed. Stewart J. Cooke (New York: Norton, 1998), 214–16.

Burney, Frances. *Evelina, or, The History of a Young Woman's Entrance into the World*. Norton Critical Edition. Edited by Stewart J. Cooke. New York: Norton, 1998.

5. A translation

5. Jovette Marchessault, *Mother of the Grass,* trans. Yvonne M. Klein (Vancouver: Talon, 1989), 112.

Marchessault, Jovette. *Mother of the Grass*. Translated by Yvonne M. Klein. Vancouver: Talon, 1989.

Chic 42b

6. An anonymous work

6. *The Dorling Kindersley World Reference Atlas* (London: Dorling Kindersley, 2005), 150–51.

The Dorling Kindersley World Reference Atlas. London: Dorling Kindersley, 2005.

7. A later edition

7. Dwight L. Bolinger, *Aspects of Language,* 2nd ed. (New York: Harcourt Brace Jovanovich, 1975), 20.

Bolinger, Dwight L. *Aspects of Language*. 2nd ed. New York: Harcourt Brace Jovanovich, 1975.

8. A work in more than one volume

Citation of one volume without a title:

8. Abraham Lincoln, *The Collected Works of Abraham Lincoln,* ed. Roy P. Basler (New Brunswick, NJ: Rutgers University Press, 1953), 5:426–28.

Lincoln, Abraham. *The Collected Works of Abraham Lincoln.* Edited by Roy P. Basler. Vol. 5. New Brunswick, NJ: Rutgers University Press, 1953.

Citation of one volume with a title:

8. Linda B. Welkin, *The Age of Balanchine,* vol. 3, *The History of Ballet* (New York: Columbia University Press, 1969), 56.

Welkin, Linda B. *The Age of Balanchine.* Vol. 3 of *The History of Ballet.* New York: Columbia University Press, 1969.

9. A selection from an anthology

9. Leslie Duer, "Portraits, Effigies, and the Narrative Impulse," in *Literature and Ethics: Essays Presented to A. E. Malloch,* ed. Gary Wihl and David Williams (Kingston: McGill-Queen's University Press, 1998), 38–39.

Duer, Leslie. "Portraits, Effigies, and the Narrative Impulse." In *Literature and Ethics: Essays Presented to A. E. Malloch,* edited by Gary Wihl and David Williams, 32–45. Kingston: McGill-Queen's University Press, 1988.

Chic 42b

10. A work in a series

10. Ingmar Bergman, *The Seventh Seal,* Modern Film Scripts, no. 12 (New York: Simon and Schuster, 1968), 27.

Bergman, Ingmar. *The Seventh Seal.* Modern Film Scripts, no. 12. New York: Simon and Schuster, 1968.

11. An article in a reference work

Chicago does not require publication information for well-known reference works (except for the edition if it isn't the first). The abbreviation "s.v." stands for the Latin *sub verbo,* "under the word."

11. *Merriam-Webster's Collegiate Dictionary,* 11th ed., s.v. "reckon."

Merriam-Webster's Collegiate Dictionary, 11th ed., s.v. "reckon."

Periodicals: Journals, magazines, newspapers

12. An article in a journal

    12. Janet Lever, "Sex Differences in the Games Children Play," *Social Problems* 23 (1996): 482.

Lever, Janet. "Sex Differences in the Games Children Play." *Social Problems* 23 (1996): 478–87.

    12. June Dacey, "Management Participation in Corporate Buy-Outs," *Management Perspectives* 7, no. 4 (1998): 22.

Dacey, June. "Management Participation in Corporate Buy-Outs." *Management Perspectives* 7, no. 4 (1998): 20–31.

13. An article in a magazine

    13. Margaret Talbot, "The Bad Mother," *New Yorker,* August 9, 2004, 32.

Talbot, Margaret. "The Bad Mother." *New Yorker,* August 9, 2004, 31–37.

14. An article in a newspaper

    14. Alexandra Lopez Pacheco, "Health Lessons Start at Home," *National Post,* August 11, 2003, SR6.

Lopez Pacheco, Alexandra. "Health Lessons Start at Home." *National Post,* August 11, 2003, SR6.

15. A review

    15. John Gregory Dunne, "The Secret of Danny Santiago," review of *Famous All over Town,* by Danny Santiago, *New York Review of Books,* August 16, 1994, 25.

Dunne, John Gregory. "The Secret of Danny Santiago." Review of *Famous All over Town,* by Danny Santiago. *New York Review of Books,* August 16, 1994, 17–27.

Chic 42b

Electronic sources

The Chicago Manual's models for documenting electronic sources derive mainly from those for print sources, with the addition of a Digital Object Identifier (DOI) if available (see p. 192), an electronic address (URL) if no DOI is provided, or some other indication of the medium, along with any other information that may help readers locate the source.

Chicago requires the date of your access to an online source only if no other date is given or if the source could change significantly (for instance, a report on medical research). However, your instructor may require access dates for a broader range of online sources. Thus they are included in some of the following models.

Note Chicago style allows many ways to break DOIs and URLs between the end of one line and the beginning of the next: after double slashes and colons, before most punctuation marks (single slashes, periods, commas, question marks, and so on), and before or after equal signs and ampersands (&). *Do not* break after a hyphen or add any hyphens.

16. A work on CD-ROM or DVD-ROM

16. *The American Heritage Dictionary of the English Language,* 4th ed. (Boston: Houghton Mifflin, 2000), CD-ROM.

The American Heritage Dictionary of the English Language. 4th ed. Boston: Houghton Mifflin, 2000. CD-ROM.

17. A work from an online database

17. Irina Netchaeva, "E-Government and E-Democracy." *International Journal for Communication Studies* 64 (2002): 470–71, accessed December 20, 2004, http://www.epnet.com.

Netchaeva, Irina. "E-Government and E-Democracy." *International Journal for Communication Studies* 64 (2002): 467–78. Accessed December 20, 2004. http://www.epnet.com.

Chic 42b

For news and journal databases, including those to which your library subscribes, you may omit the name of the database and instead provide a URL if one is identified as stable; otherwise, include the database and, in parentheses, any identifying number given.

18. An online book

18. Jane Austen, *Emma,* ed. Ronald Blythe (1816; Harmondsworth, UK: Penguin, 1972; Oxford Text Archive, 2000), chap. 1, accessed December 15, 2004, http://ota.ox.ac.uk/public/english/Austen/ emma.1519.

Austen, Jane. *Emma.* Edited by Ronald Blythe. 1816. Harmondsworth, UK: Penguin, 1972. Oxford Text Archive, 2000. Accessed December 15, 2004. http://ota.ox.ac.uk/public/english/Austen/emma.1519.

19. An article in an online journal

19. Andrew Palfrey, "Choice of Mates in Identical Twins," *Modern Psychology* 4, no. 1 (1996): 28, http://www.liasu/edu/modpsy/palfrey4(1).htm.

Palfrey, Andrew. "Choice of Mates in Identical Twins." *Modern Psychology* 4, no. 1 (1996): 26–40. http://www.liasu/edu /modpsy/palfrey4(1).htm.

20. A journal article published online and in print, with DOI

20. Ioannidis, John P. A. "Why Most Published Research Findings Are False." *PLoS Medicine* 2, no. 8 (2005): e124, doi:10.1371/journal.pmed.0020124.

Ioannidis, John P. A. "Why Most Published Research Findings Are False." *PLoS Medicine* 2, no. 8 (2005): e124. doi:10.1371/journal.pmed.0020124.

21. An article in an online newspaper

21. Lucia Still, "On the Battlefields of Business, Millions of Casualties," *New York Times on the Web,* March 3, 2002, http://www.nytimes.com/specials/downsize/03down1 .html.

Still, Lucia. "On the Battlefields of Business, Millions of Casualties." *New York Times on the Web,* March 3, 2002. http://www.nytimes.com/specials/downsize /03down1.html.

22. An article in an online reference work

22. *Encyclopaedia Britannica Online,* s.v. "Wu-ti," accessed December 23, 2004, http://www.eb.com:80.

Encyclopaedia Britannica Online. S.v. "Wu-ti." Accessed December 23, 2004. http://www.eb.com:80.

23. An online audio or visual source

Chic 42b

A work of art:

23. Jackson Pollock, *Shimmering Substance,* oil on canvas, 1946, Museum of Modern Art, New York, Web- Museum, accessed March 12, 2004, http://www.ibiblio.org /wm/paint/auth/Pollock/pollock.shimmering.jpg.

Pollock, Jackson. *Shimmering Substance.* Oil on canvas, 1946. Museum of Modern Art, New York. WebMuseum. Accessed March 12, 2004. http://www.ibiblio.org/wm /paint/auth/Pollock/pollock.shimmering.jpg.

A sound recording:

23. Ronald W. Reagan, State of the Union address, January 26, 1982, Vincent Voice Library, Digital and Multimedia Center, University of Michigan, http://www.lib .msu.edu/vincent/presidents/reagan.html.

Reagan, Ronald W. State of the Union address. January 26, 1982. Vincent Voice Library. Digital and Multimedia Center, University of Michigan. http://www.lib.msu.edu/vincent/presidents/reagan.html.

A film or film clip:

23. Leslie J. Stewart, *96 Ranch Rodeo and Barbecue* (1951), 16 mm, from Library of Congress, *Buckaroos in Paradise: Ranching Culture in Northern Nevada, 1945–1982,* MPEG, accessed January 7, 2005, http://memory/loc.gov/cgibin/query/ammem/ncr:@field (DocID+@lit(nv034)).

Stewart, Leslie J. *96 Ranch Rodeo and Barbecue.* 1951, 16 mm. From Library of Congress, *Buckaroos in Paradise: Ranching Culture in Northern Nevada, 19451982.* MPEG. Accessed January 7, 2005. http://memory/loc.gov/cgi-bin/query/ammem/ncr:@field(DocID+@lit(nv034)).

24. A posting to an online discussion group

24. Michael Tourville, "European Currency Reform," e-mail to International Finance Discussion List, January 6, 2004, accessed January 12, 2004, http://www.weg.isu/finance-dl/archive/46732.

Tourville, Michael. "European Currency Reform." E-mail to International Finance Discussion List. January 6, 2004. Accessed January 12, 2004. http://www.weg.isu/finance-dl/archive/46732.

Chic 42b

25. Electronic mail

25. Michele Millon, "Re: Grief Therapy," e-mail message to author, May 4, 2004.

Millon, Michele. "Re: Grief Therapy." E-mail message to author. May 4, 2004.

Other sources

26. A government publication

See "A government publication," pages 179–80.

26. Library of Parliament, *The War Paintings in the Senate Chamber* (Ottawa, 2002), 3.

Canada. Library of Parliament. *The War Paintings in the Senate Chamber.* Ottawa, 2002.

26. House Committee on Ways and Means, *Medicare Payment for Outpatient Physical and Occupational Therapy Services,* 108th Cong., 1st sess., 2003, H. Doc. 409, 12–13.

US Congress. House. Committee on Ways and Means. *Medicare Payment for Outpatient Physical and Occupational Therapy Services.* 108th Cong., 1st sess., 2003. H. Doc. 409.

27. A published letter

27. Mrs. Laura E. Buttolph to Rev. and Mrs. C. C. Jones, June 20, 1857, in *The Children of Pride: A True Story of Georgia and the Civil War,* ed. Robert Manson Myers (New Haven, CT: Yale University Press, 1972), 334.

Buttolph, Laura E. Mrs. Laura E. Buttolph to Rev. and Mrs. C. C. Jones, June 20, 1857. In *The Children of Pride: A True Story of Georgia and the Civil War,* edited by Robert Manson Myers. New Haven, CT: Yale University Press, 1972.

28. A published or broadcast interview

28. Donald Rumsfeld, interview by William Lindon, *Frontline,* PBS, October 13, 2004.

Rumsfeld, Donald. Interview by William Lindon. *Frontline.* PBS, October 13, 2004.

29. A personal letter or interview

29. Ann E. Packer, letter to author, June 15, 2004.
Packer, Ann E. Letter to author. June 15, 2004.

29. Vera Graaf, interview by author, December 19, 2004.
Graaf, Vera. Interview by author. December 19, 2004.

sidebar
Chic 42b

30. A work of art

30. Tom Thomson, *Snow in October*, oil on canvas, 1916–17, National Gallery of Canada, Ottawa.

Thomson, Tom. *Snow in October.* Oil on canvas, 1916–17. National Gallery of Canada, Ottawa.

31. A film or video recording

31. George Balanchine, *Serenade,* San Francisco Ballet (New York: PBS Video, 1985), VHS.

Balanchine, George. *Serenade.* San Francisco Ballet. New York: PBS Video, 1985. VHS.

 32. Antonio Vivaldi, *Gloria*, Matthias Maute, Ensemble Caprice, Analekta AN 2 9917, 2008, compact disc.

Vivaldi, Antonio. *Gloria*. Mathias Maute. Ensemble Caprice. Analekta AN 2 9917, 2008, compact disc.

Shortened notes

To streamline documentation, Chicago style recommends shortened notes for sources that are fully cited elsewhere, either in a complete list of works cited or in previous notes. Ask your instructor whether your paper should include a list of works cited and, if so, whether you may use shortened notes for first references to sources as well as for subsequent references.

A shortened note contains the author's last name, the work's title (minus any initial *A*, *An*, or *The*), and the page number. Reduce long titles to four or fewer key-words.

Complete note

 8. Janet Lever, "Sex Differences in the Games Children Play," *Social Problems* 23 (1996): 482.

Complete works-cited entry

Lever, Janet. "Sex Differences in the Games Children Play." *Social Problems* 23 (1996): 478–87.

Shortened note

 12. Lever, "Sex Differences," 483.

Chic 42b

You may use the Latin abbreviation "ibid." (meaning "in the same place") to refer to the same source cited in the preceding note. Give a page number if it differs from that in the preceding note.

 12. Lever, "Sex Differences," 483.

 13. Gilligan, *In a Different Voice,* 92.

 14. Ibid., 93.

 15. Lever, "Sex Differences," 483.

Chicago style allows for in-text parenthetical citations when you cite one or more works repeatedly. In the following example, the raised number 2 refers to the source information in a note; the number in parentheses is a page number in the same source.

British rule, observes Stuart Cary Welch, seemed as permanent as Mount Everest."[2] Most Indians submitted, willingly or not, to British influence in every facet of life (42).

42c   Chicago paper format

The following guidelines come mainly from Turabian's *Manual for Writers*, which offers more specific advice than *The Chicago Manual* on the format of students' papers. See the next two pages for illustrations of the following elements. And see pages 15–21 for advice on type fonts, lists, illustrations, and other elements of document design.

Margins and spacing Use minimum one-inch (2.5 cm) margins on all pages of the body. (The first page of endnotes or works cited begins two inches [5 cm] from the top; see p. 213.) Double-space your own text and between notes and works-cited entries; single-space displayed quotations (see below) and each note and works-cited entry.

Paging Number pages consecutively from the first text page through the end (endnotes or works cited). Use Arabic numerals (1, 2, 3) in the upper-right corner.

Title page On an unnumbered title page, provide the title of the paper, your name, the course title, your instructor's name, and the date. Use all-capital letters, and centre everything horizontally. Double-space between adjacent lines, and add extra space between elements as shown on the next page.

Poetry and long prose quotations Display certain quotations separately from your text: three or more lines of poetry, and two or more sentences of prose. Indent a displayed quotation four spaces from the left, single-space the quotation, and double-space above and below it. *Do not add quotation marks.*

Gandhi articulated the principles of his movement in 1922:

> I discovered that pursuit of truth did not permit violence being inflicted on one's opponent, but that he must be weaned from error by patience and sympathy. For what appears to be truth to one may appear to be error to the other. And patience means self-suffering.[9]

42d Sample pages in Chicago style

Title page

INDIAN NATIONALISM IN INDIAN ART

AFTER WORLD WAR I ← Double-space

REYNA P. DIXON

ART HISTORY 236

MS. PARIKH > Double-space

DECEMBER 16, 2010

First page of paper with footnotes

1" (2.5 cm)   1

1" (2.5 cm)   World War I was a transformative event for every partici-   1"(2.5 cm)
pant, not least for faraway India. Though at first unified around

In 1001, Madras, Bengal, and Punjab were a few of the huge

Indian provinces governed by the British viceroy.[1] British rule,

observes Stuart Cary Welch, "seemed as permanent as Mount

1" (2.5 cm)   Everest."[2] Most Indians submitted, willingly or not, to British   1" (2.5 cm)

———————————————— ← Line

5 spaces
      1. Martin Gilbert, *Atlas of British History* (New York:] Single-
Dorset, 1968), 96.   ] space
                         ← Double space
      2. Stuart Cary Welch, *India: Art and Culture* (New York:] Single-
Metropolitan Museum of Art, 1995), 42.   ] space

1" (2.5 cm)

Endnotes

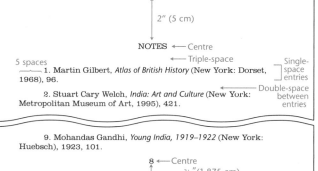

2" (5 cm)

NOTES ← Centre
                          ← Triple-space
5 spaces   ] Single-
      1. Martin Gilbert, *Atlas of British History* (New York: Dorset,   ] space
1968), 96.   ] entries
                                                    —— Double-space
      2. Stuart Cary Welch, *India: Art and Culture* (New York: between
Metropolitan Museum of Art, 1995), 421.   entries

      9. Mohandas Gandhi, *Young India, 1919–1922* (New York:
Huebsch), 1923, 101.

8 ← Centre
3/4"(1.875 cm)

Chic 42d

Bibliography

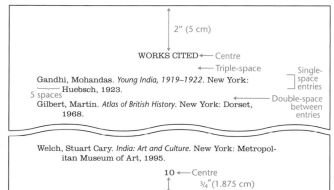

2" (5 cm)

WORKS CITED ← Centre
                          ← Triple-space
                                                          ] Single-
Gandhi, Mohandas. *Young India, 1919–1922.* New York:] space
      Huebsch, 1923.   ] entries
5 spaces
                                                    —— Double-space
Gilbert, Martin. *Atlas of British History.* New York: Dorset,   between
      1968.   entries

Welch, Stuart Cary. *India: Art and Culture.* New York: Metropolitan Museum of Art, 1995.

10 ← Centre
3/4"(1.875 cm)

43 CSE and IEEE Documentation

Writers in the life sciences, physical sciences, and mathematics rely for documentation style on *Scientific Style and Format: The CSE Style Manual for Authors, Editors, and Publishers* (7th ed., 2006). Its sponsoring organization, the Council of Science Editors, was until 2000 called the Council of Biology Editors, so you will see the style abbreviated both CSE (as here) and CBE. Electrical engineers can follow the documentation style of the IEEE (formerly Institute of Electrical and Electronics Engineers) (pp. 221–22), based on the CSE style.

While the seventh edition of *Scientific Style and Format* attempts to create common format and referencing styles for all scientific disciplines, scientific citation conventions are still evolving. The two major scientific formats—name-year style and number style—are covered here. (The CSE calls the version of number style it recommends in the seventh edition of *Scientific Style and Format* the *citation-name system*. It differs in some ways from CSE's previous style.) Both styles use a list of references at the end of the paper (opposite). Ask your instructor which style you should use. As with all citation styles, the goal is to provide enough information for your reader to locate the source.

43a CSE name-year text citations

In the CSE name-year style, parenthetical text citations provide the last name of the author being cited and the source's year of publication. At the end of the paper, a list of references, arranged alphabetically by authors' last names, provides complete information on each source. (See 43c opposite.)

The CSE name-year style closely resembles the APA name-year style detailed on pages 184–87. You can follow the APA examples for in-text citations, making several notable changes for CSE:

- Do not use a comma to separate the author's name and the date: (Baumrind 1968, p. 34).

Visit www.mycanadiancomplab.ca for
added help and exercises on citing sources.

- Separate two authors' names with "and" (not "&"): (Pepinsky and DeStefano 1997).
- Use either "et al." or "and others" for three or more authors: (Rutter et al. 1996).
- With an anonymous work, begin the citation with the first word or few words of the title followed by an ellipsis mark (Health care . . . 2004).

43b CSE numbered text citations

In the CSE number style, raised numbers in the text refer to a numbered list of references at the end of the paper.

Two standard references[4,6] use this term.

These forms of immunity have been extensively researched[3].

Assignment of numbers The number for each source is the same as its number in the reference list; sources in the reference list are listed alphabetically and numbered in their alphabctical order.

Reuse of numbers When you cite a source you have already cited and numbered, use the original number again. This reuse is the key difference between the CSE numbered citations and numbered references to footnotes or endnotes.

Citation of two or more sources When you cite two or more sources at once, arrange their numbers in sequence and separate them with a comma and no space, as in the first of the preceding examples.

43c CSE reference list

For both the name-year and the number styles of in-text citation, provide a list, titled "References," of all sources you have cited. Format the page as shown for APA references on page 199 (but you may omit the shortened title before the page number).

Spacing Single-space each entry, and double-space between entries.

Arrangement In both the name-year and number styles, arrange entries alphabetically by authors' last names. Arrange multiple items by the same author according to year in the name-year system and according to alphabetical order of titles in the number system.

Format Begin the first line of each entry at the left margin and indent subsequent lines.

216 CSE and IEEE documentation

Authors List each author's name with the last name first, followed by initials for first and middle names. Do not use a comma between an author's last name and initials, and do not use periods or space with the initials. Do use a comma to separate authors' names.

Placement of dates In the name-year style, the date follows the author's or authors' names. In the number style, the date follows the publication information (for a book) or the periodical title (for a journal, magazine, or newspaper).

Journal titles Do not underline or italicize journal titles. For titles of two or more words, abbreviate words of six or more letters (without periods) and omit most prepositions, articles, and conjunctions. Capitalize each word. For example, *Journal of Chemical and Biochemical Studies* becomes J Chem Biochem Stud.

Book and article titles Do not underline, italicize, or use quotation marks around a book or an article title. Capitalize only the first word and any proper nouns.

Publication information for journal articles The name-year and number styles differ in the placement of the publication date (see above). However, both styles end with the journal's volume number, any issue number in parentheses, a colon, and the inclusive page numbers of the article, run together without space: 28:329–30 or 62(2):26–40.

The following examples show both a name-year reference and a number reference for each type of source.

CSE REFERENCE MODELS

Books
1. A book with one author *217*
2. A book with two to ten authors *217*
3. A book with more than ten authors *217*
4. A book with an editor *217*
5. A selection from a book *218*
6. An anonymous work *218*
7. Two or more cited works by the same author *218*

Periodicals: Journals, magazines, newspapers
8. An article in a journal with a volume or issue number *218*
9. An article in a journal that numbers each issue beginning with page 1 *218*
10. An article in a newspaper *219*
11. An article in a magazine *219*

Books

1. A book with one author

Gould SJ. 1987. Time's arrow, time's cycle. Cambridge: Harvard University Press. 222 p

1. Gould SJ. Time's arrow, time's cycle. Cambridge: Harvard University Press; 1987. 222 p.

2. A book with two to ten authors

Hepburn PX, Tatin JM. 2002. Human physiology. New York: Columbia University Press. 1026 p.

2. Hepburn PX, Tatin JM. Human physiology. New York: Columbia University Press; 2002. 1026 p.

CSE
43c

3. A book with more than ten authors

Evans RW, Bowditch L, Dana KL, Drummond A, Wildovitch WP, Young SL, Mills P, Mills RR, Livak SR, Lisi OL, et al. 1998. Organ transplants: ethical issues. Ann Arbor: University of Michigan Press. 498 p.

3. Evans RW, Bowditch L, Dana KL, Drummond A, Wildovitch WP, Young SL, Mills P, Mills RR, Livak SR, Lisi OL, et al. Organ transplants: ethical issues. Ann Arbor: University of Michigan Press; 1998. 498 p.

4. A book with an editor

Jonson P, editor. 2005. Anatomy yearbook. Los Angeles: Anatco. 628 p.

4. Jonson P, editor. Anatomy yearbook. Los Angeles: Anatco; 2005. 628 p.

218 CSE and IEEE documentation

5. A selection from a book

Krigel R, Laubenstein L, Muggia F. 2002. Kaposi's sarcoma. In: Ebbeson P, Biggar RS, Melbye M, editors. AIDS: a basic guide for clinicians. 2nd ed. Philadelphia: WB Saunders. p. 100–26.

5. Krigel R, Laubenstein L, Muggia F. Kaposi's sarcoma. In: Ebbeson P, Biggar RS, Melbye M, editors. AIDS: a basic guide for clinicians. 2nd ed. Philadelphia: WB Saunders; 2002. p. 100–26.

6. An anonymous work

Health care for multiple sclerosis. 2004. New York: US Health Care. 86 p.

6. Health care for multiple sclerosis. New York: US Health Care; 2004. 86 p.

7. Two or more cited works by the same author

Gardner H. 1973a. The arts and human development. New York: J. Wiley. 406 p.

Gardner H. 1973b. The quest for mind: Piaget, Lévi-Strauss, and the structuralist movement. New York: A.A. Knopf. 492 p.

Gardner H. 1993. Frames of mind: the theory of multiple intelligences. New York: Basic. 440 p.

1. Gardner H. The arts and human development. New York: J. Wiley; 1973. 406 p.

2. Gardner H. Frames of mind: the theory of multiple intelligences. New York: Basic; 1993. 440 p.

3. Gardner H. The quest for mind: Piaget, Lévi-Strauss, and the structuralist movement. New York: A.A. Knopf; 1973. 492 p.

Periodicals: Journals, magazines, newspapers

8. An article in a journal with a volume or issue number

Kim P. 1996 Feb. Medical decision making for the dying. Milbank Quar 64(2):26–40.

8. Kim P. Medical decision making for the dying. Milbank Quar 1996 Feb;64(2):26–40.

9. An article in a journal that numbers each issue beginning with page 1

Rosenthal E. 2003 Feb. Emerging drugs in the fight against HIV disease. HRSA Careaction:1–8.

9. Rosenthal E. Emerging drugs in the fight against HIV disease. HRSA Careaction. 2003 Feb:18.

**CSE
43c**

10. An article in a newspaper

Kolata G. 2001 Jan 7. Kill all the bacteria! New York Times. Sect. B:1 (col. 3).

10. Kolata G. Kill all the bacteria! New York Times. 2001 Jan 7;Sect. B:1 (col. 3).

11. An article in a magazine

Scheiber N. 2002 Jun 24. Finger tip: why fingerprinting won't work. New Republic:15–6.

11. Scheiber N. Finger tip: why fingerprinting won't work. New Republic. 2002 Jun 24:15–6.

Electronic sources

12. A source on CD-ROM or DVD-ROM

Reich WT, editor. 2005. Encyclopedia of bioethics [DVD]. New York: Co-Health. 1 disk: colour, 4 3/4 in. System Requirements: 400 MHz or faster Intel-compatible CPU, videocard with AGP architecture and 4 MB onboard RAM, 128 MB system RAM, Windows 98 SE/2000/Me/XP, Microsoft DirectX, DVD-ROM drive.

12. Reich WT, editor. Encyclopedia of bioethics [DVD]. New York: Co-Health; 2005. 1 disk: colour, 4 3/4 in. System Requirements: 400 MHz or faster Intel-compatible CPU, video card with AGP architecture and 4 MB onboard RAM, 128 MB system RAM, Windows 98 SE/2000/Me/XP, Micro-soft DirectX, DVD-ROM drive.

Give the medium, a physical description, and, if possible, notes to assist users of the source.

CSE 43c

13. An online journal article

Grady GF. 2003. The here and now of hepatitis B immuniza-tion. Today's Med [Internet]. [cited 2004 Dec 7];6(2):39–41. Available from: http://www.fmrt.org/todaysmedicine/Grady050293.pdf6

13. Grady GF. The here and now of hepatitis B immuni-zation. Today's Med [Internet]. 2003 [cited 2004 Dec 7];6(2): 39–41. Available from: http://www.fmrt.org/todaysmedicine/Grady050293.pdf6

Give the date of your access, preceded by "cited," in brackets: [cited 2004 Dec 7] in the models above.

14. An online book

Ruch BJ, Ruch DB. 2001. Homeopathy and medicine: resolving the conflict [Internet]. New York: Albert Einstein College of Medicine [cited 2005 Jan 28]. [about 50 p.]. Available from: http://www.einstein.edu/medicine/books/ruch.html

14. Ruch BJ, Ruch DB. Homeopathy and medicine: resolving the conflict [Internet]. New York: Albert Einstein College of Medicine; 2001 [cited 2005 Jan 28]. [about 50 p.]. Available from: http://www.einstein.edu/medicine/books/ruch.html

15. A source retrieved from an online database

McAskill MR, Anderson TJ, Jones RD. 2002. Saccadic adaptation in neurological disorders. Prog Brain Res. 140:417–31. In: PubMed [Internet]. Bethesda (MD): National Library of Medicine. [cited 2004 Mar 6]. Available from: http://www.ncbi.nlm.nih.gov/PubMed; PMID: 12508606.

15. McAskill MR, Anderson TJ, Jones RD. Saccadic adaptation in neurological disorders. Prog Brain Res 2002; 140:417–31. In: PubMed [Internet]. Bethesda (MD): National Library of Medicine. 1996– [cited 2004 Mar 6]. Available from: http://www.ncbi.nlm.nih.gov/PubMed; PMID: 12508606.

16. A website

Canadian Medical Association [Internet]. 2009. Ottawa: Canadian Medical Association; [cited 2009 Jan 2]. Available from: http://www.cma.ca

16. Canadian Medical Association [Internet]. Ottawa: Canadian Medical Association; 2009 [cited 2009 Jan 2]. Available from: http://www.cma.ca

17. Electronic mail

Millon M. 2004 May 4. Grief therapy [Internet]. Message to: Naomi Sakai. 3:16 pm [cited 2004 May 4]. [about 2 screens].

17. Millon M. Grief therapy [Internet]. Message to: Naomi Sakai. 2004 May 4, 3:16 pm [cited 2004 May 4]. [about 2 screens].

18. A posting to a discussion list

Stalinsky Q. 2002 Aug 16. The hormone-replacement study. In: Women Physicians Congress [Internet]. [Chicago: American Medical Association]; 9:26 am [cited 2004 Aug 17]. [about 8 paragraphs]. Available from: ama-wpc@ama-assn.org

18. Stalinsky Q. The hormone-replacement study. In: Women Physicians Congress [Internet]. [Chicago: American Medical Association]; 2004 Aug 16, 9:26 am [cited 2004 Aug 17]. [about 8 paragraphs]. Available from: ama-wpc@ama-assn.org

Other sources

19. A government publication

Olkowski AA. 2009. Livestock water quality. Ottawa: Agriculture and Agri-Food Canada. 180 p.

19. Olkowski AA. Livestock water quality. Ottawa: Agriculture and Agri-Food Canada; 2009. 180 p.

Committee on Science and Technology, House (US). 1999. Hearing on procurement and allocation of human organs for transplantation. 106th Cong., 1st Sess. House Doc. nr 409.

19. Committee on Science and Technology, House (US). Hearing on procurement and allocation of human organs for transplantation. 106th Cong., 1st Sess. House Doc. nr 409; 1999.

20. A nongovernment report

Warnock M. 2001. Report of the Committee on Fertilization and Embryology. Baylor University, Department of Embryology. Waco (TX): Baylor University Report nr BU/DE.4261.

20. Warnock M. Report of the Committee on Fertilization and Embryology. Baylor University, Department of Embryology. Waco (TX): Baylor University; 2001. Report nr BU/DE.4261.

21. A sound recording, video recording, or film

Teaching Media. 2000. Cell mitosis [videocassette]. White Plains (NY): Teaching Media. 1 videocassette: 40 min, sound, black and white, 1/2 in.

21. Cell mitosis [videocassette]. White Plains (NY): Teaching Media; 2000. 1 videocassette: 40 min, sound, black and white, 1/2 in.

IEEE 43d

43d   IEEE numbered text citations

IEEE (formerly the Institute of Electrical and Electronics Engineers) recommends a documentation style based on the CSE number style, but using square brackets instead of raised numbers in the text. Cite multiple source numbers within the same brackets, separated by a comma but without a space. If three or more source numbers occur in a sequence, cite the first and last number separated by a hyphen.

These forms of immunity have been extensively researched [1].

Two standard references [2,3] use this term.

Four studies disagree with these findings [2–5].

As with the CSE style, these numbers refer readers to a reference list numbered in the order you refer to the sources (not listed alphabetically by author), as described in 43b. Reuse numbers each time you refer to the source. For more detailed examples, see *http://www.ecf.utoronto.ca/ ~writing/handbook-docum1b.html,* or consult Lannon and Klepp, *Technical Communication,* 5th Can. ed. (Toronto: Pearson, 2011).

IEEE
43c

PART VII

Other Forms of Communication

PEARSON
mycanadiancomplab

Visit the **Composing** space in MyCanadianCompLab to research, draft, and revise your written work and assignments. You can view instructor, peer, and tutor comments on your work, pulling together all the feedback you will need to produce better writing samples and get better marks.

44 Writing Online

The main forms of online writing—electronic mail and web compositions—dramatically expand your options as a writer. This chapter addresses some special concerns of writing online.

44a Electronic mail

The guidelines below apply to various e-mail functions, from conversing with friends to conducting serious research.

Sending messages

- *Give your message a subject heading that describes its content.* Then your reader knows what priority to assign the message—a particular help for readers who receive many messages a day. A clear subject heading distinguishes your message from spam (junk e-mail). Make your subject line work: not "Notice of meeting" but "Budget meeting Tuesday."
- *Compose a message that is concise and relevant to your recipients' concerns.* Adjust the formality of your message to your writing situation. In the message below, the writer knows the recipients well and yet has serious information to convey to them, so he writes informally while stating his points carefully.

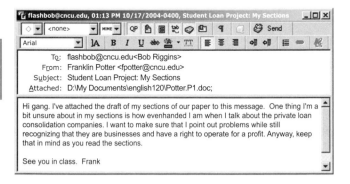

44a

Visit www.mycanadiancomplab.ca for added help and writing samples.

- *Use short paragraphs with blank lines between them.* For long messages—which recipients can review only one screen at a time—a tight structure, a clear forecast of the content, and a clear division into parts (using headings if necessary) not only improve effectiveness but also show courtesy.
- *Proofread* all but the most informal messages for errors in grammar, punctuation, and spelling.
- *Be aware that file attachments are not always readable.* If you have trouble with attachments, consult the technology advisers at your school or office.

Note Some e-mail programs don't allow underlining, italics, and boldface. Even if you can use such highlighting, you should assume that your recipients will not be able to see it in your messages. For alternatives, use underscores to indicate _underlining_ or asterisks to provide *emphasis*.

Responding to messages

- *Check that your reply has an appropriate subject heading.* Most e-mail programs label a response with the same subject heading as the original, preceded by *Re:* (from Latin, meaning "in reference to"). If your response indeed continues the same subject, then *Re:* indicates as much. If, however, you raise a new issue, you should rewrite the subject heading to say so.
- *Use quoted material from earlier messages critically.* By weaving your replies into the material quoted from someone else's message, you can respond to the author point by point, as you would in conversation. However, delete from the original anything you are not responding to so that your recipient can focus on what you have to say without wading through his or her own words.

44a

Observing netiquette

You won't always see others observing **netiquette**, or Internet etiquette, but you will see that those who do observe it receive the more thoughtful and considerate replies.

- *Pay careful attention to tone.* Refrain from **flaming**, or attacking, correspondents. Don't use all-capital letters, which SHOUT. And use irony or sarcasm cautiously: in the absence of facial expressions, they can lead to misunderstandings.

- *Avoid participating in flame "wars,"* overheated dialogues that contribute little or no information or understanding. If a war breaks out in a discussion, ignore it: don't rush to defend someone who is being attacked and don't respond even if you are under attack yourself.
- *Be a forgiving reader.* Avoid nitpicking over spelling or other surface errors. And because attitudes are sometimes difficult to convey, give authors an initial benefit of the doubt: a writer who at first seems hostile may simply have tried too hard to be concise; a writer who at first seems unserious may simply have failed at injecting humour into a worthwhile message.
- *Forward a message only with the permission of the author.* Delete third-party addresses when forwarding messages to preserve the privacy of others and protect them from spam.
- *Avoid spamming.* With a few keystrokes, you can broadcast a message to many recipients at once. Occasionally you may have important information that everyone on a list will want to know. But flooding whole lists with irrelevant messages—called **spamming**—is rude and irritating.

44b   Web composition

Unlike traditional documents, which are meant to be read in sequence from start to finish, most websites are intended to be examined in whatever order readers choose as they follow links within the site and to other sites. A website thus requires careful planning of the links and thoughtful cues to orient readers:

44b

- *Sketch possible site plans before getting started,* using a branching diagram to show major divisions and connections.
- *Plan a menu for each of the site's pages* that overviews the organization and links directly to other pages.
- *Distill your text* to include only essential information, and use headings to break the text into accessible chunks. Readers have difficulty following long, uninterrupted text passages onscreen.
- *Standardize elements of the design* so that readers know what to expect and can scan your pages easily.
- *Use icons, photographs, artwork, and other visual elements for a purpose, not merely for decoration.* Use captions to relate the visuals to your text.

Most web pages are created using hypertext markup language, or HTML, and an HTML editor that works much as a word processor does. For information about HTML editors and added help with creating websites, visit this book's Web site at *www.pearsoned.ca/aaron.*

45 Making Oral Presentations

Oral communication is similar to written communication, but this chapter explains how to adapt your message for oral delivery.

45a   Written vs. oral communication

Since listeners cannot skim or review a speech as they can an essay, oral presentations require a more explicit structure and a greater use of repetition to compensate.

Organization: Introduction, conclusion, transitions

Like an essay or report, a speech has an introduction, a body, and a conclusion. (See Chapter 1 for more discussion of thesis, introduction, body, and conclusion.)

The introduction of a speech, however, provides a more explicit statement of the thesis (the idea or message conveyed by the speech). It also features a preview of the organization of the speech (the division of the topic).

Use the introduction to set an appropriate tone and to motivate your audience. Use more frequent and explicit transitional expressions° as well as more repetition in the form of summaries and previews. Use more signposting than you would when writing:

Written
: Louis Riel was found guilty of high treason and hanged on November 16, 1885. Today many Canadians look upon him as a hero, a patriot, a founding father of the nation. Thus, a traitor for one age becomes a hero for another. Clearly, the way we interpret history depends on who we are, where we live, and what we believe.

45a

Visit www.mycanadiancomplab.ca for added help and writing samples.

Oral   On November 16, 1885, Louis Riel was found guilty of high treason and hanged, yet today many Canadians look upon him as a hero, a patriot, and a founding father of the nation. I want to talk to you about how we interpret history. Specifically, I'll discuss how our view of history depends on who we are, where we live, and what we believe. I'll look at the case of Louis Riel, show how opinions about him have evolved over the last century, and, finally, suggest some contemporary figures whose reputations may go through surprising changes before the year 2100.

Transition   I'll begin by reminding you of the historical record of Riel and the North-West Rebellion.

Signal the approach of your conclusion:

"Before concluding, I will add one further example . . ."

"To sum up . . ."

Visualization

Use vivid language and concrete examples to help your audience visualize what you are describing.

Not   Among the schoolchildren in this city, 34.5 percent do not receive sufficient nourishment at breakfast and lunch.

But   Right now Alice is sitting in her Grade 3 classroom with a rumbling stomach. She'll go hungry at recess and lunch hour because her mum was out of peanut butter this morning. In our city's schools, every third child, like Alice, comes to school hungry.

Audiovisual presentation aids are also useful, but they are no substitute for vivid writing.

45a   Diction

Use vocabulary appropriate to your audience. Since listeners cannot consult a dictionary or glossary, avoid technical language unless you are addressing experts. If you can't avoid terms that your audience may not know, define the words as you use them (see Chapter 9). Avoid distracting slang, blasphemy, profanity, or offensive terms.

Statistics

In oral delivery, round off statistics.

Not   48.73 percent of votes
But   nearly half the votes

Documentation

Provide oral footnotes:

According to a recent Statistics Canada study, the population of our town is expanding.

The newly elected head of the CMA told *The Globe and Mail* last week that Canadian medical care is in crisis.

Note Be prepared to provide detailed citations if someone questions your sources.

45b   Oral delivery

Methods of oral delivery

Reading

Reading prevents effective eye contact and encourages a monotonous delivery. Avoid reading a prepared speech to an audience.

If you *must* read a speech, print it out in a large font, double-spaced, and add cues to remind yourself to smile at the audience, tell a joke, pause, slow down, or ask a question.

Memorization

A memorized speech can be deadly to listen to and deadlier to give, especially if your memory dries up. Unless you are an accomplished actor, a memorized delivery also sounds unnatural. Avoid memorizing a text for delivery.

Extemporaneous delivery

Extemporaneous public speaking is the most difficult form to master, but with practice it is the easiest and most effective to use. An extemporaneous speech is thoroughly researched, planned, and rehearsed, but it is not memorized, nor is it written out in sentences to be read.

Instead, speak from brief notes, preferably a few key words jotted down on cue cards, or possibly displayed on *PowerPoint* (see "Presentational aids" below), to remind you of your next point. You are thus *thinking* about your ideas, not just *reciting* them. You are looking at your *audience*, not your *script*. Your sentences may not be as perfectly crafted as if you were reading—although with practice you will gain confidence and fluency—but what you lose in correctness you gain in communication with your audience. It's a worthwhile trade.

45b

Techniques of oral delivery

Eye contact

Look at your audience. Sweep the room with your eyes. Glance briefly at your notes when necessary, but maintain regular eye contact.

Posture and body language

Assume a comfortable but dignified posture. Avoid leaning on a lectern, slouching, random arm waving, constant weight shifting, restless pacing. Do not chew gum, twirl hair, jangle bracelets, rustle notes, or click pens. Adjust your facial expression to the tone and content of your speech.

Voice

Speak loudly enough to be heard without shouting. Vary your pitch and pace to avoid boredom. Avoid a singsong or repetitive inflection. Drop your voice, slow down, or pause occasionally for emphasis, but do not speak so slowly that listeners lose the thread of what you are saying. (Our minds can process words faster than most speakers can say them.) Enunciate clearly, especially consonants. If necessary, exaggerate slightly for clarity.

Presentational aids

Practise using props, projectors, computer graphic displays, DVDs, MP3s, or other presentational aids you intend to use in your speech. Cue recorded material and check equipment, including focus and sound levels, before your speech begins. Introduce aids only when needed to illustrate your speech: explain their significance, then turn them off or put them away to avoid distracting your audience.

PowerPoint software can help you to integrate visual aids with your speaking notes, but be careful to create readable slides that enhance rather than distract from your presentation. For visibility, use light text on a dark background (e.g., white on dark blue) and large fonts: 28–32 points for text, 36–44 points for headings. Avoid distracting features such as flying, fading, or zooming graphics, multiple font styles, or text that echoes what you are speaking. Keep graphics simple and clear to reinforce your ideas.

45b

Confidence

Confidence comes with experience. Control stage fright in the following ways:

- Breathing: Breathe deeply to slow down an adrenaline rush.
- Muscle relaxation: Systematically flex and relax muscle groups to reduce tension before speaking.
- Visualization: Practise imagining yourself speaking eloquently to an appreciative audience.
- Thorough preparation: Prepare thoroughly so you will feel confident.

If you lose your train of thought or make a mistake, keep talking: chances are the audience won't know you've made a mistake unless you tell them. If all else fails, summarize what you've said so far. You'll probably remember where your speech was heading, and you'll soon be back on track. Above all, remember that your listeners want you to succeed: they want to relax for the duration of your speech while you take charge.

45c Listening

We spend many more hours listening in class, at work, and in social situations than we do speaking. Learn to be an effective listener:

- *Do not* fake listening while you are really thinking about something else, such as your approaching presentation or your shopping list.
- *Do not* prejudge the speaker or dwell on his or her speech habits or bad fashion sense.
- *Do not* let yourself be distracted by physical noise (a banging door, the scene outside the window), psychological noise (your private thoughts), or semantic noise (your misunderstanding of, or emotional reaction to, the speaker's choice of words).
- *Do* motivate yourself to listen by asking yourself, "What can this speaker teach or offer me?"
- *Do* concentrate on the sequence of ideas being presented, listening critically for details that logically support the ideas.
- *Do* take notes to help focus your attention.

We all perform better for a responsive audience. Good listeners encourage good speakers.

46 Writing for Business

The principles of document design covered in Chapter 4 apply to most business writing. This chapter discusses business letters, résumés, and business memos. For help with electronic mail, see pages 224–26.

The sample documents in this chapter do not accurately depict the proportions of actual business documents. Be sure to follow the instructions provided for setting up your documents on 8½″ × 11″ (21 cm × 28 cm) paper.

Visit www.mycanadiancomplab.ca for added help and exercises on writing.

Job-application letter

In any letter to a businessperson, you are addressing someone who wants to see quickly why you are writing and how to respond to you. For a job application, see the sample on the next page and use the following guidelines.

Content

- *Interpret your résumé for the particular job.* Instead of reciting your job history, highlight and reshape only the relevant parts.
- *Announce at the outset what job you seek and how you heard about it.*
- *Include any special reason you have for applying,* such as a specific career goal.
- *Summarize your qualifications for the job,* including relevant facts about education and employment and emphasizing notable accomplishments. Mention that additional information appears in an accompanying résumé.
- *Describe your availability.* At the end of the letter, mention that you are available for an interview at the convenience of the addressee, or specify when you will be available.

Format

- *Use standard paper,* either unlined white paper measuring 8½ inches by 11 inches (21 cm x 28 cm) or letterhead stationery with your address printed at the top of the sheet.
- *Type the letter single-spaced.* Use double space between elements and paragraphs. Use only one side of a sheet. Align all elements with the left margin.
- *Address your letter to a specific person.* Call the company or department to ask whom to address. If you can't find a person's name, then use a job title (*Dear Human Resources Manager*) or a general salutation (*Dear Smythe Shoes*).
- *Close the letter with an expression that reflects the formality of the situation. Respectfully, Cordially,* and *Sincerely* are more formal than *Best wishes* or *Regards*.
- *Use an envelope that will accommodate the letter once it is folded horizontally in thirds.* Show your name and address in the upper-left corner and the addressee's name, title, and address in the centre.

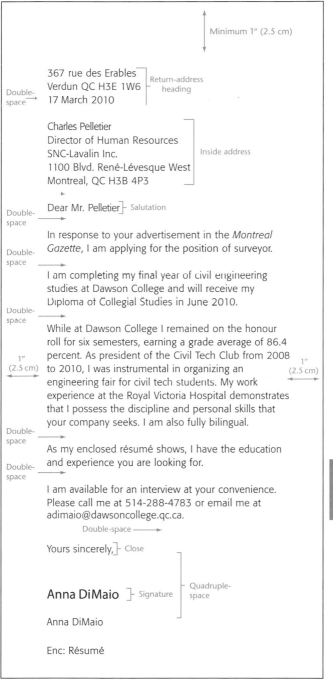

Minimum 1" (2.5 cm)

367 rue des Erables
Verdun QC H3E 1W6   Return-address heading
17 March 2010

Double-space →

Charles Pelletier
Director of Human Resources
SNC-Lavalin Inc.   Inside address
1100 Blvd. René-Lévesque West
Montreal, QC H3B 4P3

Double-space → Dear Mr. Pelletier — Salutation

Double-space → In response to your advertisement in the *Montreal Gazette*, I am applying for the position of surveyor.

Double-space → I am completing my final year of civil engineering studies at Dawson College and will receive my Diploma of Collegial Studies in June 2010.

Double-space → While at Dawson College I remained on the honour roll for six semesters, earning a grade average of 86.4 percent. As president of the Civil Tech Club from 2008 to 2010, I was instrumental in organizing an engineering fair for civil tech students. My work experience at the Royal Victoria Hospital demonstrates that I possess the discipline and personal skills that your company seeks. I am also fully bilingual.

1" (2.5 cm) ← → 1" (2.5 cm)

Double-space → As my enclosed résumé shows, I have the education and experience you are looking for.

Double-space → I am available for an interview at your convenience. Please call me at 514-288-4783 or email me at adimaio@dawsoncollege.qc.ca.

Double-space →

Yours sincerely, — Close

Anna DiMaio — Signature   Quadruple-space

Anna DiMaio

Enc: Résumé

46a

46b Résumé

For the résumé that accompanies your letter of application, you can use the sample on the next page and the following guidelines.

- *Provide the appropriate information in table form:* your name and address, career objective, education, employment history, any special skills or awards, and information about how to obtain your references.
- *Use headings to mark the sections of the résumé.* Space around the headings and within sections so that important information stands out.
- *Use capital letters conventionally.* Passages with many capitals can be hard to read. Do use capitals for proper nouns (pp. 109–10), but drop them for job titles, course names, department names, and the like.
- *Limit your résumé to one page so that it can be quickly reviewed.* However, if your experience and education are extensive, a two-page résumé is preferable to a single cramped, unreadable page.

Employers often want an electronic copy of a résumé so that they can add it to a computerized database of applicants. They may scan a paper copy to convert it to an electronic file, or they may request an electronic copy from you in the first place. If you think a potential employer may use an electronic version of your résumé, follow these additional guidelines:

- *Keep the design simple* for accurate scanning or electronic transmittal. Avoid images, unusual type, more than one column, vertical or horizontal lines, and highlighting (boldface, italic, or underlining). If its highlighting were removed, the traditionally designed sample opposite could probably be scanned or transmitted electronically.
- *Use concise, specific words to describe your skills and experience.* The employer's computer may use keywords (often nouns) to identify the résumés of suitable job candidates, and you want to ensure that your résumé includes the appropriate keywords. Name your specific skills—for example, the computer programs you can operate—and write concretely with words like *manager* (not *person with responsibility for*) and *reporter* (not *staff member who reports*). Look for likely keywords in the employer's description of the job you seek.

Anna DiMaio
367 rue des Erables
Verdun, QC H3E 1W6
Telephone: 514-288-4783
email: adimaio@dawsoncollege.qc.ca
Languages: English, French, Italian, some Spanish

Position desired
Surveyor, with possibility of career development, including
university studies in civil engineering.

Education

2007–10 **Civil Engineering Technology, Dawson College**, D.E.C. to be completed June 2010
President, Civil Tech Club 2008–10
Honour Roll

2002–07 **Centennial Regional High School**, Greenfield Park, Quebec
DES completed June 2007

Technical Knowledge

Surveying: Theodolites, Levels, Transits, Total Stations
Drafting: manual, computer (AutoCAD LT 2011)
Estimating: quantity take-offs
Software: Microsoft Office 2010, Timberline (Estimating), Primavera (Project Management), Softdesk 8

Laboratory testing: concrete, soils, asphalt, aggregates

Employment History

2009–10 **Assistant Laboratory Technician, Dawson College**
Organized and directed laboratory affairs, monitored laboratory tests, cleaned and reorganized after laboratory tests

2008–10 **Admitting and Discharge Clerk, Royal Victoria Hospital**
Admitted patients, booked surgery time for patients, booked beds for patients

References

Academic: Mr. Howard Babcock, Chair
Civil Engineering Technology Dept.
Dawson College
3040 Sherbrooke Street West
Westmount, QC H3Z 1A4

Employment: Ms. Lise Dufresne
Royal Victoria Hospital
687 Pine Avenue West
Montreal, QC H3A 1A1

Personal: Dr. Carole Adilman
9871 Gouin Blvd. West
Pierrefonds, QC H8Y 1R9

46b

46c	Business memo

Business memos (short for "memorandums") address people within the same organization. A memo can be quite long, but more often it deals briefly with a specific topic, such as an answer to a question, a progress report, or an evaluation. Frequently it has more than one recipient. Both the content and the format of a memo aim to get to the point and dispose of it quickly, as in the sample on the next page.

- *State your reason for writing in the first sentence.*
- *Make your first paragraph work.* Concisely present your solution, recommendation, answer, or evaluation.
- *Deliver the support in the body of the memo.* The paragraphs may be numbered or bulleted so that the main divisions of your message are easy to see. In a long memo, you may need headings (see pp. 17–18).
- *Suit your style and tone to your audience.* For instance, you'll want to address your boss or a large group of readers more formally than you would a co-worker who is also a friend.
- *Use a conventional memo heading.* Include the company's name, the addressee's name, the writer's name (initialled in handwriting), the date, and a subject description or title.
- *Type the body of the memo single-spaced.* Double-space between paragraphs, with no paragraph indentions.
- *List the people receiving copies of the memo* two spaces below the last line.

Bigelow Wax Company

TO: Aileen Rosen, Director of Sales
FROM: Patricia Phillips, Territory 12   *PP*
DATE: February 12, 2010
SUBJECT: 2009 sales of Quick Wax in Territory 12

Since it was introduced in January of 2009, Quick Wax has been unsuccessful in Territory 12 and has not affected the sales of our Easy Shine. Discussions with customers and my own analysis of Quick Wax suggest three reasons for its failure to compete with our product.

1. Quick Wax has not received the promotion necessary for a new product. Advertising—primarily on radio—has been sporadic and has not developed a clear, consistent image for the product. In addition, the Quick Wax sales representative in Territory 12 is new and inexperienced; he is not known to customers, and his sales pitch (which I once overheard) is weak. As far as I can tell, his efforts are not supported by phone calls or mailings from his home office.

2. When Quick Wax does make it to the store shelves, buyers do not choose it over our product. Though priced competitively with our product, Quick Wax is poorly packaged. The container seems smaller than ours, though in fact it holds the same 250 grams. The lettering on the Quick Wax package (red on blue) is difficult to read, in contrast to the white-on-green lettering on the Easy Shine package.

3. Our special purchase offers and my increased efforts to serve existing customers have had the intended effect of keeping customers satisfied with our product and reducing their inclination to stock something new.

Copies: L. Marchand, Director of Marketing
         P. MacGregor, Customer Service Manager

46c

Glossary of Usage

This glossary provides notes on words and phrases that often cause problems for writers. The recommendations for standard written English are based on current dictionaries and usage guides. Items labelled *nonstandard* should be avoided in final drafts of academic and business writing. Those labelled *colloquial* and *slang* appear in some informal writing and may occasionally be used for effect in more formal academic and career writing. (Words and phrases labelled *colloquial* include those labelled *informal* by many dictionaries.) See Chapter 9 for more on levels of language.

a, an   Use *a* before words beginning with consonant sounds: *a historian, a one-o'clock class, a university.* Use *an* before words that begin with vowel sounds, including silent *h*'s: *an orgy, an L, an honour.*

The article before an abbreviation depends on how the abbreviation is read: *She has an NSRC grant.* (*NSRC* is read as one word beginning with the vowel sound *"en."*) *He is writing an SAT exam tomorrow.* (*SAT* is read as three separate letters beginning with the vowel sound *"ess"*).

See also pp. 70–72 on the uses of *a/an* versus *the.*

accept, except   *Accept* is a verb° meaning "receive." *Except* is usually a preposition° or conjunction° meaning "but for" or "other than"; when it is used as a verb, it means "leave out." *I can accept all your suggestions except the last one. I'm sorry you excepted my last suggestion from your list.*

advice, advise   *Advice* is a noun,° and *advise* is a verb.° *Take my advice; do as I advise you.*

affect, effect   Usually *affect* is a verb,° meaning "to influence," and *effect* is a noun, meaning "result": *The drug did not affect his driving; in fact, it seemed to have no effect at all.* (Note that *effect* occasionally is used as a verb meaning "to bring about": *Her efforts effected a change.* And *affect* is used in psychology as a noun meaning "feeling or emotion": *One can infer much about affect from behaviour.*)

all, always, never, no one   These absolute words often exaggerate a situation in which *many, often, rarely,* or *few* is more accurate.

all ready, already   *All ready* means "completely prepared," and *already* means "by now" or "before now": *We were all ready to go to the movie, but it had already started.*

all right   *All right* is always two words. *Alright* is a common misspelling.

all together, altogether   *All together* means "in unison," or "gathered in one place." *Altogether* means "entirely." *It's not altogether true that our family never spends vacations all together.*

allusion, illusion   An *allusion* is an indirect reference, and an *illusion* is a deceptive appearance: *Paul's constant allusions to Shakespeare created the illusion that he was an intellectual.*

a lot   *A lot* is always two words, used informally to mean "many." *Alot* is a common misspelling.

always   See *all, always, never, no one.*

among, between   In general, use *between* only for relationships of two and *among* for more than two.

amount, number   Use *amount* with a singular noun that names something not countable (a noncount noun°): *The amount of food varies.* Use *number* with a plural noun that names more than one of something countable (a count noun°): *The number of calories must stay the same.*

and/or   *And/or* indicates three options: one or the other or both (*The decision is made by the mayor and/or the council*). If you mean all three options, *and/or* is appropriate. Otherwise, use *and* if you mean both, *or* if you mean either.

anxious, eager   *Anxious* means "nervous" or "worried" and is usually followed by *about.* *Eager* means "looking forward" and is usually followed by *to.* *I've been anxious about getting blisters. I'm eager* [not *anxious*] *to get new cross-training shoes.*

anybody, any body; anyone, any one   *Anybody* and *anyone* are indefinite pronouns°; *any body* is a noun° modified by *any; any one* is a pronoun° or adjective° modified by *any.* *How can anybody communicate with any body of government? Can anyone help Amy? She has more work than any one person can handle.*

any more, anymore   *Any more* means "no more"; *anymore* means "now." Both are used in negative constructions: *He doesn't want any more. She doesn't live here anymore.*

anyways, anywheres   Nonstandard for *anyway* and *anywhere.*

are, is   Use *are* with a plural subject° (*books are*), *is* with a singular subject (*book is*). See pp. 57–60.

as   Substituting for *because, since,* or *while, as* may be vague or ambiguous: *As we were stopping to rest, we decided to eat lunch.* (Does *as* mean "while" or "because"?) *As* should never be used as a substitute for *whether* or *who: I'm not sure whether* [not *as*] *we can make it. That's the man who* [not *as*] *gave me directions.*

as, like   See *like, as.*

at this point in time   Wordy for *now, at this point,* or *at this time.*

awful, awfully Strictly speaking, *awful* means "inspiring awe." As intensifiers meaning "very" or "extremely" (*He tried awfully hard*), *awful* and *awfully* should be avoided in formal speech or writing.

a while, awhile *Awhile* is an adverb°; *a while* is an article° and a noun.° *I will be gone awhile* [not *a while*]. *I will be gone for a while* [not *awhile*].

bad, badly In formal speech and writing, *bad* should be used only as an adjective°; the adverb° is *badly*. *He felt bad because his tooth ached badly.* In *He felt bad,* the verb *felt* is a linking verb° and the adjective *bad* modifies the subject° *he,* not the verb *felt.* See also pp. 67–68.

being as, being that Colloquial for *because,* the preferable word in formal speech or writing: *Because* [not *Being as*] *the world is round, Columbus never did fall off the edge.*

beside, besides *Beside* is a preposition° meaning "next to." *Besides* is a preposition meaning "except" or "in addition to" as well as an adverb° meaning "in addition." *Besides, several other people besides you want to sit beside Dr. Christensen.*

between, among See *among, between.*

bring, take Use *bring* only for movement from a farther place to a nearer one and *take* for any other movement. *First, take these books to the library for renewal, then take them to Mr. Daniels. Bring them back to me when he's finished.*

can, may Strictly, *can* indicates capacity or ability, and *may* indicates permission: *If I may talk with you a moment, I believe I can solve your problem.*

climatic, climactic *Climatic* comes from *climate* and refers to weather: *Last winter's temperatures may indicate a climatic change. Climactic* comes from *climax* and refers to a dramatic high point: *During the climactic duel between Hamlet and Laertes, Gertrude drinks poisoned wine.*

complement, compliment To *complement* something is to add to, complete, or reinforce it: *Her yellow blouse complemented her black hair.* To *compliment* something is to make a flattering remark about it: *He complimented her on her hair. Complimentary* can also mean "free": *complimentary tickets.*

conscience, conscious *Conscience* is a noun° meaning "a sense of right and wrong"; *conscious* is an adjective° meaning "aware" or "awake." *Though I was barely conscious, my conscience nagged me.*

continual, continuous *Continual* means "constantly recurring": *Most movies on television are continually interrupted by commercials. Continuous* means "unceasing": *Some cable channels present movies continuously without commercials.*

could of See *have, of.*

criteria   The plural of *criterion* (meaning "standard for judgment"): *Our criteria are strict. The most important criterion is a sense of humour.*

data   The plural of *datum* (meaning "fact"). Though *data* is often used with a singular verb, many readers prefer the plural verb and it is always correct: *The data fail* [not *fails*] *to support the hypothesis.*

device, devise   *Device* is the noun,° and *devise* is the verb°: *Can you devise some device for getting his attention?*

different from, different than   *Different from* is preferred: *His purpose is different from mine.* But *different than* is widely accepted when a construction using *from* would be wordy: *I'm a different person now than I used to be* is preferable to *I'm a different person now from the person I used to be.*

disinterested, uninterested   *Disinterested* means "impartial": *We chose Pete, as a disinterested third party, to decide who was right. Uninterested* means "bored" or "lacking interest": *Unfortunately, Pete was completely uninterested in the question.*

don't   *Don't* is the contraction for *do not*, not for *does not: I don't care, you don't care,* and *he doesn't* [not *don't*] *care.*

due to   *Due* is an adjective° or noun°; thus *due to* is always acceptable as a subject complement°: *His grey hairs were due to age.* Many object to *due to* as a preposition° meaning "because of" (*Due to the holiday, class was cancelled*). A rule of thumb is that *due to* is always correct after a form of the verb *be* but questionable otherwise.

eager, anxious   See *anxious, eager.*

effect   See *affect, effect.*

elicit, illicit   *Elicit* is a verb° meaning "bring out" or "call forth." *Illicit* is an adjective° meaning "unlawful." *The crime elicited an outcry against illicit drugs.*

emigrate, immigrate   *Emigrate* means "to leave one place and move to another": *The Chus emigrated from Korea. Immigrate* means "to move into a place where one was not born": *They immigrated to Canada.*

enthused   Sometimes used colloquially as an adjective° meaning "showing enthusiasm." The preferred adjective is *enthusiastic: The coach was enthusiastic* [not *enthused*] *about the team's victory.*

etc.   *Etc.*, the Latin abbreviation for "and other things," should be avoided in formal writing and should not be used to refer to people. When used, it should not substitute for precision, as in *The government provides health care, etc.,* and it should not end a list beginning *such as* or *for example.*

everybody, every body; everyone, every one   *Everybody* and *everyone* are indefinite pronouns°: *Everybody* [or *Everyone*] *knows Tom steals. Every one* is a pronoun° modified by *every*, and *every body* a noun° modified by *every*. Both refer to each thing or person of a specific group and are typically followed by *of*: *Every body of water in the province has been tested, so everybody can swim safely this summer.*

everyday, every day   *Everyday* is an adjective° meaning "used daily" or "common"; *every day* is a noun° modified by *every*: *Everyday problems tend to arise every day.*

everywheres   Nonstandard for *everywhere*.

except   See *accept, except*.

explicit, implicit   *Explicit* means "stated outright": *I left explicit instructions. Implicit* means "implied, unstated": *We had an implicit understanding.*

farther, further   *Farther* refers to additional distance (*How much farther is it to the beach?*), and *further* refers to additional time, amount, or other abstract matters (*I don't want to discuss this any further*).

feel   Avoid this word in place of *think* or *believe: She thinks* [not *feels*] *that the law should be changed.*

fewer, less   *Fewer* refers to individual countable items (a plural count noun°), *less* to general amounts (a noncount noun,° always singular): *Skim milk has fewer calories than whole milk. We have less milk left than I thought.*

further   See *farther, further*.

get   *Get* is easy to overuse; watch out for it in expressions such as *it's getting better* (substitute *improving*), *we got done* (substitute *finished*), and *the mayor has got to* (substitute *must*).

good, well   *Good* is an adjective,° and *well* is nearly always an adverb°: *Larry's a good dancer. He and Linda dance well together. Well* is properly used as an adjective only to refer to health: *You look well.* (*You look good*, in contrast, means "Your appearance is pleasing.") See also pp. 67–68.

hanged, hung   Though both are past-tense forms° of *hang*, *hanged* is used to refer to executions and *hung* is used for all other meanings: *Louis Riel was hanged* [not *hung*]. *I hung* [not *hanged*] *the picture you gave me.*

have, of   Use *have*, not *of*, after helping verbs° such as *could, should, would, may*, and *might: You should have* [not *should of*] *told me.*

he, she; he/she   Convention has allowed the use of *he* to mean "he or she," but most writers today consider this usage inaccurate and unfair because it excludes females. The construction *he/she*, one substitute for *he*, is awkward and objectionable to many readers. The better choice is to recast the sentence in the plural, to rephrase, or to use *he or she*. For instance: *After infants learn to creep, they progress to crawling. After learning to creep, the infant progresses to crawling. After*

Usage

the infant learns to creep, he or she *progresses to crawling.* See also pp. 41 and 64–65.

herself, himself See *myself, herself, himself, yourself.*

hisself Nonstandard for *himself.*

hopefully *Hopefully* means "with hope": *Freddy waited* hopefully. The use of *hopefully* to mean "it is to be hoped," "I hope," or "let's hope" is now very common; but since many readers continue to object strongly to the usage, you should avoid it. *I hope* [not *Hopefully*] *Eliza will be here soon.*

idea, ideal An *idea* is a thought or conception. An *ideal* (noun°) is a model of perfection or a goal. *Ideal* should not be used in place of *idea: The idea* [not *ideal*] *of the play is that our ideals often sustain us.*

if, whether For clarity, use *whether* rather than *if* when you are expressing an alternative: *If I laugh hard, people can't tell whether I'm crying.*

illicit See *elicit, illicit.*

illusion See *allusion, illusion.*

immigrate See *emigrate, immigrate.*

implicit See *explicit, implicit.*

imply, infer Writers or speakers *imply,* meaning "suggest": *Jim's letter implies he's having a good time.* Readers or listeners *infer,* meaning "conclude": *From Jim's letter I infer he's having a good time.*

irregardless Nonstandard for *regardless.*

is, are See *are, is.*

is when, is where These are faulty constructions in sentences that define: *Adolescence is a stage* [not *is when a person is*] *between childhood and adulthood. Socialism is a system in which* [not *is where*] *government owns the means of production.*

its, it's *Its* is the pronoun° *it* in the possessive case°: *That plant is losing its leaves. It's* is a contraction for *it is: It's likely to die if you don't water it.* See also p. 92.

kind of, sort of, type of In formal speech and writing, avoid using *kind of* or *sort of* to mean "somewhat": *He was rather* [not *kind of*] *tall.*

Kind, sort, and *type* are singular: *This kind of dog is easily trained.* Errors often occur when these singular nouns are combined with the plural adjectives° *these* and *those: These kinds* [not *kind*] *of dogs are easily trained. Kind, sort,* and *type* should be followed by *of* but not by *of a: I don't know what type of* [not *type* or *type of a*] *dog that is.*

Use *kind of, sort of,* or *type of* only when the word *kind, sort,* or *type* is important: *That was a strange* [not *strange sort of*] *statement.*

lay, lie *Lay* means "put" or "place" and takes a direct object°: *We could lay the tablecloth in the sun.* Its main forms are *lay,* *laid, laid. Lie* means "recline" or "be situated" and does not take an object: *I lie awake at night. The town lies east of the river.* Its main forms are *lie, lay, lain.*

less   See *fewer, less.*

lie, lay   See *lay, lie.*

like, as   In formal speech and writing, *like* should not introduce a full clause.° The preferred choice is *as* or *as if: The plan succeeded as* [not *like*] *we hoped.* Use *like* only before a word or phrase: *Other plans like it have failed.*

literally   This word means "actually" or "just as the words say," and it should not be used to intensify expressions whose words are not to be taken at face value. The sentence *He was literally climbing the walls* describes a person behaving like an insect, not a person who is restless or anxious. For the latter meaning, when he is in fact only *figuratively* climbing the walls, *literally* should be omitted.

lose, loose   *Lose* means "mislay": *Did you lose a brown glove? Loose* usually means "unrestrained" or "not tight": *Ann's canary got loose.*

may, can   See *can, may.*

may be, maybe   *May be* is a verb,° and *maybe* is an adverb° meaning "perhaps": *Tuesday may be a legal holiday. Maybe we won't have classes.*

may of   See *have, of.*

media   *Media* is the plural of *medium* and takes a plural verb.° *All the news media are increasingly visual.* The singular verb is common, even in the media, but many readers prefer the plural verb and it is always correct.

might of   See *have, of.*

must of   See *have, of.*

myself, herself, himself, yourself   The *-self* pronouns° refer to or intensify another word or words: *Paul did it himself; Jill herself said so.* In formal speech or writing, avoid using the *-self* pronouns in place of personal pronouns°: *No one except me* [not *myself*] *saw the accident. Michiko and I* [not *myself*] *planned the ceremony.*

never, no one   See *all, always, never, no one.*

nowheres   Nonstandard for *nowhere.*

number   See *amount, number.*

of, have   See *have, of.*

OK, O.K., okay   All three spellings are acceptable, but avoid this colloquial term in formal speech and writing.

people, persons   Except when emphasizing individuals, prefer *people* to *persons: the people of the North . . . ; Will the person or persons who saw the accident please notify. . . .*

percent (per cent), percentage   Both these terms refer to fractions of one hundred. *Percent* always follows a numeral

(*40 percent of the voters*), and the word should be used instead of the symbol (%) in nontechnical writing. *Percentage* usually follows an adjective (*a high percentage*).

persons   See *people, persons.*

phenomena   The plural of *phenomenon* (meaning "perceivable fact" or "unusual occurrence"): *Many phenomena are not recorded. One phenomenon is attracting attention.*

plus   *Plus* is standard as a preposition° meaning "in addition to": *His income plus mine is sufficient.* But *plus* is colloquial as a conjunctive adverb°: *Our organization is larger than theirs; moreover* [not *plus*], *we have more money.*

precede, proceed   *Precede* means "come before": *My name precedes yours in the alphabet. Proceed* means "move on": *We were told to proceed to the waiting room.*

prejudice, prejudiced   *Prejudice* is a noun° or a verb°; *prejudiced* is an adjective.° Do not drop the *-d* from *prejudiced: I knew that my grandparents were prejudiced* [not *prejudice*].

principal, principle   *Principal* is an adjective° meaning "foremost" or "major," a noun° meaning "chief official," or, in finance, a noun meaning "capital sum." *Principle* is a noun only, meaning "rule" or "axiom." *Her principal reasons for confessing were her principles of right and wrong.*

proceed, precede   See *precede, proceed.*

raise, rise   *Raise* means "lift" or "bring up" and takes a direct object°: *The Kirks raise cattle.* Its main forms are *raise, raised, raised. Rise* means "get up" and does not take an object: *They must rise at dawn.* Its main forms are *rise, rose, risen.*

real, really   In formal speech and writing, *real* should not be used as an adverb°; *really* is the adverb and *real* an adjective.° *Popular reaction to the announcement was really* [not *real*] *enthusiastic.*

reason is because   Although colloquially common, this construction should be avoided in formal speech and writing. Use a *that* clause after *reason is: The reason he is absent is that* [not *is because*] *he is sick.* Or *He is absent because he is sick.*

respectful, respective   *Respectful* means "full of (or showing) respect": *Be respectful of other people. Respective* means "separate": *The French and the Germans occupied their respective trenches.*

rise, raise   See *raise, rise.*

sensual, sensuous   *Sensual* suggests sexuality; *sensuous* means "pleasing to the senses." *Stirred by the sensuous scent of meadow grass and flowers, Cheryl and Paul found their thoughts turning sensual.*

set, sit   *Set* means "put" or "place" and takes a direct object°: *He sets the pitcher down.* Its main forms are *set, set, set. Sit* means "be seated" and does not take an object: *She sits on the sofa.* Its main forms are *sit, sat, sat.*

should of   See *have, of.*

since   *Since* mainly relates to time: *I've been waiting since noon.* But *since* can also mean "because": *Since you ask, I'll tell you.* Revise sentences in which the word could have either meaning, such as *Since you left, my life is empty.*

sit, set   See *set, sit.*

somebody, some body; someone, some one   *Somebody* and *someone* are indefinite pronouns°; *some body* is a noun° modified by *some;* and *some one* is a pronoun° or an adjective° modified by *some. Somebody ought to invent a shampoo that will give hair some body. Someone told James he should choose some one plan and stick with it.*

somewheres   Nonstandard for *somewhere.*

sort of, sort of a   See *kind of, sort of, type of.*

supposed to, used to   In both these expressions, the *-d* is essential: *I used to* [not *use to*] *think so. He's supposed to* [not *suppose to*] *meet us.*

sure and, sure to; try and, try to   *Sure to* and *try to* are the correct forms: *Be sure to* [not *sure and*] *buy milk. Try to* [not *Try and*] *find some decent tomatoes.* (*To buy* and *to find* are infinitives.°)

take, bring   See *bring, take.*

than, then   *Than* is a conjunction° used in comparisons, *then* an adverb° indicating time: *Holmes knew then that Moriarty was wilier than he had thought.*

that, which   *That* always introduces essential° clauses: *Use the lettuce that Susan bought* (the clause limits *lettuce* to a particular lettuce). *Which* can introduce both essential and nonessential° clauses, but many writers reserve *which* only for nonessential clauses: *The leftover lettuce, which is in the refrigerator, would make a good salad* (the clause simply provides more information about the lettuce we already know of). Essential clauses are not set off by commas; nonessential clauses are. See also pp. 84–85.

that, who, which   Use *that* to refer to most animals and to things: *The animals that escaped included a zebra. The rocket that failed cost millions.* Use *who* to refer to people and to animals with names: *Dorothy is the girl who visits Oz. Her dog, Toto, who accompanies her, gives her courage.* Use *which* only to refer to animals and things: *The river, which runs a thousand miles, empties into the Indian Ocean.*

their, there, they're   *Their* is the possessive° form of *they: Give them their money. There* indicates place (*I saw her standing there*) or functions as an expletive° (*There is a hole behind you*). *They're* is a contraction° for *they are: They're going fast.*

theirselves Nonstandard for *themselves*.

then, than See *than, then*.

these, this *These* is plural; *this* is singular. *This pear is ripe, but these pears are not.*

these kind, these sort, these type, those kind See *kind of, sort of, type of*.

thru A colloquial spelling of *through* that should be avoided in all academic and business writing.

to, too, two *To* is a preposition°; *too* is an adverb° meaning "also" or "excessively"; and *two* is a number. *I too have been to Europe two times.*

toward, towards Both are acceptable, though *toward* is preferred. Use one or the other consistently.

try and, try to See *sure and, sure to; try and, try to*.

type of See *kind of, sort of, type of*.

uninterested See *disinterested, uninterested*.

unique *Unique* means "the only one of its kind" and so cannot sensibly be modified with words such as *very* or *most: That was a unique* [not *a very unique* or *the most unique*] *movie.*

used to See *supposed to, used to*.

weather, whether The *weather* is the state of the atmosphere. *Whether* introduces alternatives. *The weather will determine whether we go or not.*

well See *good, well*.

whether, if See *if, whether*.

which, that See *that, which*.

who, which, that See *that, who, which*.

who, whom *Who* is the subject of a sentence or clause°: *We know who will come. Whom* is the object° of a verb° or preposition°: *We know whom we invited.*

who's, whose *Who's* is the contraction° of *who is: Who's at the door? Whose* is the possessive° form of *who: Whose book is that?*

would have Avoid this construction in place of *had* in clauses that begin *if: If the tree had* [not *would have*] *withstood the fire, it would have been the oldest in town.*

would of See *have, of*.

you In all but very formal writing, *you* is generally appropriate as long as it means "you, the reader." In all writing, avoid indefinite uses of *you*, such as *In one ancient tribe your first loyalty was to your parents.*

your, you're *Your* is the possessive° form of *you: Your dinner is ready. You're* is the contraction° of *you are: You're bound to be late.*

yourself See *myself, herself, himself, yourself*.

Glossary of Terms

This glossary defines the terms and concepts of basic English grammar, including every term marked ° in the text.

absolute phrase A phrase that consists of a noun° or pronoun° plus the *-ing* or *-ed* form of a verb° (a participle°): *Our accommodations arranged, we set out on our trip. They will hire a local person, other things being equal.*

active voice The verb form° used when the sentence subject° names the performer of the verb's action: *The drillers used a rotary blade.* For more, see *voice.*

adjective A word used to modify a noun° or pronoun°: *beautiful morning, ordinary one, good spelling.* Contrast *adverb.* Nouns, word groups, and some verb° forms may also serve as adjectives: *book sale; sale of old books; the sale, which occurs annually; increasing profits.*

adverb A word used to modify a verb,° an adjective,° another adverb, or a whole sentence: *warmly greet* (verb), *only three people* (adjective), *quite seriously* (adverb), *Fortunately, she is employed* (sentence). Word groups may also serve as adverbs: *drove by a farm, ploughed the fields when the earth thawed.*

agreement The correspondence of one word to another in person,° number,° or gender.° Mainly, a verb° must agree with its subject° (*The chef orders eggs*), and a pronoun° must agree with its antecedent° (*The chef surveys her breakfast*). See also pp. 57–60 and 63–65.

antecedent The word a pronoun° refers to: *Jonah, who is not yet ten, has already chosen the university he wants to attend* (*Jonah* is the antecedent of the pronouns *who* and *he*).

appositive A word or word group appearing next to a noun° or pronoun° that renames or identifies it and is equivalent to it: *My brother Michael, the best horn player in town, won the provincial competition* (*Michael* identifies which brother is being referred to; *the best horn player in town* renames *My brother Michael*).

article The words *a, an,* and *the.* A kind of determiner,° an article always signals that a noun follows. See p. 239 for how to choose between *a* and *an.* See pp. 70–72 for the rules governing *a/an* and *the.*

auxiliary verb See *helping verb.*

case The form of a pronoun° or noun° that indicates its function in the sentence. Most pronouns have three cases. The **subjective case** is for subjects° and subject complements°: *I, you, he, she, it, we, they, who, whoever.* The **objective case** is for objects°: *me, you, him, her, it, us, them, whom, whomever.* The **possessive case** is for ownership: *my/mine, your/yours, his, her/hers, its, our/ours, their/theirs, whose.* Nouns use the subjective form (*dog, Canada*) for all cases except the possessive (*dog's, Canada's*).

clause   A group of words containing a subject° and a predicate.° An independent or **main clause** can stand alone as a sentence: *We can go to the movies.* A dependent or **subordinate clause** cannot stand alone as a sentence: *We can go if Julie gets back on time.* For more, see *subordinate clause.*

collective noun   A word with singular form that names a group of individuals or things: for instance, *team, army, family, flock, group.* A collective noun generally takes a singular verb and a singular pronoun: *The army is prepared for its role.* See also pp. 59 and 65.

comma splice   A sentence error in which two sentences (main clauses°) are separated by a comma without *and, but, or, nor,* or another coordinating conjunction.° Splice: *The book was long, it contained useful information.* Revised: *The book was long; it contained useful information.* Or *The book was long, and it contained useful information.* See pp. 77–79.

comparison   The form of an adverb° or adjective° that shows its degree of quality or amount. The **positive** is the simple, uncompared form: *gross, clumsily.* The **comparative** compares the thing modified to at least one other thing: *grosser, more clumsily.* The **superlative** indicates that the thing modified exceeds all other things to which it is being compared: *grossest, most clumsily.* The comparative and superlative are formed either with the endings *-er* and *-est* or with the words *more* and *most* or *less* and *least.*

complement   See *subject complement.*

complex sentence   See *sentence.*

compound-complex sentence   See *sentence.*

compound construction   Two or more words or word groups serving the same function, such as a compound subject° (*Harriet and Peter punted down the river*), a compound predicate° (*The scout watched and waited*), or a compound sentence° (*He smiled, and I laughed*).

compound sentence   See *sentence.*

conditional statement   A statement expressing a condition contrary to fact and using the subjunctive mood° of the verb: *If she were mayor, the unions would cooperate.*

conjunction   A word that links and relates parts of a sentence. See *coordinating conjunction* (*and, but,* etc.), *correlative conjunction* (*either . . . or, both . . . and,* etc.), and *subordinating conjunction* (*because, if,* etc.).

conjunctive adverb An adverb° that can relate two main clauses° in a single sentence: *We had hoped to own a house by now; however, prices are still too high.* The main clauses are separated by a semicolon or a period. Some common conjunctive adverbs: *accordingly, also, anyway, besides, certainly, consequently, finally, further, furthermore, hence, however, incidentally, indeed, instead, likewise, meanwhile, moreover, namely, nevertheless, next, nonetheless, now, otherwise, similarly, still, then, thereafter, therefore, thus, undoubtedly.*

contraction A condensed expression, with an apostrophe replacing the missing letters: for example, *doesn't* (*does not*), *we'll* (*we will*).

coordinating conjunction A word linking words or word groups serving the same function: *The dog and cat sometimes fight, but they usually get along.* The coordinating conjunctions are *and, but, or, nor, for, so, yet.*

coordination The linking of words or word groups that are of equal importance, usually with a coordinating conjunction.° *He and I laughed, but she was not amused.* Contrast *subordination.*

correlative conjunction Two or more connecting words that work together to link words or word groups serving the same function: *Both Michiko and June signed up, but neither Amir nor Danuta did.* The correlatives include *both . . . and, just as . . . so, not only . . . but also, not . . . but, either . . . or, neither . . . nor, whether . . . or, as . . . as.*

count noun A word that names a person, place, or thing that can be counted (and so may appear in plural form): *camera/cameras, river/rivers, child/children.*

dangling modifier A modifier that does not sensibly describe anything in its sentence. Dangling: *Having arrived late, the concert had already begun.* Revised: *Having arrived late, we found that the concert had already begun.* See p. 74.

determiner A word such as *a, an, the, my,* and *your* that indicates that a noun follows. See also *article.*

direct address A construction in which a word or phrase indicates the person or group spoken to: *Have you finished, John? Farmers, unite.*

direct object A noun° or pronoun° that identifies who or what receives the action of a verb°: *Education opens doors.* For more, see *object* and *predicate.*

direct question A sentence asking a question and concluding with a question mark: *Do they know we are watching?* Contrast *indirect question.*

direct quotation Repetition of what someone has written or said, using the exact words of the original and enclosing them in quotation marks: *Feinberg writes, "The reasons are both obvious and sorry."*

Terms

252 Glossary of terms

double negative A nonstandard form consisting of two negative words used in the same construction so that they effectively cancel each other: *I don't have no money.* Rephrase as *I have no money* or *I don't have any money.* See also p. 69.

ellipsis The omission of a word or words from a quotation, indicated by the three spaced periods of an **ellipsis mark:** *"all . . . are created equal."* See also pp. 98–101.

essential element A word or word group that is essential to the meaning of the sentence because it limits the word it refers to: removing it would leave the meaning unclear or too general. Essential elements are *not* set off by commas: *Dorothy's companion the Scarecrow lacks a brain. The man who called about the apartment said he'd try again.* Contrast with *nonessential element.* See also pp. 84–85.

expletive construction A sentence that postpones the subject° by beginning with *there* or *it* and a form of *be: It is impossible to get a ticket. There are no more seats available.*

first person See *person.*

fused sentence (run-on sentence) A sentence error in which two complete sentences (main clauses°) are joined with no punctuation or connecting word between them. Fused: *I heard his lecture it was dull.* Revised: *I heard his lecture; it was dull.* Or: *I heard his lecture, and it was dull.* See pp. 77–79.

future perfect tense The verb tense expressing an action that will be completed before another future action: *They will have heard by then.* For more, see *tense.*

future tense The verb tense expressing action that will occur in the future: *They will hear soon.* For more, see *tense.*

gender The classification of nouns° or pronouns° as masculine (*he, boy*), feminine (*she, woman*), or neuter (*it, computer*).

generic *he He* used to mean *he or she.* Avoid *he* when you intend either or both genders. See pp. 41 and 64–65.

generic noun A noun° that does not refer to a specific person or thing: *Any person may come. A student needs good work habits. A school with financial problems may shortchange its students.* A singular generic noun takes a singular pronoun° (*he, she,* or *it*). See also *indefinite pronoun* and pp. 64–65.

gerund A verb form that ends in *-ing* and functions as a noun°: *Working is all right for killing time.* For more, see *verbals and verbal phrases.*

gerund phrase See *verbals and verbal phrases.*

helping verb (auxiliary verb) A verb° used with another verb to convey time, possibility, obligation, and other meanings: *You should write a letter. You have written other letters.*

Terms

The **modals** are the following: *be able to, be supposed to, can, could, had better, had to, may, might, must, ought to, shall, should, used to, will, would.* The other helping verbs are forms of *be, have,* and *do.* See also pp. 48–50.

idiom   An expression that is peculiar to a language and that may not make sense if taken literally: for example, *bide your time, by and large,* and *put up with.*

imperative   See *mood.*

indefinite pronoun   A word that stands for a noun° and does not refer to a specific person or thing. A few indefinite pronouns are plural (*both, few, many, several*) or may be singular or plural (*all, any, more, most, none, some*). But most are only singular: *anybody, anyone, anything, each, either, everybody, everyone, everything, neither, nobody, no one, nothing, one, somebody, someone, something.* The singular indefinite pronouns take singular verbs and are referred to by singular pronouns: *Something makes its presence felt.* See also *generic noun* and pp. 59 and 64–65.

indicative   See *mood.*

indirect object   A noun° or pronoun° that identifies to whom or what something is done: *Give them the award.* For more, see *object* and *predicate.*

indirect question   A sentence reporting a question and ending with a period: *Writers wonder if their work must always be lonely.* Contrast *direct question.*

indirect quotation   A report of what someone has written or said, but not using the exact words of the original and not enclosing the words in quotation marks. Quotation: *"The medium is the message."* Indirect quotation: *Marshall McLuhan said that the medium was the message.*

infinitive   A verb form° consisting of the verb's dictionary form plus *to: to swim, to write.* For more, see *verbals and verbal phrases.*

infinitive phrase   See *verbals and verbal phrases.*

intensive pronoun   See *pronoun.*

interjection   A word standing by itself or inserted in a construction to exclaim: *Hey! What the heck did you do that for?*

interrogative pronoun   A word that begins a question and serves as the subject° or object° of the sentence. The interrogative pronouns are *who, whom, whose, which,* and *what. Who received the flowers? Whom are they for?*

intransitive verb   A verb° that does not require a following word (direct object°) to complete its meaning: *Mosquitoes buzz. The hospital may close.* For more, see *predicate.*

irregular verb   See *verb forms.*

Terms

limiting modifier   Any word or word group, such as *almost*, *even*, *exactly*, *hardly*, *just*, *merely*, *only*, *scarcely*, and *simply*, that limits the number or intensity of the word or word group it modifies.

linking verb   A verb that links, or connects, a subject° and a word that renames or describes the subject (a subject complement°): *They are golfers. You seem lucky.* The linking verbs are the forms of *be*, the verbs of the senses (*look, sound, smell, feel, taste*), and a few others (*appear, become, grow, prove, remain, seem, turn*). For more, see *predicate*.

main clause   A word group that contains a subject° and a predicate,° does not begin with a subordinating word, and may stand alone as a sentence: *The president was not overbearing.* For more, see *clause*.

main verb   The part of a verb phrase° that carries the principal meaning: *had been walking, could happen, was chilled.* Contrast *helping verb*.

misplaced modifier   A modifier whose position makes unclear its relation to the rest of the sentence. Misplaced: *The children played with firecrackers that they bought illegally in the field.* Revised: *The children played in the field with firecrackers that they bought illegally.*

modal   See *helping verb*.

modifier   Any word or word group that limits or qualifies the meaning of another word or word group. Modifiers include adjectives° and adverbs° as well as words and word groups that act as adjectives and adverbs.

mood   The form of a verb° that shows how the speaker views the action. The **indicative mood**, the most common, is used to make statements or ask questions: *The play will be performed Saturday. Did you get tickets?* The **imperative mood** gives a command: *Please get good seats. Avoid the top balcony.* The **subjunctive mood** expresses a wish, a condition contrary to fact, a recommendation, or a request: *I wish George were coming with us. If he were here, he'd come. I suggested that he come. The host asked that he be here.*

noncount noun   A word that names a person, place, or thing and that is not considered countable in English (and so does not appear in plural form): *confidence, information, silver, work.* See p. 71–72 for a longer list.

nonessential element   A word or word group that does not limit the word it refers to and that is not essential to the meaning of the sentence. Nonessential elements are usually set off by commas: *Sleep, which we all need, occupies a third of our lives. His wife, Patricia, is a chemist.* Contrast *essential element*. See also pp. 84–85.

nonrestrictive element   See *nonessential element*.

noun   A word that names a person, place, thing, quality, or idea: *Maggie, Alberta, clarinet, satisfaction, socialism*. See also *collective noun, count noun, generic noun, noncount noun,* and *proper noun.*

noun clause   See *subordinate clause.*

number   The form of a word that indicates whether it is singular or plural. Singular: *I, he, this, child, runs, hides.* Plural: *we, they, these, children, run, hide.*

object   A noun° or pronoun° that receives the action of or is influenced by another word. A **direct object** receives the action of a verb° or verbal° and usually follows it: *We watched the stars.* An **indirect object** tells for or to whom something is done: *Reiner bought us ice cream.* An **object of a preposition** usually follows a preposition°: *They went to Gros Morne.*

objective case   The form of a pronoun° when it is the object° of a verb° (*call him*) or the object of a preposition° (*for us*). For more, see *case.*

object of preposition   See *object.*

parallelism   Similarity of form between two or more coordinated elements: *Rising prices and declining incomes left many people in bad debt and worse despair.* See also pp. 32–34.

parenthetical expression   A word or construction that interrupts a sentence and is not part of its main structure, called *parenthetical* because it could (or does) appear in parentheses: *Emily Carr (1871–1945) was a Canadian painter. Her work, incidentally, is in the museum.*

participial phrase   See *verbals and verbal phrases.*

participle   See *verbals and verbal phrases.*

particle   A preposition° or adverb° in a two-word verb: *catch on, look up.*

parts of speech   The classes of words based on their form, function, and meaning: nouns, pronouns, verbs, adjectives, adverbs, conjunctions, prepositions, and interjections. See separate entries for each part of speech.

passive voice   The verb form° used when the sentence subject° names the receiver of the verb's action: *The mixture was stirred.* For more, see *voice.*

past participle   The *-ed* form of most verbs°: *fished, hopped.* The past participle may be irregular: *begun, written.* For more, see *verbals and verbal phrases* and *verb forms.*

past perfect tense   The verb tense expressing an action that was completed before another past action: *No one had heard that before.* For more, see *tense.*

past tense   The verb tense expressing action that occurred in the past: *Everyone laughed.* For more, see *tense.*

Terms

past-tense form   The verb form used to indicate action that occurred in the past, usually created by adding *-d* or *-ed* to the verb's dictionary form (*smiled*) but created differently for most irregular verbs (*began, threw*). For more, see *verb forms.*

perfect tenses   The verb tenses indicating action completed before another specific time or action: *have walked, had walked, will have walked.* For more, see *tense.*

person   The form of a verb° or pronoun° that indicates whether the subject is speaking, spoken to, or spoken about. In the **first person** the subject is speaking: *I am, we are.* In the **second person** the subject is spoken to: *you are.* In the **third person** the subject is spoken about: *he/she/it is, they are.*

personal pronoun   *I, you, he, she, it, we,* or *they:* a word that substitutes for a specific noun° or other pronoun. For more, see *case.*

phrase   A group of related words that lacks a subject° or a predicate° or both: *She ran <u>into the field</u>. She tried <u>to jump the fence</u>.* See also *absolute phrase, prepositional phrase, verbals and verbal phrases.*

plain form   The dictionary form of a verb: *buy, make, run, swivel.* For more, see *verb forms.*

plural   More than one. See *number.*

positive form   See *comparison.*

possessive case   The form of a noun° or pronoun° that indicates its ownership of something else: *<u>men's</u> attire, <u>your</u> briefcase.* For more, see *case.*

predicate   The part of a sentence that makes an assertion about the subject.° The predicate may consist of an intransitive verb° (*The earth <u>trembled</u>*), a transitive verb° plus direct object° (*The earthquake <u>shook</u> <u>buildings</u>*), a linking verb° plus subject complement° (*The result was chaos*), a transitive verb plus indirect object° and direct object (*The government <u>sent</u> the <u>city</u> <u>aid</u>*), or a transitive verb plus direct object and object complement (*The citizens <u>considered</u> the <u>earthquake</u> a <u>disaster</u>*).

preposition   A word that forms a noun° or pronoun° (plus any modifiers) into a **prepositional phrase**: *<u>about</u> love, <u>down</u> the steep stairs.* The common prepositions: *about, above, according to, across, after, against, along, along with, among, around, as, at, because of, before, behind, below, beneath, beside, between, beyond, by, concerning, despite, down, during, except, except for, excepting, for, from, in, in addition to, inside, in spite of, instead of, into, like, near, next to, of, off, on, onto, out, out of, outside, over, past, regarding, since, through, throughout, till, to, toward, under, underneath, unlike, until, up, upon, with, within, without.*

prepositional phrase A word group consisting of a preposition° and its object.° Prepositional phrases usually serve as adjectives° (*We saw a movie about sorrow*) and as adverbs° (*We went back for the second show*).

present participle The *-ing* form of a verb°: *swimming, flying*. For more, see *verbals and verbal phrases*.

present perfect tense The verb tense expressing action that began in the past and is linked to the present: *Dogs have buried bones here before*. For more, see *tense*.

present tense The verb tense expressing action that is occurring now, occurs habitually, or is generally true: *Dogs bury bones here often*. For more, see *tense*.

principal parts The three forms of a verb from which its various tenses are created: the **plain form** (*stop, go*), the **past-tense form** (*stopped, went*), and the **past participle** (*stopped, gone*). For more, see *tense* and *verb forms*.

progressive tenses The verb tenses that indicate continuing (progressive) action and use the *-ing* form of the verb: *A dog was barking here this morning*. For more, see *tense*.

pronoun A word used in place of a noun,° such as *I, he, everyone, who,* and *herself*. See also *indefinite pronoun, interrogative pronoun, personal pronoun, relative pronoun*.

proper adjective A word formed from a proper noun° and used to modify a noun° or pronoun°: *Albertan winter*.

proper noun A word naming a specific person, place, or thing and beginning with a capital letter: *Peter Mansbridge, Mount Robson, Ottawa, Canada Post*.

regular verb See *verb forms*.

relative pronoun A word that relates a group of words to a noun° or another pronoun.° The relative pronouns are *who, whom, whoever, whomever, which,* and *that*. *Ask the woman who knows all. This may be the question that stumps her*. For more, see *case*.

restrictive element See *essential element*.

run-on sentence See *fused sentence*.

-s form See *verb forms*.

second person See *person*.

sentence A complete unit of thought, consisting of at least a subject° and a predicate° that are not introduced by a subordinating word. A **simple sentence** contains one main clause°: *I'm leaving*. A **compound sentence** contains at least two main clauses: *I'd like to stay, but I'm leaving*. A **complex sentence** contains one main clause and at least one subordinate clause°: *If you let me go now, you'll be sorry*. A

Terms

compound-complex sentence contains at least two main clauses and at least one subordinate clause: *I'm leaving because you want me to, but I'd rather stay.*

sentence fragment An error in which an incomplete sentence is set off as a complete sentence. Fragment: *She was not in shape for the race. <u>Which she had hoped to win.</u>* Revised: *She was not in shape for the race, <u>which</u> she had hoped to win.* See pp. 75–77.

series Three or more items with the same function: *We gorged on <u>ham, eggs, and potatoes.</u>*

simple sentence See *sentence.*

simple tenses See *tense.*

singular One. See *number.*

split infinitive The usually awkward interruption of an infinitive° and its marker *to* by a modifier: *Management decided <u>to not introduce</u> the new product.* See p. 73.

squinting modifier A modifier that could modify the words on either side of it: *The plan we considered <u>seriously</u> worries me.*

subject In grammar, the part of a sentence that names something and about which an assertion is made in the predicate°: *The quick, brown <u>fox</u> jumped lazily* (simple subject); *<u>The quick, brown fox</u> jumped lazily* (complete subject).

subject complement A word that follows a linking verb and that renames or describes the subject of a sentence° *The stranger was a <u>man</u>* (noun°). *He seemed <u>gigantic</u>* (adjective°).

subjective case The form of a pronoun° when it is the subject° of a sentence (*<u>I</u> called*) or a subject complement° (*It was <u>I</u>*). For more, see *case.*

subjunctive See *mood.*

subordinate clause A word group that consists of a subject° and a predicate,° begins with a subordinating word such as *because* or *who,* and is not a question: *They voted for <u>whoever cared the least</u> <u>because they mistrusted politicians.</u>* Subordinate clauses may serve as adjectives° (*The car <u>that hit Fred</u> was blue*), as adverbs° (*The car hit Fred <u>when it ran a red light</u>*), or as nouns° (*<u>Whoever was driving</u> should be arrested*). Subordinate clauses are *not* complete sentences.

subordinating conjunction A word that turns a complete sentence into a word group (a subordinate clause°) that can serve as an adverb° or a noun.° *Everyone was relieved <u>when</u> the meeting ended.* Some common subordinating conjunctions: *after, although, as, as if, as long as, as though, because, before, even if, even though, if, if only, in order that, now that, once, rather than, since, so that, than, that, though, till, unless, until, when, whenever, where, whereas, wherever, while.*

subordination Deemphasizing one element in a sentence by making it dependent on, rather than equal to, another element. Through subordination, *I left six messages; the doctor failed to call* becomes <u>Although I left six messages</u>, *the doctor failed to call* or <u>After six messages</u>, *the doctor failed to call*.

superlative See *comparison*.

tag question A question attached to the end of a statement and composed of a pronoun,° a helping verb,° and sometimes the word *not: It isn't raining, <u>is it</u>? It is sunny, <u>isn't it</u>?*

tense The verb form that expresses time, usually indicated by endings and by helping verbs. See also *verb forms*.

Present Action that is occurring now, occurs habitually, or is generally true

Simple present Plain form
or -*s* form

I *walk*.
You/we/they *walk*.
He/she/it *walks*.

Present progressive *Am, is,* or *are* plus -*ing* form

I *am walking*.
You/we/they *are walking*.
He/she/it *is walking*.

Past Action that occurred before now

Simple past Past-tense
form

I/he/she/it *walked*.
You/we/they *walked*.

Past progressive *Was* or
were plus -*ing* form

I/he/she/it *was walking*.
You/we/they *were walking*.

Future Action that will occur in the future

Simple future *Will* plus plain
form

I/you/he/she/it/we/they
  will walk.

Future progressive *Will be*
plus -*ing* form

I/you/he/she/it/we/they *will
  be walking*.

Present perfect Action that began in the past and is linked to the present

Present perfect *Have* or *has*
plus past participle

I/you/we/they *have walked*.

He/she/it *has walked*.

Present perfect progressive
Have been or *has been* plus
-*ing* form

I/you/we/they *have been
  walking*.
He/she/it *has been walking*.

Past perfect Action that was completed before another past action

Past perfect *Had* plus past
participle

I/you/he/she/it/we/they
  had walked.

Past perfect progressive
Had been plus -*ing* form

I/you/he/she/it/we/they *had
  been walking*.

Future perfect   Action that will be completed before another future action

Future perfect *Will have* plus past participle	Future perfect progressive *Will have been* plus *-ing* form
I/you/he/she/it/we/they *will have walked.*	I/you/he/she/it/we/they *will have been walking.*

third person   See *person.*

transitional expression   A word or phrase that links sentences and shows the relations between them. Transitional expressions can signal various relationships (examples in parentheses): addition or sequence (*also, besides, finally, first, furthermore, in addition, last*); comparison (*also, similarly*); contrast (*even so, however, in contrast, still*); examples (*for example, for instance, that is*); intensification (*indeed, in fact, of course*); place (*below, elsewhere, here, nearby, to the east*); time (*afterward, at last, earlier, immediately, meanwhile, simultaneously*); repetition or summary (*in brief, in other words, in short, in summary, that is*); and cause and effect (*as a result, consequently, hence, therefore, thus*).

transitive verb   A verb° that requires a following word (a direct object°) to complete its meaning: *We raised the roof.* For more, see *predicate.*

verb   A word that expresses an action (*bring, change*), an occurrence (*happen, become*), or a state of being (*be, seem*). A verb is the essential word in a predicate,° the part of a sentence that makes an assertion about the subject.° With endings and helping verbs,° verbs can indicate tense,° mood,° voice,° number,° and person.° For more, see separate entries for each of these aspects as well as *verb forms.*

verbals and verbal phrases   **Verbals** are verb forms used as adjectives,° adverbs,° or nouns.° They form **verbal phrases** with objects° and modifiers.° A **present participle** adds *-ing* to the dictionary form of a verb (*living*). A **past participle** usually adds *-d* or *-ed* to the dictionary form (*lived*), although irregular verbs work differently (*begun, swept*). A participle or **participial phrase** usually serves as an adjective: *Strolling shoppers fill the malls.* A **gerund** is the *-ing* form of a verb used as a noun. Gerunds and **gerund phrases** can do whatever nouns can do: *Shopping satisfies needs.* An **infinitive** is the verb's dictionary form plus *to: to live.* Infinitives and **infinitive phrases** may serve as nouns (*To design a mall is a challenge*), as adverbs (*Malls are designed to make shoppers feel safe*), or as adjectives (*The mall supports the impulse to shop*).

A verbal *cannot* serve as the only verb in a sentence. For that, it requires a helping verb°: *Shoppers were strolling.*

Terms

verb forms Verbs have five distinctive forms. The **plain form** is the dictionary form: *A few artists live in town today.* The **-s form** adds *-s* or *-es* to the plain form: *The artist lives in town today.* The **past-tense form** usually adds *-d* or *-ed* to the plain form: *Many artists lived in town before this year.* Some verbs' past-tense forms are irregular, such as *began, fell, swam, threw, wrote.* The **past participle** is usually the same as the past-tense form, although, again, some verbs' past participles are irregular (*begun, fallen, swum, thrown, written*). The **present participle** adds *-ing* to the plain form: *A few artists are living in town today.*

Regular verbs are those that add *-d* or *-ed* to the plain form for the past-tense form and past participle. **Irregular verbs** create these forms in irregular ways (see above).

verb phrase A verb° of more than one word that serves as the predicate° of a sentence: *The movie has started.*

voice The form of a verb° that tells whether the sentence subject° performs the action or is acted upon. In the **active voice** the subject acts: *The city controls rents.* In the **passive voice** the subject is acted upon: *Rents are controlled by the city.* See also pp. 56–57.

Terms

Index

Index

Credits

Detailed Contents